# The Last Entrepreneurs

## AMERICA'S
## REGIONAL WARS
## FOR JOBS AND DOLLARS

Robert Goodman

SIMON AND SCHUSTER
NEW YORK

Copyright © 1979 by Robert Goodman
All rights reserved
including the right of reproduction
in whole or in part in any form
Published by Simon and Schuster
A Division of Gulf & Western Corporation
Simon & Schuster Building
Rockefeller Center
1230 Avenue of the Americas
New York, New York 10020

Designed by Stanley S. Drate
Manufactured in the United States of America
1 2 3 4 5 6 7 8 9 10

Library of Congress Cataloging in Publication Data
Goodman, Robert, date.
    The last entrepreneurs.
    Includes bibliographical references.
    1. Industrial promotion—United States. 2. Indus-
tries, Location of—United States. 3. Industry and
state—United States. 4. Regional economics.
5. Socialism in the United States. I. Title.
HC110.I53G66        338'.0973        79-17076
ISBN 0-671-24057-9

# CONTENTS

# COMMENTS AND ACKNOWLEDGMENTS

I've always envied those authors who say some particular book or article of theirs wrote itself. This book certainly didn't. It was not a very serene or easy exercise in analysis. In producing the book, I found myself writing, rethinking, and rewriting more times than I like to admit.

Aside from any personal shortcomings, I might attribute these difficulties to the broad and complex subject matter I've examined. The more I probed this material, the more disturbed I became by the broad effect of business's job movement—the forced and rapidly escalating competition between ordinary people in different regions of the country for the jobs that business was willing to make available. The ripples of my initial studies of problems like New York City's fiscal crisis quickly began to grow much wider—their implications seemed much more fundamental to this country's economic future.

The notion of a competitive free enterprise system in which local governments throughout the country are the competitors as large business grows more cooperative gave me pause. That pause, repeating itself over and over again, forced me to stretch my original analysis. In doing this, I've had to immerse myself in a broader historical examination of American economics, politics, and labor history, and to rely on people with a larger range of experience in these matters than I. While I've criticized some notable writers and thinkers along the way, among them Amory Lovins and E. F. Schumacher, I have also learned much from their work.

The proposals for change presented in the latter part of this book draw on the experience and wisdom of many people. The results are as much my own as they are the collective insights I've gained from the process of study and debate with others striving toward similar goals of decentralized political democracy and the equitable sharing of the nation's wealth. In that section I attempt to explain how a particularly American form of decentralized socialism might work.

This description of explicit ideas and examples has been done, not as a precise blueprint for change, but because I'm hopeful that it might encourage the kind of criticism and debate around the issues of ordinary life that I've often found lacking in many socialist proposals for change. In this attempt I've likely opened myself to the criticism of proposing untested ideas. That consequence will be more than compensated for if people concerned with the problems I've presented are willing to tender their criticism with their own equally explicit solutions for change.

I will have to bear responsibility for the results of this book, but those who have helped me so much should be credited with having nudged, shifted, and often literally pulled apart the ideas and the writing. The process was sometimes painful, but always useful. For their patient work in reading, discussing ideas, and in helping with the research I thank Judith Cohen, Harry Brill, Julia Goodman, Sarah Goodman, Ruth Goodman, Patricia Griffith, Michael Haran, Chester Hartman, Anita Landa, G. Roy Levin, Kristine Rosenthal, Fred Stout, and Rand Wilson. For her help in redirecting my original concept of the book and her perceptive manuscript direction I thank my editor, Alice Mayhew.

To my students at the Department of City and Regional Planning at the University of California, Berkeley, and at the Urban Studies program at Stanford University, who attended the seminars covering some of the ideas in the book, I offer both my appreciation for their insights and for the time they endured in a formative, less structured exploration of the book's ideas.

For their help in providing research materials, I would like to thank members of the Amalgamated Clothing and Textile Workers Union, the Pacific Studies Center in Mountain View, California, the Boston offices of the United States Bureau of Labor Statistics and Bureau of the Census, and a host of people in economic development offices in cities and states across the country. My gratitude to Jaime Hendriquez and Barbara Sindriglis who typed and retyped the original manuscript and made many helpful corrections in the process of deciphering my handwriting.

My special thanks to all the people at the Center for the Study of Public Policy in Cambridge, Massachusetts, for providing me with warm fellowship and a comfortable place to work. A number of articles for the Center's magazine, *Working Papers for a New Society*, provided an extremely useful source of information and ideas.

Stephanie Cleverdon, my wife, not only shared in the

shaping of this work in all its many stages of research and writing, but was also my most influential critic.

And to those I haven't mentioned, but who know they should be here, my apologies and thanks.

ROBERT GOODMAN
*Cambridge, Massachusetts*

*For Stephanie Cleverdon,*
*and for my parents,*
*Fannie and Philip Goodman,*
*and the rest of America's working people*

# INTRODUCTION:
## Against Their Better
## Interests

If you didn't know who they were, it would have all
seemed quite normal. On the second floor of a New York
City motel, the operators of one enterprise were desperately trying to keep their customers by telling them how
much more they were offering than their competitors. A
short while later, on the floor just below them, the
advantages of their competitors were being touted just as
energetically, in the hope of luring these same customers
elsewhere.

In other parts of the country, an entrepreneur complaining of the competitive tactics being used against his
organization, described how he was being forced to scour
the globe to find new clients; another lamented his "high
risk business"; while a third explained the "cutthroat"
financial incentives he was using to attract new business.

These entrepreneurs were not business people; they

were government officials working for the city of New York, and the states of Pennsylvania, Vermont, and New Jersey. These officials and thousands more like them in city halls and state capitals across the country have become commanders in an intense war to lure each other's private investment dollars. This war, escalating dramatically since the early 1970s, is being fought on many fronts. At special dinners hosted by mayors and governors, corporate executives are offered financial incentives in return for jobs. The battle is extended with multicolored brochures and advertisements in business journals. "In Ohio," says the state's promotional agency, "profit is not a dirty word." New York advertises that it is "not giving business the business anymore," while Texas implores business to "Get on Board the ProfiTrain."

There are more than 15,000 promotional agencies whose major function is to entice jobs from each other's state and local areas.[1] Mayors and governors now travel all over the country and abroad with an arsenal of financial weapons to capture jobs. Companies are offered low taxes, low-cost factory buildings and loans, and free job training; as even more attractive enticements, they are offered outright public subsidies, lax environmental standards, and nonunion, low-paid, docile workers.

Over the past decade, public entrepreneuring has resulted in major regional shifts of money, jobs, and people. This shift has been characterized by some as the transfer of power from the industrial northern "cold belt" to a newly burgeoning southern "sun belt." It has been explained as the result of the new rise of southern politicians and southern industrialists; it has been described as people's preference for more benign weather and more easygoing life-styles. Some analysts have explained the change as simply another page in an old

American tradition of regional political struggle, a colorful portrait in which the vanquished South of the old Civil War reaps its final revenge against its old northern enemies.

The job war, however, represents much more profound changes in the economic fabric of this country. It is part of a process in which business is moving jobs to well-defined parts of the country, both within the North as well as to the South, and in which the nature of the United States economy, the role of business, labor, and government are undergoing profound rearrangements. As the use of business incentives by cities and states accelerates, public debt has grown, air and water quality have steadily worsened, and work conditions and job security have been severely undermined.

While business leaders have stimulated regional competition, they have not done so through any simple conspiracy: business is not inherently in favor of slums, dirty air, or dismal working conditions. The job war is the result of the accumulated actions of many business leaders, similarly forced by faltering profitability over the past ten years to shape their survival.

Business's movement, even its threats to move, is creating a historic irony. As governments entrepreneur against one another to lure business, business itself is moving in the very opposite direction. As governments assume more and more of business's financial risk, business, using government regulations, low-cost government loans, and government contracts for its products, has been able to move toward greater concentrated power and more peaceful and cooperative ways of redistributing the country's wealth among its own community. Today's move toward intense public entrepreneuring and corporate cooperation not only mocks the foundation of America's economic system, it provides a major test of its ability to survive.

The most rigid Marxist interpretation would have had American corporate business floating belly up years ago. But the crafting of New Deal welfare economics in the 1930s and the masterful control of world resources by business following that time, seemed to have pushed that day to some vague, possibly even nonexistent future. A fatter life for the majority had for some time provided a buffer against any stirrings at the margin. Middle-class workers in their suburban homesteads seemed beyond the reach of even the broadest interpretation of revolutionary dialectics.

The government's need to entrepreneur more aggressively, to take risks for business directly challenges the old assumptions. Private corporations are now attempting to survive by shifting more and more of the weight of doing business to both taxpayers and workers.

Because corporations can no longer thrive by competing among themselves, because they cannot generate enough of their own risk capital, because they cannot pay the price for the environmental destruction their production requires, and because they cannot generate demand simply by having useful and needed products, they must ignore their own precepts, and rely on massive government expenditures for their products (the military, highways, and other public works projects). They must look to government to provide welfare to maintain those they can't employ. They must depend upon government to entrepreneur in their own operations to decrease their costs of doing business.

But to pay for the growing public costs of this process, business itself must expand at a time when world political and economic conditions have made expansion more competitive and difficult. Expansion must now be made possible through domestic belt-tightening rather than world imperialism. People must be asked to accept less.

The political changes that might occur in America as a result of this situation could be extraordinary. They follow no automatic path to a new or more progressive economic system. They may take the form of Proposition 13 tax revolts where people, unable to meet the rising costs of public services, vote themselves fewer services. They may take more radical forms of pressure for government and worker takeovers of private companies and even more basically the development of an American form of socialism.

The most important question for Americans to confront in facing today's job war is whether the public entrepreneuring now occurring among states and local governments will continue to make economic competition the burden of ordinary people, and economic cooperation the privilege of corporate businesses. This book is an attempt to make these choices explicit and to present an alternative.

# 1
# PACKAGING THE PEOPLE:
## The Public Entrepreneurs

1975 was a bad year for Volkswagen. A steady rise in the value of the German mark and increased wages for VW workers pushed the price of VWs to record highs, and its United States sales to record lows. The year before, the company had lost $300 million—the largest single-year loss in the history of any corporation.

Adding to its troubles, the United States Justice Department was examining charges that the company was "dumping" its cars on the United States market. In one of the largest investigations in its history, the Department showed that VW was indeed selling cars in the United States cheaper than in Germany—an illegal practice that could mean stiff financial penalties. There was talk of abandoning VW's American operations altogether; there was talk of bankruptcy.

But in early May of the next year, the company's fortunes suddenly shifted. The Justice Department dropped any attempt at penalties, and contented itself with an official announcement that VW was indeed dumping cars, that it was a bad thing, and it should stop doing so. Then two weeks later, Pennsylvania Congressman John H. Dent announced a deal between VW and his state—the German company would move its first United States production plant to a site in the rolling farm country in his home district of southwestern Pennsylvania. Using over $100 million in state and local government help, an incomplete and abandoned Chrysler auto plant, a building shell with almost fifty acres of enclosed space, would be completed, then staffed by 5,000 workers, and scheduled to turn out fifty VW Rabbits per hour.

Several months later, at official ceremonies marking the VW deal, the Pennsylvania politicians who spearheaded the state's "win" basked in the sunshine of the bright future they described in their speeches. Governor Milton Shapp, who led the fight for VW inside the state legislature and who only a year before had said he would be the chief executive remembered for keeping the cost of using the turnpike toilets to a dime, now claimed the VW deal as the crowning achievement of his administration.[1] In addition to thousands of VW workers, the governor proclaimed that 20,000 other jobs would be created by the coming of the auto company. "We've pulled the big Rabbit out of the hat," beamed Shapp.

For the taxpayers of Pennsylvania, it was a rather costly magic act. The culmination of three years of dealing with state and local governments throughout the United States, the company had now positioned Pennsylvania into underwriting a major part of VW's development. The state would build a $10 million rail spur and a $15 million highway extension to serve the plant. It would provide the auto company with $40 million in a 1¾ percent long-term loan to finance the plant's completion, and an over $3 million subsidy to train VW workers. A state teachers' and workers' pension fund would provide another $6 million in loans for construction and when the plant was finished, local government would allow millions of dollars' worth of tax abatements. For the first two years VW would be given a 95 percent property tax abatement; in the next three years, 50 percent. During 1978, when the East Huntington plant was to produce over 50,000 cars, VW would pay local government less in taxes than the cost of a single new Rabbit.[2]

In addition to public incentives paid for by the taxpayers, workers at the VW plant would be asked to provide their own subsidies for the automaker. In negotiations between VW and the national office of the United Automotive Workers union, the company agreed to allow the union to organize the plant, but insisted its workers receive lower wages than at other UAW plants. The result were wages about 20 percent lower for VW workers and the savings of millions of dollars for the company.

The Pennsylvania deal with Volkswagen is an important economic event—not so much because it helped keep the automaker in business, but because of what it says about local government competition for business throughout America. It was a benchmark in the escalation of public economic incentives to attract business, "the greatest industrial-government courtship of all time," said one local newspaper.[3]

A host of cities, and virtually every mainland state and Puerto Rico competed against each other to lure the German firm. "Governors, mayors, state development officers and local businessmen are understandably drooling over VW," commented the *Wall Street Journal*.[4] High government officials and their trade missions followed on each other's heels to Wolfsburg, Germany, to present multimillion-dollar incentives.

The courting of VW is part of a process of economic scrambling, clawing, and shoving now taking place among all our states, tens of thousands of cities, and smaller units of government. This kind of public entrepreneuring, repeated many times with other companies, has turned free enterprise on its head, leaving government in the role of compeitor and business as welfare recipient. It is a process in which the public takes enormous financial risks, while business surveys the willing suitors and moves freely to where the public risk-taking is greatest.

In the Pennsylvania deal, company executives, aware of the intense public entrepreneuring that occurs in the United States, had for over three years positioned states and cities against one another, escalating incentives and extracting more and more benefits. Local governments, accusing one another of unfair competition, groomed themselves for VW executives. "These are meticulous people," said one fawning mayor, referring to VW's executives. "You say 10 o'clock," said the mayor who'd spent hundreds of hours in an unsuccessful bid for the plant, "and they expect you not a minute sooner or later."[5]

In the South, a consortium of states, Tennessee, Arkansas, and Mississippi, got together with the innovative idea that the winning state would encourage suppliers for VW to locate in the two losers. Puerto Rico, normally a haven for companies escaping higher United States production costs, outdid its usual competitive self putting together a tax exemption, training, and subsidy program that it called its "most attractive incentive package" in a quarter of a century.[6]

And then there was Baltimore. In a full-page *Wall Street Journal* ad, addressed to Toni Schumucker, president of VW, the mayor of Baltimore explained how he had sent his people out to check over personally VW's favored sites in Pennsylvania, Ohio, and Michigan. On a chart he demonstrated how his city's industrial workers had lower wages and were involved in fewer strikes. In addition, the mayor explained, the city could give VW a wide variety of financial incentives. "Baltimore wants you so much," the mayor unabashedly concluded, "we'll let you write your own terms."[7]

Dozens of governors traveled to Germany to persuade VW; there were meetings at corporate headquarters in Wolfsburg, on specially arranged boat trips on the Rhine, and in United States state capitals. As the competition heated up in early 1976, VW announced it had narrowed its choice to thirteen states. While company executives studied the offerings, they dropped hints to escalate the incentives.

In February, VW's president of the same year coyly said he already had a favorite.[8] By April, the leading contenders were known: an abandoned government defense plant near Cleveland (which had been used to build the prototypes of war planes that had bombed Germany in World War II) and the half-built Chrysler plant in Pennsylvania. With the official announcement only a short time away, a VW vice-president announced mysteriously, "It's possible we could name a site that hasn't been discussed publicly."[9]

Even after announcing the Pennsylvania "winner" in May, VW carefully and publicly held on to its second-place Ohio choice. As VW executives hammered out the details of its deal with Pennsylvania officials that summer, the company continued to send people to Ohio to keep up discussions with that state's officials. At one point, as the Pennsylvania negotiations appeared headed toward a deadlock over details of the state's aid plan, VW Vice-President Arthur Railton announced, "VW could go out and get the money ourselves. But if we are forced to that," he warned, "the question then becomes whether Pennsylvania still looks more attractive than Ohio."[10]

## Legal Bribery

This public entrepreneuring exposes a new side of the American myth of a private market. The first side of this myth claims that business survives by producing products that respond directly to consumers' demand. But billions of dollars in business-promoted government expenditures for military products, highways, and urban renewal have shown that business survival has become rooted in the process of artificially stimulating needs and markets.[11]

Business's need to stimulate markets has already outrun its ability to lobby effectively through legal channels and has forced corporate leaders into illegal methods. Bribes to government officials by prominent United States companies like Gulf, ITT, Textron, and Lockheed are symptomatic of business's growing difficulty in finding markets through normal government subsidies.

Public entrepreneuring is a different and apparently more legal form of bribery. It is a public payment to business in exchange for business's promise to remain in an area or to relocate to a new one. The bribe makers in this case are government officials, not corporate executives; the offers are not made in dark corners of foreign capitals, through laundered checks or whispered conversations. They are often made in full view, indeed, shouted by public officials as loudly as possible so that would-be recipients are able to hear them above the din of other offers.

For business, the more open and public this bribing process becomes, the more likely the amount of the inducements will escalate. Commenting on the VW competition among the states, Chrysler Corporation Chairman John Riccardo said in June, 1978, his own company, rather than use its old practice of secret negotiations with potential communities for new plants, now attempts to get these communities to bid openly against each other.[12]

When Pennsylvania officials talk freely about a $100 million "deal that VW cannot refuse," when a Baltimore mayor takes a full-page ad to tell the company it can write its own terms, when the highest elected official in New Jersey offers business free, customized training of its work force, or when state development agencies offer docile, low-paid workers and antilabor climates, they are offering bribes.

These government-initiated bribes are in some ways more insidious than private ones. In public entrepreneuring, elected officials, presumably responsible to their constituents, are involved in working out business inducements that will often lead to increased taxes and the degradation of job, wage, and environmental conditions for their constituents.

The problem is not only the moral one of public officials manipulating the lives of citizens for the private profit of business; it is in the ultimate payoff. Bribery is for a specific effect; you engage in an illegal activity, but you find yourself financially rewarded if you don't get caught. Public bribing involves a long-term payment in the form of increased local taxes for providing public services and building an infrastructure of public facilities and services. The process often has only a short-term payoff in creating jobs, and only in some communities. Over the longer period, it creates a fundamental threat to the job security of workers throughout the country. It institutionalizes public entrepreneuring so that no community can afford not to spend millions in searching for industry, setting aside land for it, building roads and other facilities. It forces the working people of the country into a fierce battle against each other which ultimately increases their taxes, drives down their wages, and degrades their working conditions and environment.

Even within the winner communities themselves, the benefits can be illusory or are obtained at severe cost. When the VW deal was announced, for example, the federal Environmental Protection Agency complained that the state already exceeded federal air pollution standards. To allow VW's pollution from its paint operations, the EPA required that some other form of industrial pollution in the area be reduced. Obligingly, the state agreed to shift to a lower-polluting, asphalt highway-repair program for southwestern Pennsylvania. Instead of resulting in cleaner air, the shift concentrated the pollution at the VW site where 8,000 pounds of hydrocarbons are pumped into the air each day.

Only two years after Governor Shapp announced the rabbit-out-of-the-hat trick, official estimates had already revised downward by half his projection of 20,000 jobs to be generated by the VW deal. At that time, only a single company, with 100 jobs, had come to Westmoreland County. Meanwhile, a 110-acre industrial park for companies supplying VW remained vacant. "The great expectations produced by VW," wrote *Business Week* in 1978, "have done little more than raise real estate values 15% within the past year."[13]

### Upping the Ante

The Pennsylvania deal with Volkswagen may be one of the more celebrated examples of public entrepreneuring, but it is hardly unique. It comes at a time when aggressive local government competition for business throughout the United States has rapidly accelerated. In the VW deal the ante has been visibly and dramatically raised, setting a higher standard for government incentives subsidies for business throughout the country.

"It's going to cost more to get development in the future," said Norval Reece, Pennsylvania's secretary of commerce, commenting on the VW deal. "You're conspicuous if you don't go after development," he said, indicating that almost a billion dollars in low-interest local government-sponsored revenue bonds for private business were made in 1977 alone. "I'll go anywhere to keep up with the competition," says Reece, "even if it's just for 200 jobs." [14]

In next-door Ohio, government officials are racing to keep up with Pennsylvania's incentives. "We've been working like crazy," said Robert Stutz, a state economic development official, "to bring Ohio up to the same competitive status with neighboring states like Pennsylvania." Sounding very much like a supermarket executive, another Ohio official says government tax incentives to attract business are very much like "loss-leaders" in stores, which are used to lure customers, in order to have them spend more once they're inside. [15]

Escalating incentives have resulted in a race for each state to do unto others, before another state does the same unto them. "We steal industry from New York," says Peter Bearse, an economic analyst for New Jersey, "and lose it to Pennsylvania." [16] Politicians in New York, complaining of job losses, have called for a more competitive posture; the state estimated that about 50 percent of the jobs leaving New York in the ten to twelve years before 1974 were relocating in New Jersey. [17] "What the South has been doing to New Jersey for 15 years," said New Jersey's chief official for attracting industry, "I'm now doing to New

York. It's cutthroat, regrettably," he added, "but it's every state for itself."[18]

It is not only cutthroat, but apparently sometimes even illegal. It is normal, for example, for state government to single out particular industries for special treatment. According to Linda Liston of the Industrial Development Research Council, a research organization specializing in corporate expansion, "You can always sell business some land below cost and figure nobody's going to know about it. This kind of thing is still going on," says Liston, "but they just don't talk about it. There's very big legal risk— jail."[19]

David M. Reeves, president of the same council and an executive of the Ralston Purina Company, recognizes the problem, but also considers it a normal way of doing business. "If you bring industry to a community," he says, "even if you've had some bending of the law it's hard to call that a bad thing."[20]


## Knocking the Competition

Local governments haven't been at all shy in announcing their abilities to outdo each other. All states, most large cities, and even many smaller ones now have advertising campaigns funded by tax dollars. In many ways these public campaigns are more aggressive and competitive than those of private business.

Interstate badmouthing contrasts virtues with competitor's flaws. Typically, economic development agencies compile charts which might include wage rates, levels of unionization, measures of profitability, numbers of strikes, and favorable business laws. Self-promotion sometimes involves outright sniping at other states. Describing New Hampshire as "What America was," a state brochure explains, "[o]ne is constantly reminded of the exodus of manufacturing plants from our surrounding states by reading the newspapers of neighboring states which constantly bemoan the loss of their good industries to New Hampshire. As the saying goes, we must be doing something right." Joining the popular baiting of New York City as a place that "pays out more than it takes in," New Hampshire in turn extols its own good management.[21]

In Kansas, the state's economic development secretary offers what he calls "the best revenue bond law among the states," and "a better transportation system than neighboring states."[22] Nevada's Department of Economic Development produces a letter from a corporate executive to show its worker turnover rate is lower than neighboring California.[23] New York State proclaims it has "one of the best tax incentive programs in America,"[24] and its record of "man-days idle" between 1975 and 1978 is better than Alabama, Arizona, Connecticut, Louisiana, New Jersey, Tennessee, Texas, and Virginia.[25] Michigan attempts to lure its neighbors' industries by claiming better tax advantages. "Think it over," says a state advertisement. "If your plant is in Ohio, Indiana, Illinois, Wisconsin, Minnesota, or Pennsylvania—Michigan is just a short distance away."[26] Another advertisement cartoons a harried executive, pointing a gun at his head; a pile of Pennsylvania state tax forms are scattered over his desk. "Two things in life are certain," says the Michigan ad, "death and taxes. At least in Michigan the taxes won't kill you."

Feeling the pressure of Michigan's competition, Ohio's Governor James Rhodes traveled to Michigan in 1976 to talk with business people about moving to Ohio. "We're back in the raiding business," said Rhodes.[27] Meanwhile, that same year, New York State's Governor Hugh Carey, complaining about the anti-New York campaigns of New

Jersey and Connecticut, called for more cooperation among neighbors. "When we think of New Jersey," he told a meeting of the three state's officials, "we don't talk about your mosquitos, we brag about your tomatoes."[28] But little more than a year later, New York was taking full-page ads to extol its business incentives against its neighbors and other states.[29]

Since the early 1950s, incentive escalation between governments has grown. At that time only a handful of states offered business low-interest bonds for private development; now almost every state offers them. Today, some states offer business what the *Wall Street Journal* calls "a candy store of tax incentive programs."[30] Between 1966 and 1975, the number of states offering tax exemptions on new equipment jumped from fourteen to twenty-seven; state financing for plant expansions went from fifteen to twenty-seven.[31] In Michigan, state tax officials estimate that by 1986, tax incentives alone—a small part of what governments usually offer business—will cost state and local governments $80 million per year in revenues.[32] In Ohio, local communities can grant industry up to twenty years of tax abatements.[33] New York City, chastened by its mid-1970s financial crisis, offered business what it called "the most comprehensive package of financial incentives of any city in America." By using tax abatements, tax waivers, and interest rate reductions, said the city's Industrial Development Agency (IDA), savings to business could "equal or even surpass the initial project cost."[34]

Public entrepreneuring includes national and international finance, the geographic shift of billions of dollars in production facilities and payrolls, and the use of billions more in new government and private facilities to accom-

modate the needs of business. The extent and complexity
of these operations can be numbing to contemplate. A
simpler metaphor for beginning to understand this process might be the operation of professional sport teams,
where local governments also compete to underwrite the
profits of private ventures.

Most sports teams are comparatively small in their
earning ability compared with national corporate firms.
But most, contrary to the we-do-it-for-the-love-of-the-
game myths promoted by the owners, are profit-making.
These profits sometimes don't show up on Internal
Revenue forms, but according to Roger Noll, who headed
a study for the Brookings Institution, all of the major
sports leagues, with the exception of the recently defunct
World Hockey League (WHL), have shown substantial
profits. In the early 1970s, the benefits of ownership for
all leagues (excluding the WHL) were, according to the
Brookings Institution study, approximately $2.7 billion.
In 1977, fifteen baseball teams were reported to have
made record profits. A year later, F.A.N.S., a Ralph
Nader group, projected an average pretax profit of
almost $4 million for each National Football League
team.[35] "By one means or another," said a *Sports Illustrated*
study of team financing in 1978, "almost all professional
franchises make money."[36]

A few professional teams like the Milwaukee Bucks
and the Seattle Supersonics are run as business corporations, with their stock traded on the stock market. More
typically, sports team owners are comprised of syndicates,
headed by business people, who have made their fortunes
in other ventures. The San Diego Padres is controlled by
McDonald's magnate Roy Kroc; the New York Yankees by
George Steinbrenner, the chief executive of a shipbuilding company; the Oakland As by Charles O. Finley, a
health insurance executive; the Kansas City Royals by

Elving Kaufman, a drug company owner; and the Houston Oilers by oil millionaire Kenneth Stanley Adams, Jr.[37]

Losing teams that are unable to attract fans can be taken as a tax loss against the more profitable ventures of business people. Sports players, like pieces of equipment in factories, can be depreciated by their owners as they grow older. A White Sox president once explained that buying a baseball team was buying the right to depreciate.[38]

For city residents the costs of providing facilities for these private industries is real and undepreciable against taxes, since their taxes must be used to pay the debt and the operating deficits of the stadiums. As in the case of competing for other private industries, the cost of keeping private sports teams in action is subsidized by taxpayers, while profits accrue to the business owners.

## The Sporting Life of Taxpayers

At the second game of the 1977 World Series, played under the bright lights of a newly remodeled Yankee Stadium, 55,000 fans at the game and millions more watching on TV were to see a spectacle they had not expected. Beyond the geometry of the bright green playing field, above the outfield stands, large clouds of smoke billowed from a nearby building fire. As the fire raged and sirens mingled with the cheers of spectators, the Dodgers hit three home runs into the smoke-draped stands to defeat the Yankees 6 to 1.

Yankee Stadium is in the South Bronx—and the fire that night was only one of an average of ten per day that are reported in that section of New York. In 1978 former mayor John V. Lindsay, who helped put an original $24 million stadium-remodeling package together when he was in office, justified the final $100 million cost as necessary for community improvement. "If the Yankees had left it would have been a disaster for the city and particularly the Bronx. . . . Brooklyn never recovered when the Dodgers left the city."[39]

Lindsay's notions about baseball teams' influence on a city's future may be historically simplistic. But his view of how a city responds to "save" itself from the threat of a migrating sports business is revealing. By threatening or actually moving to another city, sports teams, like other private businesses, have been able to play off government against government to win enormous public subsidies.

During the next twenty years taxpayers will spend close to a billion dollars to pay the operating costs and deficits of these new sports facilities.[40] Seventy percent of all professional sports stadiums in America are now publicly owned, including almost all the stadiums built since 1960. Most of the more than fifty sports facilities built or remodeled in recent years were supposed to provide the citizens of cities or states with revenue; instead many of them are adding to their taxes.[41]

Politicians in cities that are suffering from serious and, in some cases, catastrophic fiscal problems have eliminated financial risk for team owners, while strapping taxpayers with public debt. Between 1975 and 1978, Pontiac, Michigan, a small city of predominantly poor people, thirty miles north of Detroit, subsidized $6 million in costs for its new "Silver Dome." The stadium houses the privately owned Detroit Lions football team, the Detroit Pistons basketball team, and the Detroit Express soccer team. In 1978, the city used almost 90 percent of the $2.4 million additional taxes it raised to pay for its stadium debt. Since its opening, the stadium's financial burden has forced the city to freeze all new public construction and public hiring, in addition to a battery of other austerity measures.[42]

In 1966, business people and politicians persuaded Louisiana voters that a new sports stadium would help put New Orleans, a sun belt city with a higher per capita debt than either Newark or Detroit, back on its feet. The city ranks forty-fourth nationally in per pupil spending for education; in some black ghettos the recent unemployment rate for blacks was 60 percent. A new sports stadium, said its business and political supporters, would be self-supporting, requiring nothing from taxpayers.

The New Orleans Superdome was completed in 1976 at a cost of $163 million, $130 million more than the original estimate. It is one of the most expensive sports facilities ever created. With interest being paid into the next century, the building will eventually cost over $300 million. In 1977, the building, which was to cost Louisiana nothing, lost $13 million.[43]

In a 1971 deal to keep the Yankees from moving to a new stadium in New Jersey, New York City committed itself to rebuilding Yankee Stadium at an estimated cost of $24 million. A clause in the contract between the Columbia Broadcasting System and the city, which insisted the stadium "be equivalent in all respects with the best features of the new stadia at Pittsburgh, Philadelphia and Cincinnati," eventually forced the city's cost to $100 million.

Two years after the deal between the city and CBS, CBS sold the Yankees to a business syndicate headed by George Steinbrenner, the chief executive officer of the American Shipbuilding Company in Cleveland and an investor in various Florida business enterprises. In 1977, the year the Yankees won the World Series, the Steinbrenner syndicate grossed about $15 million after taxes. But as a result of its "keep the Yankees" contract, which allowed the owners liberal maintenance deductions against rent, the city received $171,000. The amount was about one-tenth of 1 percent of what Steinbrenner's group received, and a fraction of the millions the city paid for its yearly stadium debt. The year before, with the Yankees winning the league pennant, the city had to pay the owners $10,000.

Meanwhile, two new parking garages built by the city to the custom standards of the Yankees' owners were proving another financial burden to residents already suffering one of the worst financial crises faced by any modern city. Several years after the garages were built, the private company leasing them hadn't collected enough, according to the terms of their lease, in parking fees to justify any payments to the city at all. The area surrounding the stadium was so pockmarked with vacant land left by burned-out and demolished buildings, thousands of fans arriving at games by car had little trouble finding parking spaces.[44] New York City, it might seem, could be forced to rebuild the neighborhood around Yankee Stadium, simply to get some income from its parking garages.

Sports stadiums, parking and transportation facilities have been built and maintained at enormous public expense to house what are called "home teams." The teams, however, have been anything but at home in the cities. Encouraged by public subsidies, owners have moved teams from city to city.[45] As taxpayers absorb the costs of providing the physical facilities for private teams, the owners of these teams often sell the TV rights to the games played in these publicly subsidized settings. In 1960, the National Football League teams received $30 million for the rights to televise their games; by 1978 the figure jumped to $162 million. TV rights for football alone in the next four years are estimated to be worth $656 million.[46]

What a city loses in TV rights is not simply money, but the opportunity to see "its" team play. In a form of electronic extortion, owners will often "black out" a home game on TV in order to persuade people to pay admission. During some sellout games owners may beneficently lift their blackout and let residents watch their team.

Public entrepreneuring in sports resembles the relationship of local government to any migratory industry. Private companies set the terms of the arrangement, while the public pays. Local governments compete with one another to make their incentives more attractive—a new stadium, a weatherproof dome, parking garages, lower rentals, tax abatements, low-interest loans, or new roads. In return the company will stay, as long as it continues to make better profits.

As governments escalate their incentives, companies move to new locations—or threaten to do so in order to extort more favors from the "home" team or industry's current taxpayers. To pay for the vacated and subsidized facilities, governments must either raise taxes or cut back on public services for their citizens.

## Both Sides of the Street

The rapidly accelerated use of public incentives and the varying strengths of organized labor in different regions have created a more complex decision process for business executives looking for new locations. Corporate location consulting has grown into a healthy business. These experts-without-a-country, moving freely between business and government clients, live off business mobility and governments' frantic reactions. Working both sides of the street, they profit from helping to create a problem, and then from trying to solve it.

The Fantus Company, a subsidiary of Dun and Bradstreet, the financial community's premier credit-rating company, has become the country's leading advisor to migrating corporations. In the sixties and seventies, the New York and Chicago-based firm was one of the principal groups of experts suggesting that New York City firms move away from the city. In 1976, after years of helping companies move out, the company's experts were then hired by a private New York foundation created by city industry and government leaders to help keep industry from leaving and to attract new industry.[47]

The experts' advice to New York City was to exhort the city to compete more strongly against other governments. "As location consultants for thousands of corporate clients," they explained, "Fantus is keenly aware of the strategies utilized by competitive cities for the attracting of an expanding or relocating industry. At this point in time, New York City cannot offer, to a prospective client, the quality and array of services available in other United States cities."

While New York was behind, it could catch up by more aggressive competition with the "complex financing arrangement and novel incentives" offered businesses by other cities. A new public-private "economic development corporation" would investigate the inducements industry had found attractive elsewhere, and then lobby for state laws to allow them in New York City. Some of what are described as "more sophisticated development weapons" include selling urban renewal land to developers "at less than fair market value," the "lease of urban renewal land at or below fair market value," and a proposal that the city "completely fund from its own revenue sources the construction of public improvements necessary for some development."

The new economic development corporation, the Fantus report suggests, would be given special governmental powers "to deliver financial incentives and development stimuli to interested developers. . . . At least two-thirds of the appointed members," it states, "should be from the business community. . . . Its legal status as a quasi-public, non-profit corporation provides it with powers to which public agencies or officers are not entitled. These include the ability to make direct loans to private business, share in ownership and risk, issue bonds, and buy, sell or lease property *without cumbersome public hearings or approvals"* (my emphasis). Economic development corporations, they explain, "are insulated more politically than city departments. Elected officials are not as directly responsible for an EDC as they are for a city department."[48]

In 1975, Fantus became a "hired gun" in the Illinois Manufacturers' Association's lobbying effort to undermine the gains of the state's labor organizations and lower-income residents. Using such selected indicators as corporate taxes, state welfare payments, and legislative protection of unions, Fantus prepared a report in which every state's business climate was ranked by an elaborate numerical system. The purpose, according to Fantus President Maurice Fulton, was to give corporate clients a "feel" for where they might invest their money.

The effect of the report was to attack states such as Illinois, where labor and residents had won more job security, better wages, and more progressive social programs than in other states. According to the report, "Those states with a right-to-work law are considered favorable to management and are ranked highest." States that have created a local government agency to protect workers' rights are conversely given bad marks: "Those which have a labor relations law calling for a state labor relations board are considered favorable to labor and are ranked lowest."

States making more meager payments for workers injured in accidents go to the head of the class, as do states that make union organizing difficult. "The higher the degree of regulation of unions, the more favorable is this to management." An additional markdown was earned by states making higher welfare payments or collecting higher corporate taxes. "The greater the proportion of the state's income which comes from corporations, the greater the likelihood that the legislature has adopted the philosophy of letting business and industry carry the load for the improvement and enlargement of state services."[49]

The states with the worst antilabor policies and those that provide their residents fewest social services tend to find themselves at the top of the list. Since being issued, the report has been touted by states on the "top" as evidence of their attractive climate for business, and by business leaders in the "bottom" states as evidence of the need for more government antilabor measures.

The state of Alabama, for example, sends prospective businesses a "Special Report" from the state's chamber of commerce which proclaims, "Alabama ranked second in the nation . . . (by) one of the country's most respected consulting firms. . . ."[50] The Illinois Manufacturers' Association, in a lobbying effort against labor which blitzed all the state's media and legislators, says, "Illinois ranks a poor 35th among the 48 adjacent states in attractiveness to business according to . . . nationally recognized plant relocation consultants. . . ." The report, which the association suggested business people distribute to their employees and local news media, was a graphic threat that business had thirty-four states they could move to. "Illinois is increasingly considered by employers as being pro-union and anti-business," said the manufacturers, denouncing improved unemployment benefits for workers. "Many of the actions by state regulatory authorities," they continued, "particularly in pollution control, are considered [by business] excessive in requirements and costs and exhibiting an anti-industry bias."[51]

A colorful example of the shifting expert-without-a-country is David A. "Sonny" Werblin, a wealthy, show-business agent turned sports promoter. In a period of little more than ten years, Werblin was able to use public entrepreneuring to reshape the sports activities of New Jersey and New York.

Sonny Werblin first gained prominence in the early 1960s when he bought a major share in a relatively unknown football team called the New York Titans. He renamed them the Jets and signed a young University of Alabama quarterback named Joe Namath to an unprecedented $427,000 contract. In the late sixties, shortly after selling his share in the rising team for a million-dollar profit, he convinced state officials in New Jersey to build a $300 million sports complex in the Meadowlands, a swampy bird sanctuary about eight miles from the George Washington Bridge.

Werblin, named chairman of New Jersey's Sports and Exposition Authority in 1971, proceeded to make financial arrangements that would move three of New York's biggest sports teams to New Jersey: first the Giants football team, then the Cosmos soccer team, with multi-million-dollar star attraction Pelé, and finally, with an offer to build a 20,000 seat arena, the Nets basketball team.

He offered the Yankees a lucrative arrangement to move to New Jersey, but the deal failed when the Yankees parlayed the offer into a New York City commitment to rebuild Yankee Stadium. He tried to move his old New York Jets football team across the Hudson, but again, more aggressive financial bargaining by New York City prevailed.

A new Meadowlands horse-racing track built at Werblin's suggestion has shifted attendance to New Jersey, cutting New York State's income from betting at Roosevelt Raceway and Yonkers Raceway by 30 to 40 percent. The new Meadowlands indoor arena, to be built for the Nets basketball team, promises to siphon off not only basketball attendance from Madison Square Garden in New York, but also makes space for hockey games, rock concerts, wrestling title fights, and other special events now housed at the Garden.

In December, 1977, while New York State officials were wringing their hands over lost betting revenues, while New York fans were still denouncing the various team owners for leaving, and while the New York Knickerbockers were suing the new New Jersey Nets for infringing on their territory, Sonny Werblin took a new job. This time he was moving back to New York to become President of the Madison Square Garden Corporation, the same company that owned the Knickerbockers and Roosevelt Raceway and the same company so affected by Werblin's New Jersey activities. His new job, for a reported $225,000 yearly income, was to repair the financial damage produced by his own efforts.

People like Sonny Werblin and companies like Fantus have been kept in their lucrative trade by government economic weakness and business's dependence on that weakness. What distinguishes these experts is their adeptness in positioning companies, whether they are sports teams or giant conglomerates, in the midst of government economic scrambling. The location experts can adapt themselves to any phase of the battle—advising business or government either how to fight or how to take advantage of the fight. They can work for a private sports team like Sonny Werblin did in New York, shift to a public agency, then shift back to the private world. The shifting is not so contradictory as might first appear. Whether working for a public or private agency their goals are not really very different—to give business an opportunity to take maximum advantage of the public entrepreneurs.

The interchangeability of public and private decision makers is mirrored in the education of the new public entrepreneurs. The skills required for work in private and public enterprise have become so interchangeable that in 1975, Yale University created an entirely new graduate school based on that premise. William H. Donaldson, the school's first director, described the function of the education program as serving people "in government interested in working into the private sector, or anyone in government charged with regulating business or thinking of going into business." The school would develop "a whole new kind of manager," he said. "[P]eople who want to make a lot of money and still have a diversity of careers." "I think the lines between the private and public sectors are blurring more and more," said Donaldson, who among his own private and public careers made a $10 million fortune in Wall Street in the 1960s, and was Vice-President Nelson Rockefeller's chief architect in 1975 for a now defunct proposal to use $100 billion in government-backed financing to stimulate energy development by private companies.[52]

As those who control private capital need more direct access to public decision making, the distinctions between private executives and public entrepreneurs blur. Staffing public offices with executives from private business is a well-established custom, from the smallest levels of government in which real estate developers sit on town zoning boards to the federal government, in which the highest ranking members of regulatory agencies are often alumni of the industries they regulate.

One of the most dramatic examples of the business-government interchange happened in the early 1970s. As the public pressure for environmental control increased, forty states created antipollution boards. Thirty-five included officials who worked for some of the biggest industrial polluters in the country. On some, industry representatives were the majority—four out of five on Ohio's Pollution Control Board. All six industry representatives on Alabama's pollution agency board were executives of companies involved in pollution legal proceedings. In Pennsylvania, the only "public" representative of the pollution agency was a former steel company vice-president.[53]

## Education and the Public Entrepreneurs

A government's ability to attract business depends not only on a political climate that offers financial incentives such as tax abatements and industrial financing, but on a hospitable setting for directing the constituency's education toward the new needs of business. As declining profitability forces business to attack benefits at the work place, it provokes it to attack benefits in the schoolhouse.

Following World War II, the expanding economy for the first time allowed a certain expansion in the educational system. Aided by increased automation and by low energy costs, fewer production workers were needed to produce the country's wealth. An increasing number of people could be supported through long periods of nonproductive (in an economic sense) schooling. The Sputnik trauma of the fifties, when Russia seemed to have pulled ahead technically, prompted greater federal aid to higher education, especially in the science and engineering curricula.

During this period more and more students were placed on the ladder toward higher and higher levels of education. More teachers were hired, colleges were expanded, an enormous number of junior colleges were built, and enrollments exploded. Between 1957 and 1965, enrollment in higher education climbed by over 80 percent.[54] The long held dream of rising through the educational system to personal enlightenment and high economic position was given flesh and substance. More sons and daughters of blue-collar workers, it now seemed, had a realistic chance for more privileged lives than their parents.

In the late sixties, a leaner economic outlook prompted business to shift its gears. The economic system was not producing enough high-level jobs for all those being trained for them, nor was it producing the wealth that can maintain people in schools for long periods of time. By 1971, 36 percent of the males graduating from college couldn't find professional or managerial jobs. It is not at all uncommon now for college graduates to find themselves in low-level jobs that a short time before they would have rejected.

This rather expensive education for low-level jobs produced a shift in government policy. A tighter rein is being kept on the educational system in an attempt to gear educational policy more precisely to the needs of business expansion. The more ephemeral and rapidly expanded programs of the fifties which might lead students to broader choice of careers are, in the nomenclature of Washington, no longer operative.

The new policy is another "giveback" being asked of the American people, who are being told, in essence, that the production system can no longer support their rising educational expectations. In 1974, President Gerald Ford explained the dilemma to a graduating class at Ohio State University. "Your professors tell you that education unlocks creative genius and imagination and that you must develop your human potential. With your Masters or Ph.D.s," he continued, "you go out and look for a job and now they say you are overqualified. . . . The fact of the matter is that education is being strangled—by degrees."[55]

The dour picture Ford painted for the college graduates of '74 was a twist in the commencement speaker decorum which prescribes an extolling of the virtue of education, ever upward and onward. It reflected basic shifts that were occurring in the nation's education policies. In 1965, all local governments in the country were spending $200 million a year on their vocational programs. By 1976, the figure had jumped to $3 billion.[56]

In the competition between public entrepreneurs, governments will often tout their vocational training programs to business. State promotional agencies explain that more students are now being channeled into vocational education programs (VOC-ED), and the schools are adaptable to specific business needs. North Carolina proclaims, "[w]e in North Carolina are proud to lead the nation in the proportion of residents enrolled in vocational education programs." Nebraska demonstates to business that between 1965 and 1976 it increased its VOC-ED students by 170 percent. Pennsylvania says that over 40 percent of its upper-level high-school students in 1974 were in such programs.

In addition to increasing public commitment to vocational education, states now spend more to train workers directly for specific businesses. In the sixties, few states offered subsidies for business training programs. Now, after years of escalating incentives, almost every state offers business trained workers at little or no cost.

"Profit from free, customized training of your own work force," New Jersey Governor Brendan Byrne tells business. "We'll survey your needs, plan the training, secure the funds and facilitate, screen and recruit workers—and train the workers precisely to your needs."[57] Not only will Texas provide all the buildings, equipment, and teachers, in their "ProfiTrain" program, but the state will even pay to hire the company's own instructors to train their prospective workers.

Texas' training program, paid for by the public as most state programs are, was developed in the early 1970s when, according to the state's industrial commission, Texas was trying to make itself more competitive with other locations. "No other program in the country can touch us," the commission now boasts, referring to its "total orientation to the profit advantage." Workers are trained "on their own time," says the commission, "and the company hires only those it chooses." "It's all done to your specifications, but at our expense and the expense of the trainees."

In 1976, Texas claimed it could save a firm up to $2000 in training cost for every worker it trained. Tennessee's Department of Education made similar claims for its training program, suggesting companies could benefit further by being able to set higher production quotas for its state-trained workers. The department also claimed companies could save an additional $200 to $400 per worker through worker "turnover" during the state-paid training period, rather than after a plant went into operation.[58]

Oklahoma's Governor David Boren, unwilling to be outdone by competitor governments, boasts that "No state can match our network of technical schools." "The beauty of it," says Boren, "is that we are set up flexibly to use these facilities. . . . For example, Goodyear is coming into the state. We took around 20,000 square feet at the Vo-tech school in the Lawton area and brought in the Goodyear tire-making equipment. The State of Oklahoma—at our expense, with their equipment, is training these people.[59]

"Imagine your very first day of operations in New Bedford," says the city's development commission. "You open your doors and greet a complete, fully trained staff of workers. They're ready and able to start producing immediately and you haven't done a thing to train them."[60]

Tracking students toward careers, according to their ability to perform useful tasks for business, is a well-traveled road in American public education. Yet within the confines of such sorting, there has been the veneer, and occasionally the substance, of humanistic and critical education—especially as more students were able to spend more time in higher education programs. But with the state now shifting more directly to industry job training, the remnants of an objectivity that separates public and industrial education is being further eroded.

In their zeal to attract business, the public entrepreneurs often view people as parts to be engineered into an efficient piece of production equipment. Their promotional language reveals the product orientation. Texas claims "workers are trained to meet or exceed company's specifications."[61] Alabama says "workers can be trained to the manufacturer's specifications while the plant is under construction." Their training program, "will insure the trainee will make a minimum of mistakes."[62] Minnesota claims it is producing "super skilled, highly productive and readily trainable folks whose minds and muscles can make your company grow." Its vocational schools, says the state, provide workers with skills, its health-care program provides them with strength, and the state has "more than 15,000 lakes and four full seasons of recreation to keep them happy."[63]

Lest the company worry that the workers will wander beyond the narrowly specified areas, government entrepreneurs explain how precisely structured their programs are—usually toward company dedication, company loyalty, and the ability to handle simple skills. "The training's value to the company," Alabama stresses to prospective businesses, "depends upon results and not complex ideas and individual philosophy. . . . The training process," it says, "must be simple . . . the job must be well defined." "[A] program will be designed," says the state, "to develop positive attitudes in supervisors and subordinates toward their jobs, their employees and the organization." The training program will "[a]void all those items which would be nice-to-know and include only special features to develop the necessary skills and abilities to do the job, with an emphasis on progressing each trainee at a maximum rate geared to each individual's abilities."

Texas, which boasts of its antiunion laws and low wages, claims it produces "dedicated workers" through its orientation programs. "Included," says the Texas Industrial Commission, "is trainee orientation on the free enterprise system and its value to the worker in order to make workers better persons, and their jobs more rewarding."[64] A Commission audio and slide show tells workers:

> We own more automobiles, TV sets, radios, boats, and almost more of everything than all the rest of the people combined. . . . Today, because of the efforts of some groups of social reformers, consumer advocates and other people who find fault with the American

way of life, we are in danger of losing many of the benefits we take for granted. . . . The problem is, when wages go up, the company's bills go up. So in order to still compete with other companies, employees must produce more—work more efficiently—in order to make up the difference.[65]

From billions in tax incentives to subsidized sports stadiums, from job training to industrial revenue financing, our cities and states have become the nation's premier entrepreneurs. But as attractive as these kinds of public bribes may be, they tell only part of the story of what local government does to package people for business. These are the gestures of welcome, only "a kiss" as one General Motors executive described tax abatement. In addition to the incentives of using people's taxes and tailoring their educational system to the needs of business, government officials are now entrepreneuring with another side of people's lives. The vastly different work conditions across the many regions of an immense country are the setting for this even more important act of public entrepreneuring.

# 2
# WHERE THE JOBS
# HAVE GONE:
## The Corporate Geography

Today's aggressive state chase after business has been popularly described by the media as a kind of second coming of the Civil War—the reincarnation of old battles in which the South, remembering its century-old humiliation, finally makes good on its pledge to rise up against the descendants of northern carpetbaggers. Shivering, energy-starved industries are presumably migrating southward in droves, toward a balmy climate and plentiful power, as vengeful "Freeze a Yankee" bumper stickers urge more terror against northern neighbors.

A burgeoning "sun belt," embracing the lower half of the United States and stretching roughly from North Carolina to California, is heralded as the preeminent region of industrial growth, while a frigid northern "cold belt," with its older cities and obsolete industries, is relegated to old-age stasis and permanent decline.

Like an inexhaustible Lazarus, the South has been resurrected again and again. A "New South" was proclaimed after the Civil War, another in the 1920s, and yet another after World War II. The term "New South" now runs the risk of becoming our regional equivalent of the perpetual going-out-of-business sale.

There is however a good deal of truth to the most recent description of southern resurgence. Over the past ten years, and even earlier, the sun belt as a whole, by important measures like rate of job increase, has grown faster relative to the North as a whole. But this broad generality based on climatological "belts" is misleading. To understand regional job shift more accurately one must look at what is happening in individual states.

Over the past eight years many cold belt states grew faster than their sun belt counterparts. Total jobs in North and South Dakota, for example, grew at a faster rate than those in North Carolina, Georgia, or Tennessee. New Hampshire's work force grew faster than every southeastern state including Florida, while Idaho's and Wyoming's grew faster than every sun belt state except Nevada. Manufacturing jobs have followed similar regional patterns of growth.

The growth in absolute numbers of jobs in some northern states may not be as high as some in the South. But rates of job growth, rather than absolute numbers, are a more revealing index of how well a state is doing relative to its population. One hundred thousand new jobs over eight years in a large state like New York is close to stagnation; in New Mexico, it would represent an economic boom.

The most prominent cause for job shifts is not warm climate, but labor conditions and the willingness of state and local governments to make those conditions attractive to industry. There is a persistent correlation between the level of a state's job-growth rate and its level of unionization. Over the past ten years, most of the job growth has shifted to the least unionized parts of the country, both

North and South. 'While government incentives like tax breaks and job training may help to influence where a business decides to locate, labor conditions, especially wages and the level of union power, play an even more prominent role. No state government, North or South, has been able to ignore business's struggle to improve its profitability by dampening the demands of workers.

With labor costs a major factor for many industries, corporate executives tend to search for regional locations where local economic and physical conditions encourage low wages. "Except to expand into new markets or to exploit newly available sources of materials," says *Corporate Financing,* a trade journal of corporate executives, "industry locates (or relocates) plants primarily to obtain the most favorable labor environment." In many southern and northern rural areas, business is able to find a lack of organized labor strength, long distances to jobs, and a lack of work opportunities. These conditions provide what John Greene and Allan Gussak, two New York-based business consultants, recommend as "insularity"—the isolation of workers, physically, mentally, and socially, from influences that might induce them to ask for higher wages.

To achieve "insularity," they advise business executives to look for places with "relative lack of manufacturing employment within easy community distance . . . no high-wage industry within the labor drawing area," and "low-median income, due to seasonality of wage scales." In rural antiunion states, they suggest companies can find large numbers of farmers, hired hands, sharecroppers, recent high-school graduates, dropouts, workers and unemployed . . . "a surplus of population over local job opportunites . . . these populations rarely disappoint."[1]

## Selling Labor Conditions

Business's ability to force workers to accept lower wages and worse conditions has been helped by the aggressive packaging and then merchandising of regressive labor policies by these governments. Advertising as the most eligible candidates for business location, competing governments proudly wear their antilabor positions on their sleeves. "Right-to-Work" states in all regions of the country boast legal restrictions against unions. Workers are described as loyal, hard-working, and most prominently, nonmilitant, nonunion, and low paid.

States barking their antilabor wares through promotional brochures could virtually be using the same format. "Labor- management relations are excellent," says Oklahoma. ". . . Wage rates are considerably below those found in major manufacturing areas."[2] Oklahoma's low level of unionization is then compared with "selected" states like Pennsylvania, Michigan, and New York, where considerably higher percentages of the work force are unionized.

"Work stoppages are almost nil," says South Dakota. "Only 14.4 percent of the working force belong to unions, compared with a national average of 28.4 percent."[3] Texas, comparing its low level of unionization with that of other states, boasts, "The average hourly labor rates are consistently lower than those for the U.S. as a whole . . . only in the petrochemical field does Texas experience rates higher than the national average. . . . Texas has statutes prohibiting union security contracts."[4]

"Virginia is one of the least unionized of the more industrial states," says a publication from the governor's office. "Only six states had a smaller percentage of their non-agricultural work force unionized than Virginia."[5]

"[An] attribute of Utah's labor market," says a state promotional brochure, "is its low labor cost. . . . Utah, with 13.1 percent of the total nonagricultural workers affiliated, has the smallest percentage of union-affiliated workers of any Rocky Mountain state other than Wyoming."[6] A chart points out that in Salt Lake City, secretaries, janitors, laborers, maintenance and construction workers tend to earn less than in a number of other cities in nearby states.

Florida tells prospective business its workers' wages average between 10 to 30 percent less than the rest of the United States. "Labor cost savings," says the state, "whether direct, such as wages and salaries, or indirect, such as the unemployment compensation rate or other supplementary costs, can be realized by locating in Florida."[7]

Colorado, which cannot boast an antilabor "Right-to-Work" law, nevertheless takes pride in its severely restricted union shops. "The Colorado Act," says the state, "is more restrictive than the federal act regarding union shops, requiring 75% of the employees who vote in the bargaining unit to vote for a union shop before an agreement can be entered into requiring union membership as a condition of continued employment."[8]

One of the most blatant antilabor positions of state government is taken by North Carolina. Prospective businesses are sent data to demonstrate the state had less than 7 percent of its nonagricultural workers in unions in 1974 (making it the least unionized state in the country). During the same year, North Carolina's manufacturing workers had the biggest gap in their weekly earnings from the national manufacturing average of any state in the union—these workers earned almost 30 percent less than the average American worker. Construction workers in the state did even worse, taking home a weekly paycheck of about 40 percent less than the national average for similar work.[9]

North Carolina, which is one of the most industrialized of the agricultural states, publicly proclaims the antilabor virtue of its "Right-to-Work" law. The "Right-to-Work" promotion brochure begins by announcing that the law "GUARANTEES employee freedom." Its real antiunion bias then follows. The local law, says North Carolina, "PRESERVES right to manage," "CURBS union monopoly power," "LESSENS union abuses and violence," "REDUCES feather bedding," "INDUCES unions to fulfill contracts," and "FREES employees from labor boss domination."[10] Not surprisingly, with this kind of government-supported vehemence against labor, North Carolina has become a favorite location for an increasing number of industries rotating out of the unionized regions of the country.

Vigorous antilabor competition among the states has had its effect. Now on the defensive, some of the more unionized states are quick to point out that their unionism has "matured," that their unionized workers understand business needs, and that unionism is declining and there is still plenty of cheap labor available within their borders.

Michigan says, "Although hourly labor costs in Michigan are slightly above the national average due to the concentration of large employers in the auto industry, wage rates for placements through the Michigan Employment Security Commission are substantially lower."[11] Oregon, another of the more unionized states, indicates it had less time lost in strikes in the sixties than Washington State, Nevada, or Arizona, and that it has workers willing to start at $2.25 to $3.00 per hour.[12]

The city of New Bedford in Massachusetts labels its people "workers not complainers." Citing a consultant's report that called labor-management arrangements "stable and responsible," it explains, "New Bedford's entry-level wages average $.75 to $1.20 below the national average for many occupational skills." [13] The city's labor relations, says the city's Economic Development Agency, "almost sounds like some utopian fairy tale. . . . Of eight non-union company elections since 1966, two were organized." [14]

Illinois proudly notes, "About 35 percent of the non-agricultural employees are unionized, a percentage that has been declining in recent years." To stress the point, an illustration in the state's promotional brochure depicts a mammoth worker, representing 65 percent of the state's nonunion workers, towering over a small one, representing the 35 percent that are unionized. They also explain that "[b]etween 1972 and 1974, Illinois had the lowest average percentage of union victories in NLRB elections of any state in our upper midwest area." [15]

Some governments package their localities by promoting profit opportunities offered by the special cultural backgrounds or sex of their workers. The Corpus Christi Industrial Commission (Texas), for example, claiming for itself a share in "the last frontier where labor is willing to work," boasts a "large pool of female labor" which it describes as "low cost, unskilled, trainable, with dexterity." [16] The Texas Industrial Commission emphasizes the fact that the number of women in the labor force grew from 27 percent in 1950 to 39 percent in 1970. Arizona, meanwhile, noting its wage rates are below the national average, claims, "The reservation Indian population—the largest in the U.S.—constitutes a substantial and virtually untapped labor pool."

Arizona sells the "innovation" of access to even

cheaper labor across its Mexican border. "The opportunities for investment and production in our sister state
of Sonora [Mexico] are numerous," says the Arizona
governor's office. "Lower labor costs and an untarnished
work ethic make our border areas logical candidates for
those with 'off-shore' production requirements."[17]

New Mexico, which borders the Mexican state of
Chihuahua, makes the incentives of locating near Mexico
more explicit. The two states, says New Mexico in a joint
statement with Chihuahua, work together to help industry
"establish labor intensive operations in Chihuahua and
capital intensive operations in New Mexico. Such across-
the-border businesses profit from Chihuahua's lower costs
and wage rates, along with New Mexico's proximity to
management and markets. The continued advantages and
cooperative services of New Mexico and Chihuahua include low costs and taxes, unemployment rates high
enough to create strong competition for jobs. . . ." The
two development agencies note the Mexican state's "large
and productive labor force available at wages as much as
60 percent lower than American rates." The majority of
the population, they explain, are young and mostly out of
work (48 percent unemployed), providing a prospective
employer with "a long-term labor base."[18]

Officials in some states emphasize high unemployment
rates and other difficulties people have in finding work as
a key attraction to business. In Vermont, where labor
salaries are among the lowest in New England, jobs
increased by over 25 percent during the past eight years—
about the same rate as North Carolina. To outsiders,
Vermont often seems a land of cheese, maple syrup, and
skiing. Actually the state depends on manufacturing as its
most important economic activity; over 25 percent of the
total goods and services produced in Vermont comes

from manufacturing, as against 13 percent from tourism and only 5 percent from agriculture.[19]

Norman Cushman, a state industrial representative, claims that some of the state's success in attracting business is because "people have to drive 30 or 40 miles in rural Vermont and are happy to have jobs." In addition, he says, "We don't have the same problem as other parts of New England. . . . Unions are fragmented, there are small pockets here and there . . . compared with other states we don't have a labor problem." Indeed the state has less than 18 percent of its labor force in unions, ranking it behind a number of southern states. "It is hard," said Cushman, "to get a guy who wants a job to go on strike. When that changes, we'll be like every other state."[20]

While the southern half of the United States contains some of the least unionized states, half of the nation's least unionized states include the Plains states of Kansas, Nebraska, North and South Dakota, the mountain states of Utah, Colorado, Wyoming, and Idaho, and the north-eastern states of Vermont, New Hampshire, and Maine.

South Dakota had less than 12 percent of its non-agricultural work force organized in 1972, about half the national average. In that same year, Kansas was only 15 percent organized, North Dakota 16 percent organized, New Hampshire 7 percent organized, and Vermont 18 percent organized.

In the past eight years, these unorganized regions have grown at the expense of the organized ones (see map page 42). Between 1970 and 1978, the least unionized states (those which were *less* than 20 per cent unionized in 1972) averaged a job growth of almost 40 percent. During the same period, the work force in the remaining states (those that were *more* than 20 percent unionized in 1972) grew by an average of only 23 percent;

in short, the average less unionized state grew almost twice as fast as the more unionized one.

Nationwide per capita job gain statistics support the same conclusion. Between 1970 and 1978, the least unionized states as a whole added double the number of jobs for each of their residents than did the most unionized ones; during the same period the ten least unionized states as a whole added more than *triple* the number of jobs for each of their residents than did the ten most unionized states.[21]

## The Energy Factor

An often-cited reason for regional job shifts is energy costs. But these costs are likely to be a relatively small factor in the movement of most industries. In 1974, for example, the cost of energy in high job-growth states like Florida, Georgia, North Carolina, South Carolina, and South Dakota was comparable to the cost in low job-growth Illinois, Ohio, Michigan, Pennsylvania, and New York. In fact, New Hampshire, Vermont, and Maine, which experienced rapid rates of job growth in the seventies, were also among the highest cost energy states. Job growth in oil and natural-gas-rich states like Oklahoma, Texas, and Louisiana was high during the 1970s, but no higher than that of many states without such resources. States like New Hampshire and Florida, which are not energy rich, grew faster during the 1970s than did Oklahoma, Texas, and Louisiana.

Energy costs are a critical factor in some industrial shifts, but only in a limited number of industries. Petrochemicals, basic metals (steel and aluminum), paper and paperboard, and cement, for example, are "energy-intensive" industries that require enormous quantites of fuel

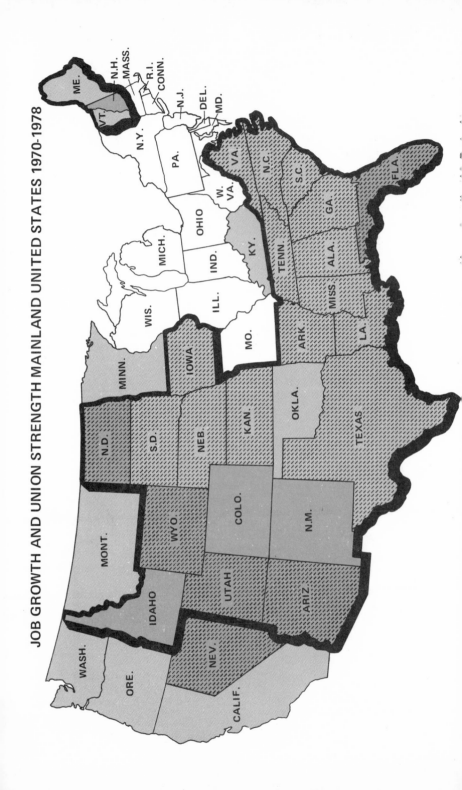

JOB GROWTH AND UNION STRENGTH MAINLAND UNITED STATES 1970-1978

and electricity. Such industries, especially in their newer plants, are more highly automated and generate fewer jobs relative to the amount of money invested in them than "labor-intensive" operations such as textiles, electronics, or services.

In 1975, the eight largest energy-using industries, including blast furnaces, petroleum refining, and industrial chemicals, used close to half of all the country's industrial energy, but employed less than 2 percent of its work force. As energy use by United States manufacturers dropped by 4 percent between 1972 and 1976, the total energy bill went up from $11.7 billion to $27.6 billion. While the number of manufacturing workers went down more than 10 percent during that same period, their total salaries went from $174.2 billion to $233.4 billion.[22]

According to a 1977 report prepared for the United States Department of Labor, "labor is the single most important input into the production of a firm, accounting for approximately sixty percent of all input payments on a

less than 24% job growth 1970-78

more than 24% job growth 1970-78

more than 40% job growth 1970-78

least unionized states
(20% or less of a state's workforce were in unions in the early 1970s)

states with antiunion shop, "right-to-work" laws

national basis."[23] If the disproportionate energy use of the energy-intensive industries is discounted, the dominance of manpower costs over energy costs becomes even greater. On a national basis, energy costs for all industries excluding the eight largest energy-using industries were approximately only 4 percent of expenses.

In looking at energy costs as a factor in regional job shift it is also important to remember that the job shift began much before the 1973 energy crisis, dating to at least 1965, and for some industries, such as textiles, furniture, and leather, even before. And in looking at warm climate as a factor it is also important to remember that for decades the migration of the rural poor from the warm South to the cold North followed basic economic motives—as did the movement of Puerto Ricans from their balmy climate to northern industrial cities. The movement of southern Europeans to the northern United States years before and the recent movement of migrant workers from southern Europe, Turkey, and the Middle East to northern European countries follow a similar motivation. Energy costs are not unimportant, but the availability of jobs has been, and continues to be, a prime reason for population shifts.

## The Green Migration

Within the overall industrial movement to antilabor regions there has been a conscious effort by many companies to locate in small rural towns. In these areas business is hoping to further avoid the labor organizing that has been traditionally centered in larger urban areas. In Georgia, for example, new plants have tended to locate in white, rural, fringe areas and small towns; in Kentucky, the state's highest manufacturing growth rates in the sixties were in smaller areas; in Texas new factories are often located in old farming communities.[24] In textiles, the migration to "green" country regions has been a flood tide; by 1970 three out of four workers in textile mills were in the countryside.[25]

Conscious of industry's new preference for rural locations, some states have nudged their local rural areas to compete more aggressively for industrial suitors. In South Carolina, for example, local communities of under 15,000 people are given special inducements to become part of what the governor's office calls its GREAT TOWN program. Admission to the program, an acronym for the Governor's Rural Economic Achievement Trophy, means a place on a "priority list" of localities which the state sends to prospective industries looking for sites. To win a place on the GREAT TOWN list, a rural community must, in addition to other projects like grooming its appearance and producing promotional brochures, create an organization to help finance private industrial development. "Once the community has completed these elements," says Robert E. Leak, director of the State Development Board, "an evaluation team made up of professional development representatives will examine what the community has accomplished. If this team agrees that the community is prepared for industrial prospects, then the community will be designated a GREAT TOWN."[26]

During the sixties urban experts prophesied a continued growth trend in America's metropolitan areas. But the prophecies were wrong; America's small cities and rural towns are now growing 40 percent faster than its metropolitan areas.[27] In just five years, between 1970 and 1975, almost 2 million people migrated to America's green areas.

Not only is the trend toward rural areas, but it is to the *most* rural of them; the highest rates of migration, according to Calvin A. Beale, a demographer for the Department of Agriculture, are to the counties which have the lowest population densities—less than ten people per square mile. The "cities" with the largest growth since 1970 have been those with less than 2,500 people.[28]

The movement of manufacturing jobs to rural areas in the South is not new; what is new is the extent to which it has accelerated. While almost three out of four Americans lived in metropolitan areas in 1970, only slightly more than half the people in the Southeast lived in these areas. Except for Florida and Georgia, job growth in southeastern metropolises during the sixties was actually less than in other cities in the rest of the nation.[29] By the early seventies, many of the formerly fast-growing central cities in the South and Southwest were actually losing population: Fort Worth lost one out of twelve residents; Atlanta lost one out of eleven.[30]

The southern trend toward rural development was visible at least as far back as 1899, when 30 percent of southern plants were in the countryside. By the 1950s, well over 40 percent of the industrial plants were in green areas; by the sixties the figure reached 50 percent. By the late sixties, cities and towns with less than 25,000 people and the less populated areas beyond them were hosting two-thirds of the South's new manufacturing growth.[31]

Not only is this greenward movement happening in traditional rural industrial states like North and South Carolina, but it is even found in the more urban states in the South like Tennessee, where industry once tended toward urban areas. Between 1950 and 1973, rural counties in Tennessee were growing almost six times as fast as metropolitan areas.[32]

The Conference Board, a New York-based research

arm of the major American corporations, recently made the rural-urban growth distinction for potential sun belt investors. With the growth rate in southern metropolitan areas declining, said the Conference Board in 1977, and increasing in its rural areas, "would-be investors should proceed cautiously and selectively before committing themselves to any metropolitan area in the South. . . . It is the *non*metropolitan South that warrants new investments, an important change from the past."[33]

While many northern metropolitan areas lost workers during the 1960s, many of its rural areas were growing rapidly. The labor force in the southern countryside grew by 21 percent during that time and the North's rural labor force was not far behind, increasing by 16 percent. By the early 1970s, the green migration in both the North and the South accelerated, as rural businesses added more than half a million workers a year, growing twice as fast as the country's metropolitan areas.

In spite of the much proclaimed decline of the Northeast, there has been sustained growth in many of the region's rural areas. The industrial boom in southern New Hampshire and in northern Vermont's Chittenden County has been especially pronounced. Low levels of unionization and low wage rates have been a prominent attraction in both states. Between 1964 and 1974, New Hampshire ranked second in the nation in relative loss of union membership, declining from 20 percent of its nonfarm workers to only 15 percent. Vermont's 18 percent unionized labor force is equally attractive to business. "A signal asset of Vermont's growth," said *The New Englander,* a business promotion journal, "is the docile, effective work force. There are few unions in the region, and the ones that operate there are far from militant."[34]

In manufacturing jobs, the green migration during the

1960s was even more dramatic. Between 1960 and 1970 production jobs in America's rural areas grew almost three times as fast as those in its metropolitan areas. By the early seventies, metropolitan areas actually began to show a net job loss, as the movement of industrial jobs to green areas continued to accelerate. By 1973, 25 percent of all American manufacturing jobs were already in the countryside.[35] If the trends continue, over a third of all manufacturing jobs will be in rural areas by 1980.

Even the dominance of the metropolis as a stronghold of service-oriented, white-collar jobs has slipped. By the 1960s, the growth of service jobs in urban areas still outpaced that in the countryside. But in the early 1970s, the situation reversed; by 1973, white-collar jobs in the countryside were growing almost 30 percent faster than in the metropolis.[36]

Jobs are shifting to more rural areas of America, not because business has suddenly discovered the attractiveness of rural life-styles and open space. Business decisions are firmly rooted in profit margins. While it may often be cheaper to build physical facilities in rural areas, the major costs of most industries, as indicated earlier, are still overwhelmingly their labor costs. Business's movement to the countryside is primarily a function of its attempt to cut these costs.

The popular explanations of America's economic crisis as an "urban crisis" or a crisis of a North-South shift are misleading and have distorted our perception of some of the country's real economic problems. They give the impression that there are "healthy" regions and "sick" regions, with the obvious solution the administration of additional plasma, through more liberal federal re-distribution formulae, to the sick regions. They follow the same empty programs, which in the 1950s and 1960s declared that an "urban crisis" was upon the land, and solutions were presented to prop up these cities as though the act of helping them would make an entire country healthy again.

Business does not need either the city or rural areas, either northern or southern regions, as the exclusive geography for its activities, but can instead move freely between areas of maximum opportunity, taking advantage of the regional competition it fosters as its migration wreaks havoc with local economic conditions. No pocket of the country, rural or urban, can remain immune to the effects of this shifting.

Today's green migration continues business's historic tradition of avoiding any specific regional, urban, rural, or size bias in its strategies; it has instead carefully tried to locate its operations in the most profitable geography for the historic moment. Just as business now tends to locate in rural areas, no amount of open space or country lifestyle will keep it from shifting back to urban areas, if wages and public incentives in these urban areas are made attractive enough. Successful business people are neither liberal nor conservative, urban- nor rural-oriented, North- nor South-oriented; they are business people, and they move their operations where the action suits them best. Success for business has historically meant avoiding simple ideological commitments to either smallness or bigness, to city or countryside, but a pragmatic adherence to the rule of profit.

As a result, problems supposedly the exclusive preserve of big city life have now moved to the country, or more accurately, they've become homogenized throughout the land. Lost in the drama of New York City is the fact that some of New York state's greatest unemployment and welfare problems were in the more rural upstate areas. The state's budget division in 1976 reported the home relief case load was rising almost three times as much upstate as it was in the city.[37] The 1970 census showed almost 10 percent of the state's rural population living below the poverty line, with the number rising.[38] In 1974, a presidential report to the Congress stated that government per capita expenditures for human resources, primarily for welfare and Social Security, were highest in the country's rural areas.[39] Between 1973 and 1974 the number of people on welfare in Chicago, Detroit, Houston, Los Angeles, Philadelphia, and New York has gone down, while rising in the nation's smaller cities and rural areas.[40] In 1977 almost 10 million people below the official poverty line were living in the countryside, over 650,000 more than in the central cities.[41]

The myths of "upstate" and "downstate" interests, separate urban and rural economies, life-styles, and politics have made for the popularization of urban problems as though they were some unique disease quarantined from the problems of Appalachia, rural Vermont, and the industrialized hinterlands of the South. Supposedly conservative rural states like Iowa, Kansas, North Dakota, Idaho, and Vermont make per capita welfare payments to their recipients that are as high as more urbanized "liberal" New Jersey, Pennsylvania, Ohio, Massachusetts, Connecticut, Rhode Island, and Michigan. Nebraska, Iowa, Oklahoma, Texas, North and South Dakota, and Montana all provide for higher Medicaid payments than either Massachusetts, Ohio, or New Jersey.[42]

The national crisis today has been caused by industrialization and business expansion into rural and urban regions throughout America. The regional homogenization of economic problems climaxes the long-term shift from a nation characterized by family farming and small-scale individual entrepreneurship to a nation dominated by wage earners, concentrated private economic power, and government entrepreneurship on a massive scale.

As business continues its green migration, the ways and economic life of the countryside are coming to mirror those of the city. The tableau of the farm worker leaving the homestead to find better economic opportunity in the big city is already a picture of the distant past. What more accurately portrays both urban and rural life now are dependence on corporate factory jobs, maintenance and office work, and dependence on government unemployment compensation, public "workfare" jobs, welfare, and Medicaid. Government housing subsidies have become as necessary in the countryside as they are in the cities; our urban slums now find their rural counterparts in the mobile homes of the new aluminum ghettos.

# 3
# REGIONAL ROTATION:
# Harvest of the Losers and Winners

". . . Senator Daniel Patrick Moynihan, his face red and his arms flailing, said that the S.E.C. [Securities and Exchange Commission] owed the banks 'an apology.' He added that the S.E.C.'s bias against Wall Street and the banking and investment community, as expressed in the report looked as if it came from 'a teaching aid provided for a Moscow school system.'

"The Senator said that the banks were only 'guilty of innocence' during the 1975 city crisis."
> —*New York Times* Report of Hearings before the Senate Banking Committee, December 16, 1977.[1]

"People don't want housing in the South Bronx, or they wouldn't burn it down."
> —Press Conference, Senator Daniel P. Moynihan[2]

"I'm a liberal Democrat with a quarter-century involvement in the politics of this party and with the inevitable experience of having found that a great many things we thought and believed in didn't turn out to be."
> —Senator Daniel P. Moynihan[3]

52

In the early 1960s, as the cities edged precipitously toward economic crisis, architects and planning experts were enlisted by business leaders and politicians in an attempt to unravel a difficult paradox; while business needed a population of low-paid workers in these cities, it wished at the very same time they weren't there at all. Workers were needed for factories, and increasingly, to service office buildings, apartment houses, stores, and restaurants. Business also needed a pool of lower-paid and unemployed workers as a visible threat to higher paid ones; "a reserve army," as Marx called it, that could always replace higher paid workers, should their demands become too great.

But not only was the housing for a vast number of poor people physically unattractive, the entire process of maintaining the poor had become increasingly dangerous. The poor were becoming more vocal and visible in their actions, threatening the established social order. The problems of safety and urban attractiveness were important ones for managerial and professional personnel who were filling roles in a growing marketing, government, and service economy that was coming to characterize cities across the country. The planning experts' dilemma was essentially how to make the poor most useful and invisible.

Their solution was to give the middle class a choice of locations in both the cities and the suburbs, while at the same time attempting to diffuse the social and visual impact of the poor by means of welfare programs and slum beautification. Entire city neighborhoods were to be recycled from poor to middle and upper class, while access to the suburbs was to be improved with massive programs for new urban highways. Those of the poor who were relocated and those low-income communities that remained were to be spruced up with "poverty wars,"

Model City, and anticrime programs. The poor would remain, but pacified and hidden behind a facade of social reconstruction.

The now-you-see-them, now-you-don't approach was perhaps epitomized by a 1960s' proposal, supervised by an American Institute of Architects urban design team. Illustrated with attractive sketches of tree-lined highways slicing through the slums, the proposal suggested that these sections, euphemistically called "gray areas" and "gray zones," be shielded from the view of people driving to and from the city.

"Gray areas are vital functional and physical adjuncts to the center of the city," said the proposal. "Perhaps the real defect of the gray zone is that we see too much of it. . . . If the gray area is too frequently visible, too depressing because it is too much in our presence, perhaps we can arrange our major routes to avoid it, to bypass it, to give us views of the parts of the city we hold in high esteem."[4]

These urban-design efforts were not very effective. Despite the best efforts of the planners, the poor stubbornly remained visible, both physically and especially politically. Neighborhood groups, often with the help of leftist organizers, fought and became increasingly successful at disrupting urban renewal programs, zoning changes, rent increases, and highway projects that would have forced them out.

In New York City, a highway plan promoted by David Rockefeller for lower Manhattan was stopped; an enormous $400 million convention center in San Francisco delayed for more than ten years; a half-billion-dollar, six-lane highway that would have circled Boston and other inner cities halted; and an enormous downtown Boston development project delayed for years. Rent strikes and actions by tenants' groups in that city had been so effective that the city's biggest housing developer brought a legal conspiracy case against hundreds of his tenants, charging they were depriving him of his property rights.

In Chicago, Philadelphia, Baltimore, and other cities all over the country, scores of attempts to remodel cities to fit business needs were met with pitched battles. In the early seventies, Anthony Downs, chairman of one of the country's more influential real estate research corporations, stated: "local political resistance to large scale renewal will remain so intense in the future that few local governments will begin new projects."[5]

## A Shift in Urban Programs

At the same time that community opposition to urban renewal was growing, the federal dollars to fund these programs began to dry up. Faced with an increasing bill for the war in Vietnam and the decline of the national economic growth that generated federal tax dollars, Washington's urban presence began to fade. By the mid-sixties David Rockefeller, one of the prime financial supporters of urban renewal, had already sounded the retreat; between the needs of the cities and the needs of the war, he informed a congressional committee in 1966, the war should take precedence.[6] Nixon, a more conservative standard-bearer, was elected none too soon; he would rescue the faltering economy from the liberals' Vietnam debacle and rearrange their ailing urban strategy.

The formulation of the new urban approach was charged to Daniel P. Moynihan, Nixon's top urban advisor. Moynihan's political career is characterized not so much by any philosophical consistency as by his astute ability to drift easily and quickly to political ideas on the ascendance. When Kennedy generated a poverty war in the cities, Moynihan rode that wave, supporting and administering federal aid to the urban poor. When Kennedy, and later Johnson, moved the nation deeper into war in Vietnam, Moynihan responded with a proposal to channel the poor toward the war effort. "I would hold," he said, in 1966, as the bloodshed in Vietnam escalated, "that a whole generation of poor Negroes and Whites are missing their chance to get in touch with American society. Once they pass through and beyond the Selective Service screen," Moynihan continued, "they are very nearly done for in terms of the opportunity to become genuinely functioning, self-sufficient individuals. . . . Very possibly our best hope is seriously to use the armed forces as a socializing experience for the poor—particularly the Southern poor—until somehow their environments begin turning out equal citizens."[7]

Later, as a Nixon advisor, Moynihan adroitly adopted the conservative ideas of Edward Banfield, his former Harvard colleague (who would also become a Nixon advisor), to develop his famous "benign neglect" approach to the problems of the urban poor. Banfield's ideas became the theoretical underpinning for the Moynihan-Nixon disassembly of the liberal policies of the previous administrations, many of which Moynihan himself had once championed.

Banfield called for replacing government poverty programs with what he called the "powerful accidental forces" of the economy. "Because capital tends to increase by geometric progression," wrote Banfield, "a rich country becomes exceedingly rich in the span of a few years." Through continued economic growth, he explained, the city's poor would automatically be pushed into the middle class. Inside a generation, poverty as we know it, said Banfield, would disappear.

The key to this program was a drastic reduction in welfare and a new respect for low wages to fuel the city's historic mission of economic growth: ". . . a ceasing to harass private employers who offer low wages and unattractive (but not unsafe) working conditions for workers as an alternative to unemployment."

The liberals' concern for upgrading the conditions of the poor, *while they were poor,* according to Banfield, was misguided. The city, in fact, *had* to have slumlike qualities in order to house the poor who were needed in business and industries. "In order to grow fast," he said, "the city had to become a center of warehouses, shops, and factories, which meant it had to have a plentiful supply of housing that such labor could afford. If all the housing had been decent by the standards of the time," said Banfield, "some of the labor required for the city's growth could not have afforded to live in the city at all."

The nature of economic growth in the cities meant each city competing against other cities, attempting to maintain the lowest standards possible in order to attract business growth. No city, said Banfield, "could have added very much to its wage bill without worsening its economic position vis-a-vis other areas."[8]

Banfield's callous urban strategy was based on an accurate reading of the historic role of the city's low-wage labor force. His approach was adopted by Nixon in the late sixties, and has become the most pragmatic politics of the present. It is openly adopted not only by conservatives, but liberals whom the press dubbed "fiscal conservatives." Many liberal politicians who once mocked such approaches have learned to make political capital out of exhorting constituents to think about less, to accept the imperatives of economic growth, and to increase public competition to aid business.

Liberal support for this strategy was caused by the

failure of economic projections like Banfield's. American hegemony over world markets has been weakened—Banfield's facile prediction of sustained economic growth didn't come true. Through "benign neglect," the number of urban poor in the cities did not shrink, but continued to grow. By 1974, in spite of reduced populations in most big cities, the number of people in them living below the poverty level had increased beyond what it had been ten years before.[9] And by 1977, the percentage of all Americans officially living below the poverty line remained about the same as it was in 1969.[10]

## The Shape of Regional Rotation

The chance that a new sleight of hand can make the cities a pacified holding area for the poor, while creating an urban "renaissance" for the middle class is now much less possible than it was in the sixties. With the decline in economic growth rates, the new face of the business-supported urban policy has become much leaner and more harsh; its slums must be cheaper than rural slums, its workers must be more willing to accept lower salaries than low-paid workers in other parts of the country. Business has now stepped up its strategy of holding jobs in one region hostage to those in another; the "new respect for low wages" that Banfield thought necessary through official government policy can be achieved simply by getting local governments themselves, in different regions, to compete against each other with conditions that drive wages down. By either threatening to, or actually moving from city to rural area or suburb, or from one state to another, business is attempting to create more hospitable conditions for itself in all regions of the country.

The process resembles crop rotation, a farming technique where total crop yield is increased by leaving some lands fallow while others are planted for harvest. By leaving the fallow regions, business adds to the reserve of low-paid and unemployed workers and poorly maintained communities in the country. Far from being abandoned, the cities and states in these fallow regions are being put through a process of enrichment for later use on more favorable terms to business.

The effect of withdrawing the older, higher wage and higher public-service-cost areas from their former prominence in the production system is to make them more disciplined and manageable places for future production. As business migrates or threatens to migrate, these more mature cities and regions take on the economic and psychological qualities of losers, in their entrepreneurial battles against the expanding "winner" cities and regions. Forced to abandon their former drive for better wages, working conditions, and public services, the losers must concentrate instead on the essentials of survival by offering business more public subsidies, tax abatements, no-strike pledges, and lower wages in competition with similar offers from the winners.

Like crop rotation, the process is not a static one. As the winner cities and regions expand, they too will begin to resemble the current mature areas; rising expectations in the winners will result in demands for better wages, improved environmental conditions, and public services. At this point, with land costs in the losers lowered, with their remaining workers hungrier, business's interest is likely to be rekindled. As the demands of the winners increase, the current losers can be rotated back as production centers at a more primitive state of economic demand; alternatively, business can threaten to move back to the losers, in order to reduce the demands of the winners.

Business has found it relatively easy to get people and their governments to participate in this rotation process. There are vast regions of the country where unemployment is high, where organized labor is weak, where enormous numbers of people live outside the mainstream economy, and where three dollars an hour is more than most adults ever made in their lives. When business moves to these new regions it not only gains an immediate source of cheaper labor, but more importantly, it promotes an advantageous longer-term antagonism between workers, environmentalists, and politicians in all regions. As workers compete against each other for the available jobs, they check each others' demands for higher wages or for costly business investments to improve their working or environmental conditions. And as politicians compete with each other to attract industry, they escalate the financial, environmental, and antilabor incentives they must each offer.

It was not long after job growth stalled in New York, New Jersey, and Pennsylvania that officials in these states began to announce the curtailment of environmental progress. When steel companies threatened to close in 1978, Pennsylvania politicians declared a delay in the pollution control timetable for that industry. In New York the state responded to job growth loss with a vigorous new attitude. "It will do little good if we rescue our environment at the expense of our economy," said Governor Hugh Carey. "Anyone who doesn't agree with that principle," he threatened, "won't be working for this administration." At about the same time in neighboring New Jersey, Governor Brendan Byrne announced plans to lower air pollution standards in certain parts of South Jersey, arguing he was convinced the state could still meet federal standards, "while lowering the cost of doing business."[11]

The need for local politicians to attract and keep their always movable private jobs makes them attempt to position their competitors as permanent loser regions. This becomes especially important as the national economy tightens, and as the costs of providing public services increase. As this occurs, each winning government is forced to protect its own low level of public expenditures for social services, and increasing costs for business incentives, by making sure other governments are not able to obtain more public money to be used to compete against them.

When New York City was trying to get federal aid during its mid-seventies financial crisis, for example, politicians from competing regions, joining with business leaders, used the opportunity to force the city to reduce its budget and cut back on public services. "This is not a divorce proceeding, you know," said Georgia's Governor George D. Busbee, "where you're going to give alimony to the wife according to the manner of living she's become accustomed to." "You can't sustain what you're accustomed to now," said the Georgia governor responding to a New York State official's request for help in Washington, "and you're going to have to make some changes." [12]

With the new austerity measures taken by the losers, business is able, at least over the short future, to reap profitable rewards. The prospect of capturing a share of business's migrating jobs, or trying to hold the ones they already have, can open public treasuries for financing business ventures, marshal local opinion into antilabor actions, and force labor itself to cut wages.

It is not necessary for business actually to move to new regions to make regional rotation effective. What is important is a credible ability to move to them. By demonstrating it can move at will—not only to new regions in this country, but to other countries as well—it gives force and substance to its demands from labor, politicians, and environmentalists. Business now does not have to raise its voice very high to be heard. The precedents of places like Detroit, New York, or Youngstown, Ohio, hang conveniently and ominously over bargaining tables.

### Extortion as Fertilizer

The case of the Millers Falls Company, a hand tool producer in western Massachusetts, illustrates the terrible effectiveness of regional rotation. The hundred-year-old company, located in the small town of Greenfield, had once been one of the largest employers in that part of the state. But since the fifties, when the company employed 1,300 workers, little new investment was put into the plant and the number of workers steadily declined. In 1962, Millers Falls was bought by the multinational Ingersoll-Rand. In the fall of 1976, with only half the 1950s' work force remaining, Millers Falls president James Mitchell publicly announced he was looking at sites in North Carolina and Connecticut and was considering moving.

His announcement brought a quick visit by Massachusetts Governor Michael Dukakis. The company president explained that property taxes and wages were higher in Massachusetts than in alternative states. "If we are going to invest in a replacement," said Mitchell, after the meeting with the governor, "should we invest in Massachusetts?"

The meeting was followed by a promise of state assistance from the governor. The state helped persuade the union at Millers Falls to negotiate new wage and benefit conditions, and offered $285,000 in state money to secure another $775,000 from the federal government's Economic Development Administration to help prepare a new building site. Meanwhile, Deerfield, an adjacent town, offered the company thirty acres, ten more than the company itself was asking for. The town also agreed to use its tax-exempt status to help Millers Falls raise a million dollars at low interest to pay for part of a new $3.7 million plant. "We decided to give the Sunbelt a run for the money," said John F. Ciesla, chairman of Deerfield's industrial development commission.

It was the Millers Falls workers who would be asked to run most for their money. The company's president, after announcing the possible move, then suggested his workers take a $1.50 an hour pay cut and agree to givebacks in their worker-incentive program. The union, the United Electrical, Radio, and Machine Workers of America (UE), whose members were already earning forty cents an hour less than the average for southern New England, refused to negotiate.

The company, meanwhile, continued its threats to leave. At one point Mitchell called the workers together on the factory floor. "We told them face to face it wasn't a bluff," he later explained. "We said that unless the union at least agreed to talk to us we'd all lose."

Three months later, after bitter negotiations, the union backed off its hard line. It agreed to the givebacks in the worker-incentive program (though less severe than the company originally proposed) and to a four-year contract with no pay increases. The union's decision represented the union's forced choice to preserve jobs in exchange for a smaller paycheck. "We feel we submitted to extortion," said UE organizer John Cage. "The company says you submit or we throw you out and turn this town into a ghost town."[13]

After the settlement, Millers Falls president Mitchell

claimed that after four years, his workers will be within fifty cents an hour of competitive workers in the South. One sixty-one-year-old welder, who earned about $160 per week before the settlement, now earned about $145. Another worker who had been at the plant for thirty years was taking home $130 per week.

## A Budding Crop

By the early 1970s, the harvest of business's earlier regional job shifting was already producing results. Observing the accelerated movement of low-paying textile jobs back to northern states like New Hampshire, Vermont, and Maine, two partners of Industry Research, a plant-location consulting firm, explained the advantages of regional abandonment and reclamation in disciplining local attitudes toward business. "[I]ndustry is returning," they said, "in many cases attracted, ironically enough, by the low levels to which industry's defection ultimately depressed wages. And the old militant unionism that many people blamed for the disaster is remembered as a bitter not-to-be-repeated lesson. . . . Such moves argue at least a new-found economic equivalence with the South for such footloose, labor-intensive industries."[14]

By the late 1970s, apparel jobs, while declining overall in New England, had selectively increased in the states where they were least unionized and lowest paid. In Maine, New Hampshire, and Vermont, apparel manufacturing jobs increased by 30 percent between 1972 and 1979.[15] Meanwhile, other states and cities in the late 1970s were also beginning to emerge as a bountiful crop of regional rotation.

In New York City, the drying up of construction work during the mid-1970s dampened construction workers' demands. By the end of 1977 the bricklayers' union had taken a 14 percent cut. During that same year, Peter Brennan, president of the Building and Construction Trades Council of Greater New York, accompanying New York's Mayor Abraham Beame to Houston, told oil executives that the city's construction unions would be willing to produce no-strike pledges for companies locating in the city. The mayor himself held out offers of tax forgiveness, low-cost loans, and the public construction of facilities needed by the oil companies.[16]

By 1976, the declining wage rates of factory workers in New York were being touted by city officials as an inducement to industry. During that year, manufacturing jobs reversed their enormous six-year decline and even began to show modest increases. According to Herbert Bienstock, the regional head of the Bureau of Labor Statistics, the rise resulted from New York's workers receiving fewer wage gains and becoming more competitive with the rest of the country.[17] At the end of 1977, New York City's Business Marketing Corporation, created to lure firms to that city, was able to extol the fact that wages for clerical workers were declining relative to other cities.[18]

In 1978 business leaders continued to promote the city's new ability to compete. Noting that manufacturing wage rates in New York City were rising more slowly than the rest of the country, Karen Gerard, a Chase Manhattan Bank vice-president, explained that the city's manufacturing jobs had begun to rise. "[C]lerical wage rates are also increasing less rapidly than in the nation," said Gerard, "and are now comparable with those in many competing communities."[19] By mid-1978, wages in New York City had increased only 1.6 percent, compared to almost 8 percent in the West and more than 8 percent in the South.[20]

In New Jersey, where four business taxes were repealed and where wage rates trailed the national average by 20 percent, new businesses were incorporated in 1978 at a record pace, with job gains across most of the state's industries.[21] By the end of 1978, Camden, New Jersey, a city with half its population on either welfare or Social Security, reported a net gain of seven new industries. Citing the narrowing labor, tax, and land-cost differences between Camden and other parts of the country, and "the kind of incentives the Southern states use to entice industry out of the North," the financial pages of the *New York Times* explained that "Camden and other cities like it have found that hell may have a floor."

In the bleak, vacant-lot-pocked topography of Camden, where unemployment was double the national rate, business had the option of a large pool of low-wage labor, industrial land for as little as $1,000 an acre, twenty-five-year-old factories selling for a tenth the cost of building new ones, and long periods of public tax abatements.[22]

In Connecticut, regional rotation brought increased pressure to escalate state incentives for business. At the beginning of 1978, Governor Ella T. Grasso proposed doubling the $500 the state gave industry for every new private job created, a 25 percent reduction in corporate tax on new investment, and a state and local government offer of an 80 percent real estate tax break for new business.

New York State promised even more. "Who says the grass is greener in Greenwich?" the state proclaimed in full-page ads in several business magazines. "Up until a few years ago," the state Department of Commerce confessed, "wherever a businessman looked, the grass was always greener outside New York. And to a large degree it was. But not anymore." New York was now offering a host of tax incentives that many states, especially southern states, weren't.[23]

The abandonment of Pennsylvania as an investment region was also beginning to produce results. By 1978, the state, with the nation's next to lowest record of job growth in the preceeding eight years, was providing industry with low-interest revenue bonds worth almost a billion dollars a year, in addition to sizable tax abatements and other incentives. "I'm not even going to wait till I take office to sell the 'New Pennsylvania' to business," the state's governor-elect Richard Thornburgh announced in early 1979, promising business continued public incentives and still lower corporate taxes.[24]

Meanwhile, at the Volkswagen plant in New Stanton, Pennsylvania, where the state was providing the company with incentives worth over $100 million, union workers were being forced to accept wages 20 percent lower than elsewhere in the auto industry. Six months after the factory opened its doors, in October, 1978, 2,000 workers went on a wildcat strike in defiance of the national UAW's agreement with the company. They were forced back to work with few gains, when the company threatened to close the state-subsidized plant.[25]

## Stop and Go Jobs with the Taxpayer's Help

The process of regional rotation now occurring among the regions of this country is actually part of a broader pattern of job shifting and corporate investment strategies that has developed over the past fifteen years. Lured by even more attractive labor conditions and government incentives in Latin America, Asia, and other parts of the world, many American corporations have, since the mid-1960s, accelerated their movement of jobs to foreign countries. A 1976 study for the United States State Department noted that over 1 million jobs were exported during the late 1960s and early 1970s.[26]

The recent movement of jobs to new regions within America can sometimes be simply a brief stopover on the journey to even lower wage and environmentally less restrictive regions outside the country. During the early 1970s many firms, especially in the electronics industries, once content with attractive public incentives and labor conditions in some southern states, began to move their operations to even more enticing places overseas. Electronics companies in Mississippi, Arkansas, and Texas closed their United States shops and moved to Mexico. In Memphis, Tennessee, an RCA TV production plant with 4,000 employees, one of the mid-South's biggest plants, closed its doors and moved to Taiwan. The company had moved to the Memphis location only five years before, when it closed a similar plant in Bloomington, Indiana.[27]

Whether jobs are shifted to unorganized and incentive-proffering regions in this country or abroad, the basic effect is often the same: American workers and their local governments are forced to compete more vigorously, to offer more lucrative public incentives, fewer environmental regulations, and cheaper labor. And while brief regional stopovers might at first seem an expensive way of doing business, these moves, with the help of government incentives and tax programs, can be a relatively painless way to maintain profits.

When they move to a new location, companies benefit by tax lures, training, and other incentives provided by local government. Through the use of generous tax deductions for expenses, and tax credits to "stimulate" investment, companies can also write off the costs of building new facilities and abandoning old ones, transpor-

tation costs and payments to consultants and other personnel involved in finding new locations. In many cases
equipment can be saved by shipping it from the closed
plant to new locations in this country or abroad; again the
costs of this movement are taken as tax deductions—with
the public absorbing part of the costs through lost tax
revenue. Even in the few cases where abandoned workers
are compensated—as in the case of a 1962 federal
program to provide benefits to some workers losing their
jobs because of increased foreign imports—the public
again bears the brunt by having to pay for most of the
retraining and extended unemployment benefits.

## Rationalizing Rotation

When liberal planners, academics, and media people
provided respectable rationalizations for devastating urban renewal and highway building schemes during the
1950s and 1960s, they translated schemes for the wholesale destruction of low-income neighborhoods into theories of "urban renaissance." Today, a similar battery of
experts and the media are explaining business's devastating abandonment of the cities as "planned shrinkage,"
and the precursor of yet another renaissance. As segments of the media now exhort politicians and workers in
loser regions to dampen their demands and to make
themselves more competitive, many experts proclaim that
the abandonment of loser cities and regions can actually
be an attractive opportunity.

Professional urban planning theories to support abandonment and reclamation generally favor the idea of
"mothballing" parts of the cities, until these cities become
more attractive to business. A program of deliberately
cutting back on public services in the most deteriorated

(i.e., the poorest) sections of the cities is called for during the abandonment period to explicitly encourage the remaining population to leave, by moving either to low-income areas in other parts of the country, or to those parts of the cities where they can be more inexpensively taken care of by governments.

George Sternlieb, head of the Center for Urban Policy Research at Rutgers University and an influential consultant to government, posed the mothballed city to a group of financial leaders and urban planning experts. Discussing how a new federal urban development bank might approach city problems, he noted:

> . . . it should view the city very much the way we viewed the development of the bomb shelter or fallout shelter program. There is a finite possibility of a need to utilize them. The question, then, of public policy, is what is the least-cost approach that is politically feasible to preserve an infrastructure so that if, as, and when there is a public recognition, desire, and necessity to reutilize them, there is something left to reutilize?[28]

Anthony Downs, head of the Real Estate Research Board, a consultant to the federal Department of Housing and Urban Development, many city redevelopment agencies, in addition to the RAND Corporation and the Standard Oil Company, developed a similar strategy. "It's not necessarily bad," advises Downs, "for land parcels cleared in renewal areas to remain vacant for long periods of time." "Society," he said, "can be viewed as 'banking' this land for potential future use whenever changed local conditions stimulate increased demand there."

As a strategy for the future, Downs suggests what he calls "a modified form of triage," an idea he adopted from

French military strategy during World War I. At the time, French army doctors would operate only on those wounded soldiers whom they decided stood a good chance of survival. Those who would probably survive without surgery, or those whom the doctors felt were lost causes, were given pain killers and left to their own devices.

"This strategy," recommends Downs, "means there would be no large expenditures for upgrading efforts in most parts of very deteriorated areas. . . . Eventually, after the very deteriorated areas are almost totally vacant, they may be redeveloped with wholly different uses."

"Many local officials have privately admitted to me," says Downs, "that they have decided to quit spending sizeable public funds trying to upgrade the most deteriorated areas of their cities. . . . But they will almost never admit publicly they have decided to 'write off' such neighborhoods, since they would naturally infuriate the people who still live there."[29]

City officials have increasingly shown less need to be circumspect about their own forms of strategic abandonment. In late 1976, Stewart Forbes, a former real estate businessman who was deputy development director of the Boston Redevelopment Authority, picked up on an old Daniel P. Moynihan theme and told a congressional committee that "benign neglect" must be the approach used for declining neighborhoods.

Earlier that year, Roger Starr, then head of New York City's Housing and Development Administration, called for what he termed "planned shrinkage" of the city through the systematic reduction of schools, fire stations, and hospitals in poor neighborhoods.

The next year, following Jimmy Carter's dramatic walking-in-the-rubble tour of the South Bronx, Allan R. Talbot, executive director of New York City's private

Housing and Planning Council, wrote the president advising against any precipitous building undertaking. Most of the area, said Talbot, should simply be cleaned up, made into parks, open space, and other "interim uses until basic economic forces change." Defending Starr and Talbot's strategies for neighborhoods like the South Bronx (strategies vehemently denounced by local community leaders), *Business Week* commented, "In the end, planned shrinkage turns out to be anything but a counsel of despair."[30] *Fortune* editor Gurney Breckenfeld also lent support for rationalizing this process. ". . . the truly shocking aspect of city shrinkage," said Breckenfeld, "the bombed-out look of half-abandoned slums in the older metropolis, can be viewed as an opportunity, too. As a rule it means that the worst neighborhoods are emptying out because the region as a whole has ample housing (though not, in most cases, at agreeably low prices). In time the destruction of places like New York City's South Bronx will provide a chance to rebuild worn out parts of cities in patterns that better fit today's or tomorrow's technologies and living patterns."[31]

In testimony before Congress, and in discussions with other urban experts and business leaders, Herrington Bryce, vice-president of the Academy for Contemporary Problems, a liberal research organization, argued against stopping the flow of capital from some regions of the country to others. "There is some sense," said Bryce, "in capital flowing into areas where there are higher rates of return, and giving these other areas where capital is flowing [from] some opportunity to retool."[32]

Bryce later repeated his prescription at a congressional hearing, warning against federal intervention in the flow of investment between regions:

> The problem in trying to interrupt that flow often-times amounts to penalizing areas which have been

imaginative in the way they have attracted capital or which have certain natural advantages which investors are seeking at a particular time.[33]

The "natural advantages" in attracting capital have included less militant, lower-paid labor and an ability to achieve the rapid and often environmentally unsound removal of natural resources. Competing governments' "imaginative" ways of attracting migrating dollars range from free job training, subsidies to build plants, fewer social services, fewer environmental restrictions, and anti-union legislation.

Some of the country's leading media, while reporting on winning and losing, have also become cheerleaders in the process. During New York City's fiscal crisis, the *New York Times,* for example, consistently editorialized in favor of making the city more competitive with other places. The newspaper responded to wage cutbacks by the bricklayers in 1977 by urging other unions follow suit— "May their constructive concession prove instructive to others."[34] The *Wall Street Journal* proclaimed business's early success at extracting concessions from government and workers in the loser regions in 1978 as a kind of sporting comeback by competitive underdogs. "Now, hard-hit parts of the Northeast," said the *Journal,* "particularly in New England, are beginning to fight back. The state of Massachusetts, long reputed to be indifferent or even hostile to business, is trying to change its image, and state officials say they are making some headway."[35] "It is this leveling of costs, in wages and other areas," said the *Boston Globe,* describing how the Millers Falls workers were forced to take cutbacks, "that could eventually lower the cost of doing business in Massachusetts and, at least, make the state competitive enough to keep the business that is here now and encourage it to grow."[36]

## The Danger for Business

In spite of rationalization by experts and boosterism by the media, the dilemma for ordinary people remains straightforward—a continuing attack on the wages and jobs of workers in those parts of the country where they have won better conditions and an attack on environmental conditions in all parts of the country. In addition they can expect business to ask for more and more of their tax dollars as inducements to remain or to relocate.

While regional rotation has an irresistible logic for business profitability, it is a dangerous game. Vast communities of the poor in some parts of the country may keep wages down in others, but they can become an enormous threat to social stability and order. To maintain the poor in the old metropolitan areas requires reinforcing the means of social control. It means more police, more money for the "justice" system, and it means making more welfare available to buy off potential social unrest. But the less productive the older cities become, the less able they are to pay for the public social services needed to maintain the unproductive workers. To solve this problem, business leaders now argue for easing local tax burdens by federalizing welfare. Through federal subsidies, workers in the fallow regions will presumably be maintained at marginal levels, or be given low salaries for private and public "workfare" jobs, in order to keep them available for work in industry; more accurately, to pose them as a threat to the current workers in those industries.

In effect, tax dollars from workers in the productive regions are drained off to maintain a low-paid community of unproductive workers in the fallow ones. Workers in the productive regions are required to use part of their paychecks to maintain a condition that helps put a damper on their own wages.

The dependence of the nonproductive regions on the productive ones presents a fundamental dilemma for business and government. It is no mere problem of finding friendlier politicians in Washington who won't say "drop dead" to places like New York. The dependence represents a structural flaw within the American economic system; as the next chapter explains, no amount of business migration or public entrepreneuring can avoid the consequences of that defect. In fact, the more that businesses migrate and the more that governments compete against each other, the more critical the crisis for business becomes.

# 4
# THE PUBLIC ENTREPRENEUR AS POLICEMAN AND ACCOMPLICE: Dilemma of the Living Losers

The aim of the State should be clearly to improve the conditions of life rather than to promote opportunities for profit.
> —Report of the New York State Commission on Regional Planning to Governor Alfred E. Smith, 1926.

There's no such thing as zoning, there's only deals.
> —Samuel J. Lefrak, New York real estate developer, 1970.[1]

You must be good to business even if you hate rich people, even if you don't like pinkie rings, even if you detest Scarsdale and Rolls-Royce.
> —Mario C. Cuomo, Liberal party candidate for Mayor of New York, 1977.[2]

When a private business loses big, it eventually goes bankrupt and dies; governments, on the other hand, are a very special kind of competitive creature. When a government doesn't compete well, it may lose some industries, it may lose some taxpayers, it may even declare it is bankrupt, but it certainly doesn't die. This difference is crucial and lies at the heart of a corrosive situation business is shaping for itself by promoting government's imitation of a free enterprise system. The ultimate irony of this strategy is that by lifting the yoke of competition from its own shoulders, and placing it squarely on those of the public, business is helping create the conditions for its own decline.

Local governments have been forced to copy the private enterprise system with a particular vengeance. The public approach is ironically much closer to Adam Smith's model of free market competition than might be found in the operation of any large modern corporation. In contrast to the limited competition of monopolies and oligopolies that private winner corporations can establish for themselves, no single government or small group of governments can corner enough power to slacken its future need to compete. The pure, continuous, and unrestrained nature of competition by governments is an intimate part of business's own struggle for economic survival.

## Marketplace of the Two Entrepreneurs

There is logic, at least an abstract one, to competition between private businesses. The private entrepreneur risks his capital to produce a product or service he thinks will return an attractive profit on his investment. Competing against other entrepreneurs, he will make his prices as low as possible to capture as much demand as possible for his product or service. If the private entrepreneur is a "winner," he captures a greater share of the market than his competitors. He now has accumulated more money than his competitors and can invest more than they to expand production and produce even greater profits. Meanwhile, the private "losers," producing less and accumulating fewer profits, are eventually forced out of business altogether.

Aside from the moral question of "winners" and "losers" and the enormous exploitation of labor needed for private competition, there is a certain technical attractiveness and wisdom in this self-regulating system. What we are left with as the end result of pure private competition, at least theoretically, are a number of the most efficient producers. These successful producers, in order to gain even more profit and guard their position against new competitors, will improve their product lines and continue to produce at the least cost possible. Meanwhile, the marginal and otherwise unsuccessful operators, instead of drawing off money and resources in their inefficient operation, go bankrupt and self-destruct—the system, in effect, cleanses itself.

Of course in the real world the private market is not nearly so pristine, and in fact, costly, wasteful, and inefficient monopolies or oligopolies, where industries are controlled by a single or few firms, are more typical of what actually exists. The point is not that the private system has worked, but that, theoretically at least, a case can be made for the efficiency of a Darwinian marketplace in which the fittest, or at least most aggressive, survive.

The purpose of private entrepreneurship is to expand profits for stockholders. The relationship between the investor and his private company is a fickle and potentially temporary one. So long as acceptable levels of profits are maintained the investor will lend his money to the company; as soon as he can find a more profitable return elsewhere he moves his money. When there are low returns, there are few investors. When a company continues to lose, it eventually has no investors and dies. But the relationship between the public entrepreneur and its citizens is very different—the citizen doesn't expect a return in dollars, but instead looks for a continuous supply of the best public services and products in exchange for the lowest possible prices. Citizens expect their public entrepreneurs to keep taxes low while providing them with good schools, safe highways, clean streets, and protecting their property and lives. Public entrepreneuring has no automatic purging mechanism like private entrepreneuring does to improve the efficiency of the overall system; losing public entrepreneurs don't self-destruct, and losing citizens can't easily move themselves and their tax dollars to new places and to new public entrepreneurs.

## Alive and Losing

The decrease in services and increase in taxes of the loser governments will force some residents to leave, but many, if not most, will tend to stay. Family and friendship ties will hold people in these communities, older people will not be easily uprooted; others will own homes with low market values and would have to spend much more for one in a new community, while many will simply hope that local economic conditions will somehow turn around. The fact is that workers and residents, whether willingly or not, are committed to remaining in a city or town in a way in which private investors simply are not tied to their companies.

Instead of abandoning a losing city, many of its residents will use the political process to retain and expand services. With private firms leaving, they are forced to ask for more welfare, more housing assistance, and more unemployment benefits. Rather than folding, the loser government finds that at the same time its financial capacity to provide services is decreasing, the demands for maintaining and increasing services are expanding.

Faced with this political reality, the losing public entrepreneurs must not only continue to make debt payments on facilities they've already built and now have less use for, they must also continue to pay salaries to people who collect garbage, put out fires, teach children, and police the streets. Since local government has few ways to raise money other than through taxes or getting money from the federal government, it finds itself with no alternatives other than both to ask Washington for help and to turn more humbly to private firms in the hope of bringing jobs to the community, so it can tap wages from those jobs to pay for taxes. At the same time it hopes that the creation of these new jobs will reduce welfare and other costs produced by unemployment. Instead of fading, the losing government must become even more visible and compete even harder to attract business than in more prosperous times.

This kind of entrepreneuring system, in effect, not only is unable to purge itself through the self-destruction available through bankruptcy in the private system, but has to expand its capacity to produce revenue at the very point at which it is least able to do so. While technically local government can declare bankruptcy, the fact remains that bankruptcy doesn't result in the same absolution from debt that it does for the private entrepreneur. A bankruptcy for government, in contrast to one for business, has proved to be a temporary phenomenon. All of the large cities that defaulted on their debts during the 1930s' depression, had repaid them by 1938.[3] Some cities which couldn't repay at that time stretched their obligations over a longer period. Asheville, North Carolina, was still using 17 percent of its debt service money in the mid-1970s to pay for the default of its 1930s' loans.[4]

Although New York City did not formally declare bankruptcy in 1975, it was indeed bankrupt that year since it could not repay its loans. The technique that avoided official bankruptcy was a "stretch-out" arrangement by the city and state officials, and their private financial advisors, that forced debtors to wait for their money.

If it were truly possible for the public entrepreneurs to ape the real world of private enterprise, then a limited number of cities and states could retain an exclusive ability to attract business. In effect it would then be possible for at least some governments to have a kind of public monopoly or oligopoly in luring business, and find themselves with a stable and continuous access to jobs and adequate tax revenues. But it is virtually impossible for most governments to do this.

Those winner cities and states, that is, those that are able to lure a larger share of migrating corporations, will only have a temporary competitive advantage over the losers. They can use the increased tax revenues made available by more jobs, fewer welfare problems, and higher real estate values to provide more services to business in the form of more roads, vocational training programs, industrial revenue bond, tax abatements, sports stadiums, or whatever is necessary to attract even more businesses. As a growing and attractive area for business, these winners will also find themselves able to borrow money at more favorable rates than the losers, a factor that can further increase their competitive advantage in attracting more business.

But here the similarity between public and private monopoly ends; the public entrepreneur winner, at this point, in contrast to the private winner, cannot parlay its competitive advantage into a perpetually winning or monopoly situation.

The public entrepreneurs, in an ironic contrast to corporate enterprise, are forced to operate in a free market system. A government's ability to provide business with attractive financial incentives like tax abatements, industrial revenue financing, low labor rates, and lax environmental controls is not restricted to the winners. By responding in kind, a loser area is able to make "a comeback."

As the losers become hungrier, they compete more vigorously. While it is difficult for them to eliminate public services, it is not impossible to cut them to the bone. Faced with a steady deterioration of private jobs and their tax base, local governments will tend to create their own austerity programs; public employees can be fired and welfare benefits can be reduced. More antilabor legislation, as well as lowered environmental standards, can be proffered to business. Public officials can also encourage private job holders to accept lower wages in order to keep their jobs.

This ability of the losing public entrepreneur to stay alive and compete more aggressively even while it is losing means that the success of a winning public entrepreneur is always temporary. With the possible exception of those few local governments that exercise some control over extracting their unique natural resources, none have a monopoly over the conditions that will attract business; none can become the exclusive producer of a particular product and none can produce an exclusive antilabor or lax environmental climate. As jobs increase in an antilabor winner like New Hampshire, for example, labor organizing is likely to increase and New Hampshire's labor situation can come to resemble that of some of today's loser states. Conversely, a current loser like Ohio might come to resemble Texas, if Ohio's politicians are willing to take more antilabor positions in order to keep or attract industries.

Unable to form monopolies, governments must vigorously compete against each other in their own free market system. But none of them die in these battles—instead they are forced to play Sisyphus, perpetually shifting between winning and losing.

## The Costs of Public Entrepreneuring

What business hopes for in its strategy of regional rotation is that both winner and loser cities and regions will be "cost effective" in their competition with each other; the winners providing the minimum wages and public services necessary for business profitability, while the losers reduce wages and are otherwise maintained by a steady, but inexpensive supply of welfare plasma to keep them alive as competitors against the winners.

This strategy can work as long as the cost of public competition comes from changes in the living conditions of ordinary people; through their higher national and local tax dollars, through their reduced wages, or through their poorer health and higher doctor's bills to pay for deteriorating environmental conditions. Any rise in the costs of the overall system, whether in the form of welfare or wages, has to be accounted for either by an expansion of production, or by peoples' willingness to accept cutbacks in how they live. If the taxpayers in either or both the winning and losing communities are unwilling to pay for these costs, then business itself must expand its production to produce more wealth to pay for them.

Regional rotation is not a cheap system. As more loser regions are created, more welfare costs are necessary to maintain them. The more that cities and regions compete with each other, the more they duplicate each other's infrastructure facilities. As winner cities and regions build new roads, schools, and sewers, the losers must still maintain the debt and upkeep costs of the ones they already have. Maintaining underused facilities and services in loser cities and regions, while creating similar ones in the winners, adds to the financial burden of the entire nation. Whether this burden is paid for by national taxes or local ones the nation's private economy must ultimately expand to create the wealth to pay for the taxes that maintain the losers and allow the winners to grow. The only alternative to this expansion is to sharply curtail government services.

The government's maintenance of loser cities and regions is not entirely new. America's rural areas, which began to be economically abandoned more than one hundred years ago, had to be maintained by welfare and other public service programs. The nature of maintaining losers today, however, is even more expensive than it ever was in the past, confronting government with new and formidable problems.

Today, highly urbanized sections of the country with an enormous already constructed world of roads, buildings, sewers, and communication systems, and populations of millions, have been left to lie fallow by the private investment system. The cost of maintaining public services in these large urban areas is significantly higher than it is in rural areas. Tax rates become progressively higher as cities increase in size, suggesting increased per capita costs of public services in larger urban areas. In 1974, for example, local taxes per capita in cities of a million or more were over three times higher than in towns of 10,000 or less.[5]

In absolute dollars, the national burden of supporting most big cities is rising rapidly. By 1978, for example, Los Angeles and Phoenix received more than double the federal funds they did two years before; Atlanta, St. Louis, and Cleveland's share increased by three times; while Newark's rose by a factor of five.[6]

The abandonment of the older, loser cities, it might be argued, should involve proportionally lower tax costs for these cities, since abandonment presumably means less garbage to collect, fewer fires to put out, and fewer crimes committed. In fact the evidence of the big cities which have undergone major decline over the recent past indicates that government employees have not decreased in proportion to population decrease. The four cities with the highest population losses, averaging a 26 percent drop between 1960 and 1975, reduced their total police, fire, and sanitation staffs by only 12 percent.

While the cost of maintaining the losers remains high, the cost of running the entire national system of local public services has also grown dramatically. The rise in the number of public employees in the growing "winner" cities is far outdistancing their population increase. Between 1960 and 1975, four of the fastest growing cities added 43 percent more people, but over 80 percent more employees to their combined police, fire, and sanitation departments.[7] In overall terms, the national cost of maintaining both winner and loser government services has risen enormously—in less than ten years, the total expenditures of the entire country's state and local governments went up by 170 percent.[8]

What is startling about the growth of state and local government costs is not only the dollar amounts, but how much they have risen compared with private business investments. Up until the mid-1960s expenditures for private domestic investment were substantially more than those of state and local governments. In 1965, for example, the private sector spent almost 60 percent more on its investment in the United States than did local and state governments. By the early 1970s the gap had narrowed.

In 1977, local and state expenditures totaled $250 billion dollars, only 15 percent less than the total private investment in the country that year—more than double the amount state and local governments were spending in 1970. While these government expenditures have continued to rise as a percentage of the total GNP, the GNP itself has steadily deteriorated from a growth rate of 3.5 percent in 1965 to 2.4 percent in 1977.

In 1960, state and local government expenditures were 9 percent of the GNP; by 1977, they were up to 13 percent. The growth rate of state and local government costs outstripped virtually every major category of GNP including all private spending for goods and services, all private domestic investments, all of the country's net exports, and all federal spending.[9]

While the money to pay for this growing level of state and local public spending must come from expanded economic growth, the prognosis for growth is not good. In a 1977 study of 2,500 corporations in 37 industries, a research arm of Standard and Poor's reported that over a ten-year period the average rate of return on invested capital declined by over 30 percent. According to the Commerce Department, profits as a percentage of gross national product during that same period went down almost 45 percent.

"There has been a basic long-term decline," said Reginald Jones, Chairman of GE, "in the real rate of return that a businessman can expect from his investment." In some basic industries the ten-year decline in the rate of investment return has been especially dramatic; in the automobile industry the after-tax return on invested capital was down 45 percent; in metals and mining, tires and rubber, and textiles and apparel, the return was down about 60 percent.[10]

This downward shift in the *rate* of profit doesn't mean that the total dollar *amount* of a company's profits in any given year is down—in fact, the amount of a company's profits can increase at the very same time that its rate of profit goes down. Indeed it is not unusual to find many companies declaring record profits just as they complain about finding investment capital.

What declining rates of profits means, simply, is that a company must invest more money than before in order to sustain the same level of profit as before. This need for an ever-bigger "capital fix," through ever-higher levels of investment, means that business must generate even more profit, or borrow more money to stay where it was.

During the past twenty-five years, American corporations have, in fact, been forced to spend more and more of their profits or borrow money for expansion. In 1950, only 2 percent of profits were needed for expansion; by 1960 it was 6 percent. In 1974, corporations were able to raise only a fifth of their needs in the normal borrowing market, and were forced to take shorter-term, higher-cost loans for the rest. The next year, 17 percent of all profits were being used for interest payments.[11] In 1978, Richard W. Kopcke, an economist for the Federal Reserve Bank of Boston, warned:

At the same time rates of return were falling, the rising cost of financing capital assets has steadily undermined investment incentives. This is especially disquieting because attaining national economic goals requires brisk investment spending like that of the middle 1960s—when rates of return were reaching a postwar peak and capital costs were relatively low—to provide the momentum for economic growth into the 1980s.[12]

In addition to its declining rates of profit, American business is also being buffeted by losses in its productivity. American business's productivity, which is a function of its investment in new technology to improve its production efficiency, now lags behind most major industrial nations. By the end of 1978, American productivity growth was close to a standstill.

The declining economic position of American business is now reflected in the everyday lives of consumers and workers. By the end of 1978, when many government leaders were predicting a possible recession for the end of the following year, 15 percent of the country's plant capacity was already unused and over 6 million people were officially unemployed. The level of plant idleness, said the *Wall Street Journal,* exceeded that "prevailing during most of the postwar era, including some recession periods." The 6 percent unemployment level, said the *Journal,* "exceeds levels recorded during any of the six recessions that have punctuated post-World War II prosperity."[13] At about the same time, G. William Miller, Chairman of the Federal Reserve Board, predicted it would take five to eight years to reduce the near double-digit inflation to acceptable levels.[14]

In addition to the formidable impediments of slow growth and inflation to job creation, new opportunities in foreign countries have put a further squeeze on the available money for investment in this country. What has been called the "capital shortage" doesn't mean there's less total money available, but less money available to aid expansion in *this* country.

In the recent past, capital has migrated to find lucrative returns in the "developing world" nations. In 1973 the thirteen largest commercial banks in the United States received 34 percent of their combined earnings from overseas operations. Two years later, almost 50 percent of these earnings came from abroad. While earnings' growth of the leading United States banks declined or rose modestly in this country between 1970 and 1975, those in foreign countries increased substantially. Earnings of the Bank of America, for example, the largest bank in this country, grew about 5 percent here, but 38 percent abroad. Chase Manhattan's earnings in this country went down over 6 percent, but grew by 27 percent abroad. According to a recent report by a Senate subcommittee, of all the money now owed by all the developing countries that are not oil producers, approximately one-quarter to one-third is owed to United States banks.[15]

## Short Term Solutions, Long Term Problems

Increasing federal and local government subsidies to prop up the faltering investments of American business could allow for the temporary expansion and health of some winner communities. But this only delays the national problem of insufficient economic growth rather than solving it. Since these public subsidies must ultimately come from private economic expansion, they eventually contribute to what economist James O'Connor calls "the fiscal crisis of the state"[16]—the inability of private economic expansion to meet the debt created by rising public expenditures. Ultimately this debt must be called, and when the private sector cannot produce the tax revenue to pay it off, the economic system moves toward collapse.

The problem business faces in having to use regional rotation is not only to head off this economic collapse, but to dampen the social turmoil which follows in its wake. When business runs from some regions, it creates not only severe public cleanup and maintenance costs in these regions, but serious political costs as well; regional rotation produces mounting discontent and real possibilities for disruptive social upheaval. "The poor who are left behind may not accept their lot passively," warned a *Business Week* editorial, "especially when the cities' shrunken economic base impairs their ability to offer welfare or housing."[17]

Nor is it only the poor who are abandoned—and angered—by business's abandonment. Although some of the more mobile middle-class people can follow business's migration, others, tied to family, mortgages, neighborhoods, cannot. Even as the prosperity of the city around them vanishes, they still expect the high standard of living and high level of public services to which they've become accustomed. Unlike the rural population abandoned in an earlier historical period, they are neither accustomed to, nor do they have the physical resources to make do by techniques like marginal subsistence farming.

The demands by the remaining middle class for continuation of the garbage pickup, road maintenance, unemployment benefits, police protection, and other benefits that they've come to expect, coupled with the maintenance costs for the indigent population, impose an enormous strain on the system's financial resources. Faced with the higher costs to support these services in loser communities, business has no choice but to call for austerity and cutbacks.

When business cries out in unison about profligate city spending, it is not simply chastising public officials in order to publicly congratulate its own corporate efficiency. It recognizes that higher local government costs for competing, for managing the city's infrastructure, its garbage collection, welfare services, and education system will mean less money available to subsidize industry; higher salaries for municipal workers will also tend to drive up the salaries of its own workers. Business needs government to entrepreneur for its growth, it needs government to provide the welfare and policing for those it can't employ, but business would like this done under its own terms. In the new euphemism for cheap, it must be "cost effective."

Business must now at the same time improve its earnings and hold down government expenditures. For business, holding down government expenditures is problematic, since it has come to depend on these government expenditures to provide a guaranteed market for many of its products. It cannot, for example, decrease government expenditure for products like military hardware or highways, on which it can make large profits; but rather it must decrease expenditures for social services or garbage collection, which yield relatively little profit.

To control and "tune" government expenditure more precisely to its current needs, business must now find more direct ways to influence local politics. From business's perspective, local democratic political processes have interfered with cost effectiveness. Local democracy is a vestige of a time when local governments were hungrier for industrial development and did not pass enormous public expenditures for welfare and municipal salaries; in short, a vestige of a time when democracy was affordable. Today, business is forced to find new ways of leaning on government officials, in order to provide cheaper ways of maintaining services for its workers.

## New Corporate Involvement in Local Government

To help tune public expenditures more precisely to their own needs, business people have often organized, through either official government agencies or private ones, to directly influence local government policy. Organizations staffed by corporate executives and their personnel, like New York City's Emergency Financial Control Board, Boston's Financial Committee, and the Bay Area Council in San Francisco, which "watchdog" the financial condition of these urban areas, reflect direct corporate involvement in local government affairs.

In 1976, the Business Roundtable, a group of major United States corporate executives, including David Rockefeller, G.E. chairman Reginald H. Jones, and Citibank president Walter B. Wriston, called for even more direct business participation in financial planning and in the day-to-day operations of city government. The Roundtable's Task Force on Municipalities, headed by General Motor's chairman Thomas A. Murphy, urged that business leaders press for permanent "Economic Growth Commissions" in every city in the country. The commissions would be comprised primarily of representatives from the local financial community, "as well as elected officials." Not only would the growth commissions participate in local planning, but, according to the Murphy task force, they would also be encouraged to lobby in Washington and state capitals.

The more direct involvement of business leaders in

city operations is an attempt to shift at least some power over local affairs to nonelected business leaders. The task force's rationale is that business leaders' political clout in Washington and state capitals can substitute for the declining political influence of the cities resulting from their recent population losses. "Central cities, as a result of population loss, and decreased voting by their remaining residents," said the business group, "are faced with continuing erosion of their political impact. Thus, there is need for the development of municipal advocates from non-governmental sources."

On a local level, says the Roundtable group, the business community could help evaluate "The necessity, adequacy and effectiveness of the public services currently provided . . . it might be possible to eliminate some services determined to be of marginal need and cost-effectiveness to the city and its residents." It could also "assist or advise" city officials in "applying business expertise to help solve labor problems faced by many cities." Business involvement, they claim, would give municipal officials "an objective 'outside' view of policies and procedures."[18]

## The Growing Crisis for Business

As business attempts to manage the losers by making them cost-effective, it may be able to delay the reaction to the economic crisis it is creating, but it cannot forever avoid that reaction. The discontent of the large population of both poor and middle-class people who remain in the loser regions cannot easily be answered by austerity programs; if anything, these programs are likely to stir up even more social unrest. Large segments of the middle class may line up behind business-recommended cutbacks in welfare aid to the poor, but they will not as easily abide drastic cuts in police and fire services, street cleaning, education, and other services they have come to expect.

The process of creating loser regions is also likely to push more middle-class people toward an increasing dependence on government services themselves. As business mothballs loser regions for later use, middle-class workers in these regions will find their wages lowered and more of their jobs disappearing. As regional rotation shifts more private workers into dependence on government welfare services and on government-created jobs like those in the CETA program, it is also likely to generate more vigorous antibusiness attitudes on the part of these workers.

Still another problem for business in promoting austerity programs in the losers are the large numbers of government workers already in these cities and regions. Public workers, who now represent one out of every six jobs in America, have an obvious interest in preserving public services, and in doing so, add to business's political problems.[19]

Business now finds itself faced with a very different challenge to its survival than it did in the fifties and early sixties when the nation's economy was expanding. At that time it could generate the surplus dollars for government to use in middle-class programs for urban renewal, new surburbs, highways and poverty wars to pacify the poor. With an expanding economy it could offer both the poor and the middle class the prospect of rising expectations for better education, housing, and other material goods. Today, business can only offer a future of lowered expectations and fiscal austerity.

With very different economic conditions, business now faces sustained low rates of economic growth and high rates of unemployment and inflation. To counter its declining growth, business must shift its heavier burden of maintaining profits onto ordinary people, persuading, cajoling, or forcing them to accept lower wages, fewer environmental restrictions, less safe jobs, and fewer public services. For a time these kinds of austerity measures may work, as in the case of people voting themselves fewer public services through proposals like Proposition 13. But these techniques can only be successful in winner states like California which can shift a surplus in government income at the state level to pay for the services that would have been cut by tax reductions at the local level. There is little opportunity to do this in loser states, where fiscal conditions make it difficult or impossible for the state to offset massive revenue loss at the local level. And even winner entrepreneurs like California can only expect to maintain their more lucrative positions as long as those parts of the private economy that support them remain healthy, and as long as the losers remain ineffective in competing with them—two very unstable conditions.

As the economy worsens, the costs of local government may be shifted to the state or federal government. Indeed, the federal government is already supporting close to 800,000 CETA jobs, mostly to pay for public employees which local governments can't afford to hire themselves. This shifting of costs doesn't eliminate the effects of the economic crisis on the taxpayer, it only shifts the place where the taxes are paid.

As all levels of government attempt to underwrite the unprofitability of business and to unlodge a stagnant economy with higher taxes and borrowed money to pay for public works, public jobs, and tax incentives to business, inflation is accelerated. For business this process may be necessary, but at the same time extremely dangerous. Continued inflation leads to the point where people can no longer afford many goods and services; as this happens, production slows and unemployment increases. "More ominous still," warned Arthur F. Burns, former chairman of the Federal Reserve Bank, "by causing disillusionment and breeding discontent, inflation excites doubts among people about themselves, about the competence of their Government, and about the free-enterprise system itself."[20]

As regional rotation continues and the problems of loser communities grow, politicians in these communities will be turned to by their citizens, as they always have been in times of economic crisis, for better solutions. What then if anything can these politicians do?

Today, local politicians must attempt to shape their economies through a frustrating, schizophrenic attempt both to try to help business and at the same time to protect the welfare of their constituents. In addition to these requirements politicians must act upon a rigid pattern of regionally specialized economies historically shaped, not by local needs, but by industrialists who organized their enterprises on a national and worldwide scale. These two conditions, the limits of the existing governing process to act on local economies and the existing regional geography of specialized local economies, leave local politicians little room seriously to act upon and improve local conditions. The answer to the question—what can politicians do to change regional rotation?—is, very little—unless, as we will see, they are willing to change the fundamental role of government in the process of shaping our economic system.

## Policeman and Accomplice

Local governments in America operate under two very particular constraints. They have a mandate to support a political system aimed at democratic governance and the protection of the individual, and they must also support an economic system built on the needs of business. The nature of these constraints prescribes a very precise, yet schizophrenic role for politicians.

Since cities and states depend on the tax dollars produced as a result of business development, local politicians can expand public services only to the extent that business prospers. But in order to stay in power, these politicians must also maintain their legitimacy as protectors of the people's interest. This role, however, is often at odds with business growth, since such growth can involve unsafe work conditions, increased environmental pollution, insufficient wages for a decent livelihood, traffic problems, and so on.

Regardless of liberal or conservative coloring, politicians must simultaneously promote business growth, and at the same time protect citizens against hazards produced in the process of generating that growth—in effect, they have no alternative but to become both accomplice and policeman.

Pennsylvania's Governor Milton J. Shapp put this dilemma of government succinctly:

> Sometimes labor gets sore at business. Sometimes government gets sore at business. Sometimes the public gets sore at business. But nobody gets sore at jobs . . . the point is nobody can be *against* business. And those who think they are had better do a little soul-searching. Unless they're also against eating.[21]

So long as the local economy experiences continuous economic growth, mayors, governors, and other local officials can avoid dealing with the contradictions of being both policeman and accomplice. When the local economy is booming, when there are adequate jobs at decent wages, politicians can be less aggressive as accomplice in providing business financial incentives. They can continue to pay for the costs of building more schools and roads, of providing more government services by raising taxes and by more government borrowing against future taxes. Borrowing against future taxes is often more attractive to politicians since it keeps the tax rate from rising too quickly during their term in office.

The real crunch for these politicians comes when the national economy slows down. At this point, business is forced to search for more ways to cut costs and improve its profits by finding more government subsidies and lower-paid workers. Politicians, recognizing that their own survival depends on sustained or increased economic growth of their locality, offer more tax abatements and subsidies, ease environmental controls, proffer antiunion legislation, while attacking the jobs and salaries of government workers.

While playing accomplice to business becomes a necessity for all local governments, it becomes especially difficult for those loser governments being abandoned by business who must now entrepreneur even more vigorously, if they are to keep their remaining businesses or attract new ones. This need for more entrepreneuring, however, comes at the very moment when this community's ability to pay is being undercut by drastic losses in tax revenues and increased welfare and other social service costs.

It is at this moment that enormous pressures are usually brought to bear against politicians by business leaders, to initiate the kind of solutions that "Won't-cost-the-public-a-dime." These may include cutting back social welfare programs, laying off public employees, and providing the kind of "workfare" for the unemployed that allows them to replace laid-off public employees at lower salaries. These "costless" solutions may also include pressure against public employee unions to use their pension funds to underwrite tax abatements for business, as well as attempts to convince local politicians to pass labor laws restricting union power. They are also likely to include business lobbying to ease environmental controls.

By forcing local government into the role of policeman and accomplice, our economic system precludes any serious and effective possibilities for these governments to determine their own local economic planning; the very best that local politicians can hope for is to be more successful than their counterparts in other parts of the country in attracting business. In the case of the Millers Falls Company mentioned in Chapter 3, for example, the owners threatened to leave Massachusetts if the workers didn't accept cutbacks and if the state didn't offer subsidies. Given the government's limited role of policeman-accomplice, these officials saw little alternative but to urge Millers Falls workers to be more cooperative with the company, while it offered the company state subsidies.

Government officials, faced with a company's threats to move, often don't know if a company is bluffing, nor does the government's present role encourage them to devise any really effective response to the company's threats. What's called the "local planning process" is little more than gambling with taxpayers' money, in the hope of retaining an industry. "I didn't know if [the Millers Falls president] had four aces or a busted flush," said Howard Smith, Massachusetts Secretary of Commerce, "and I didn't want to know"; he saw job loss and state revenue loss which he said he simply didn't want to lose.[22]

No region is safe from having to play policeman-accomplice. Even liberal democrats, who in better times trumpeted the cause of the poor, now couch their roles as financial risk takers for private development in the name of fiscal responsibility. Supposedly progressive politicians such as California's Jerry Brown, faced with a financial crisis, proclaim that ordinary people must now learn to live with less, as social services are cut back and the banner of economic survival is raised.

The local politician is extremely limited in what he or she can do to improve a locality's economic health. Because of legal restriction and ideological climate, politicians are limited to managing certain public facilities and services such as schools, street cleaning, fire fighting, and policing. They aren't normally expected to consider, for example, the use of publicly owned production enterprises to produce goods that people need; nor are they generally expected to create public jobs to provide for these needs.

Given these restrictions, the local politician tries to do the most he or she can to create a healthy local economy. By setting aside land for commercial development and by offering incentives, they hope to attract jobs, which will give local people the ability to pay their taxes and to buy the goods and services they need. A local politician's most progressive, voter-pleasing way of doing this is to lure high-paying jobs, to find industry which has as little pollution as possible, one which will do the least environmental damage possible, and at the same time require as little as possible from the public treasury for public facilities and services to support that industry.

During this process of business hunting, government will engage in what some public economic development people call "booze and brochures." They will have special luncheons to persuade corporate executives, advertise in business journals, mail out promotional brochures, and send off trade missions to corporate headquarters. Of course not all communies get the clean industries and the high-paying jobs; in fact, many realize their best hope for attracting industry is to make it known that labor is cheap, unions are weak, and environmental regulations lax.

## The Real Planners

City officials attempt to do local public planning for their communities, but the real planning is neither *local* nor *public*. The real planning that takes place is *private* planning, and the geographic focus is *national* or *worldwide*. The most critical planning decisions for a community are not those made in the local planning office, but are those made by business leaders, deciding where to move their plants. The local economy, its environment, the jobs of its people are determined by how business utilizes the local community's jobs and exports to fit into its national or worldwide market.

Faced with the reality that local governments must respond to business to stay afloat, the themes of "home rule" and "local autonomy" become empty political slogans. Local officials may be democratically elected, but their actions are entirely circumscribed by the imperatives of economic forces over which they have no real control. With capitalism the only game in town, those who don't play simply don't survive.

The kind of "keep out zoning" that is popular in wealthy bedroom suburbs is the exception that proves the rule—people in these suburbs can afford to pay for the privilege of keeping unattractive industry from their own doors through the money they receive from their investments in other communities, which have no choice but to accept unattractive growth. It is one of the ordinary paradoxes of capitalism that the business people who cry most loudly about the necessity of economic growth are the "community leaders" in keeping growth out of their own environmentally attractive communities.

## Hopeful Anticipation

What passes for public planning in most communities is not really planning, but might more accurately be called *"hopeful anticipation."* A community or region will divide itself into different land-use categories, such as residential, commercial, offices, industrial, agricultural, and so on, then, using tax and other incentives, hopes to persuade business to locate in those places. There is no obligation on business's part to locate in any particular community or region. "The primary responsibility of a corporate head, of course, is not to boost a community, but to benefit the shareholders," explained *Corporate Financing,* a business executives' trade magazine. "Little in their corporate behavior," the magazine candidly observed elsewhere, "suggests that corporations are swayed by a sense of overriding *economic* responsibility to involved populations. Nor is anyone proposing—and a revolutionary proposal it would be—to legislate such a responsibility . . ."[23] (emphasis theirs).

In order to anticipate the movement of business, most communities set aside large pieces of land for industry or build roads and utilities for industrial parks. On the West Coast, about 75 percent of the land zoned for industry in most large metropolitan areas is vacant.[24] According to the Tennessee Department of Economic and Community Development, a "competitive surplus" of land "must be maintained over and beyond the minimum amount required for projected new plants and expansions in order to provide a variety of locational considerations to prospective industries."[25] Between 1977 and 1980, it recommended more than 6,000 acres of land be added to this surplus to meet industry's possible needs.

Local government can at best mitigate the conditions of its dependence on business; it can't destroy that dependence. Locked into "hopeful anticipation," planners preen their communities for business by attempting to become skillful in anticipating where investment dollars are flowing and what industries will be the growth leaders of the future.[26]

What results from this approach is not planning based on the needs of the community, but a grab bag of business activities, a textile factory, insurance offices, a polyvinyl plant. It is a development process that in no serious sense can be called local planning or local control; it is a process of anticipation and reaction. It is a process in which some communities may get job-creating industries and others automated plants, some communities environmentally attractive industries, and others environmentally dangerous ones. A community can try to get what it wants, and even try to fight against what it doesn't want—but eventually the community must adapt itself to the needs of private business. To paraphrase Pennsylvania's Governor Shapp, labor can get sore at business, government can get sore at business, and the public can get sore at business, but nobody can be *against* business.

## Dow Chemical and Local Planning

A recent case in California is a good illustration of the limits of local protection against business development. For two and a half years, the residents of Collinsville, a small agricultural town in the northern part of the state, waited while Dow Chemical executives, environmental groups, county, state, and federal officials, using millions of dollars in private and public funds and pounds of "impact statements," negotiated the town's future. Dow's plan was to locate a half-billion-dollar complex in Collinsville, on the banks of the Sacramento River. The development, which was to be the country's biggest petrochemical plant west of the Mississippi, would pump 40,000 pounds of hydrocarbons and oxides of nitrogen and sulfur a day into the air. According to scientists at California's Air Resource Board, its location in the path of ocean air blowing through the Carguinez Strait could make pollution in the Central valley worse than in Los Angeles.

To supply the plants, one of which was planned as the country's biggest producer of vinyl chloride (a known cause of liver cancer in workers), 10 million barrels of naphtha would have been shipped across the San Francisco Bay, up the Sacramento River, and then unloaded. In order to move ethylene, propylene, and hydrogen between its new complex and an older one on the opposite bank, Dow was planning to lay four steel pipes under the river on a site over the Antioch earthquake fault. A broken pipe could contaminate the river and the air above; the possibility of a shipping accident was not remote, even according to Dow's own consultants.

On January 19, 1977, after years of negotiations with groups and government officials opposed to the plant, Dow suddenly announced its decision to cancel the project. R. I. Brubaker, the company's general manager for the western United States, told the press they'd had enough planning. "Our supply of capital has its limits," he announced tersely.

For many people in Collinsville and the rest of northern California's Central valley, the chemical company's decision appeared to be a reprieve from what could have been a monstrous environmental disaster. That feeling of relief was likely underlined when less than a year later an accident at a Dow plant in Michigan pumped noxious chemicals into the air, causing large-scale environmental havoc.

The success of environmental and other groups in stopping the Dow plant, however, did not mean the people in northern California would be permanently protected against environmentally unattractive development. Even as Dow dropped its plans a number of other potentially hazardous industries, including a petrochemical plant by the Atlantic Richfield Company, twice the size of Dow's, were being proposed for the same area. Meanwhile business lobbyists stepped up their effort to urge laxer planning controls.

Immediately after Dow announced its withdrawal of the petrochemical project, state officials and business executives, led by Governor Jerry Brown, began a campaign to make sure the Dow phenomenon would not repeat itself. Worried that California might be seen as antibusiness as a result, the state's Office of Planning and Research was dispatched to develop a new "streamlining" process that would identify sites all over the state appropriate for industrial development. The proposal aimed to "chart the minefield" of state regulatory agencies for business by creating regional councils all over the state which would be required to develop plans to show industry where it could and could not locate. "To spur a positive and creative response," said the state's planning office, "some sanctions would be imposed on regions that failed to produce an approved industrial and commercial site plan within some reasonable time period, such as two years." In effect, local governments would be forced to formalize their processes of "hopeful anticipation."

Approval of regional plans would be the job of a select

few of the governor's cabinet officers: his secretaries of business and transportation, resources, and planning and research. Notably absent from the approval process, but whose views these cabinet people would "solicit," would be members of two state agencies which helped delay the Dow plant, the air and water control boards.

This kind of action-by-business, reaction-by-government planning is not only an ineffective way of protecting a community's social and environmental interests, it is also extremely expensive. It results in large expenditures of both public and private dollars in the anticipatory process: the time of batteries of planners, engineers, lawyers, private executives, and public officials, engaged in promoting economic development or trying to stop it. On a national level the marketplace of public entrepreneuring also leads to the duplication of human and material resources by the thousands of cities and all of the states that are being forced to compete with each other.

The people, meanwhile, pay for the process at both ends, as consumers and taxpayers. Dow Chemical, for example, may have spent millions in two and a half years of futile planning and lobbying to locate its plant. The cost of this effort is likely to show up in higher consumer costs for Dow products; the costs of paying public officials and planners, either to promote or to try to stop the plant, in its turn shows up in higher taxes.

### The Local Economy—An Unnatural Act

Existing local economies in America have been shaped or, more accurately, crippled, by the ways in which they were used by industrialists to create a market for their products and services. Whatever little control local politicians are left with has been further eroded by the constraints of a local economy that was created not to produce for local consumptions and needs, but to maximize profit through regional specialization.

The industrial growth of America is often benignly explained as a kind of Darwinian model of natural selection that sorts each function to its most economic and efficient place in the regions of America. In this scenario, Americans progressively shape new technological inventions in order to adapt to the unique geographies and the available resources and climates of America's various regions. The placement and growth of cities are presumed to be a natural response to natural geographical breaks between sea routes and land routes, between rivers and the hinterlands beyond them. The development of the Midwest is explained as the result of mechanized farming inventions and the new railroads, making it possible to harvest great quantities of food on the flat prairies and ship them east.

A more accurate portrait of regional growth is less the simple result of nature and the progress of new inventions than of conscious business decisions. Industrial leaders helped shape both private and public investments toward a regional production system of specialization and dependence. It is no natural phenomenon, for example, for the major part of America's agriculture to be in the most arid parts of this country at enormous distances from population centers; nor did nature ordain the industrial development of the North and the prolonged rural underdevelopment of the South.

Maintaining the South as a specialized cotton- and lumber-producing region, and developing the West for food production was conceived by visionary industrialists who used government subsidies to organize the transfer of goods. Private rail systems financed by local and national governments made possible the long-distance shipment of coal, lumber, and food. In the 1840s and 1850s, cities, towns, and even whole states were forced into insolvency by having to use their public funds to support private canal and railroad companies.[27] An extensive interstate highway system, again subsidized by the public, later extended the possibilities for goods shipment, as did new technologies for freezing, packaging, and preserving foods. Irrigation systems, dams, and water control projects in the West were heavily subsidized by government expenditures.

The resulting transportation, irrigation, and products-processing infrastructure created a geographical interdependency, fueling expansion in private investment and profits. Products and resources gathered from a vast continent were sorted, processed, shipped, and then distributed by a smaller and smaller number of companies growing more powerful as regional dependency increased. Railroad companies not only shipped goods, but also controlled large land holdings, including coal mines. In the late 1890s, journalist Henry Demarest Lloyd explained how railroad owners gained control of the mines.

A new law of industry is rising into view. Ownership of the highways ends in ownership of everything and everybody that must use the highways. . . . The railroads compel private owners to sell them their mines or all the product by refusing to supply cars, and by charging freight rates so high that every one but themselves loses money on every ton sent to market. When the railroads elect to have the output large, they furnish many cars; when they elect to have the output small, they furnish few cars; and when they elect that there shall be no output whatever, they furnish no cars.[28]

The transferring of goods was so lucrative that goods were sometimes shipped enormous distances in irrational patterns in order to create more profits. Stuart Chase, an early advocate of rational regional development, described a 1921 United States Geological Survey which "found Kentucky lamp coal moving into Indiana, Illinois and Ohio past mines in these states producing coal of an identical quality. . . . Equal grades of coal are solemnly moved from Illinois mines to be sold in Ohio, and from Ohio mines to be sold in Illinois."[29]

Today, New England, with some of the finest forests in the country, receives most of its plywood and building lumber from outside its borders. It contains 18 percent of the nation's forest land, yet produces only 2.5 percent of its lumber.[30] Enormous quantities of timber are being logged in the Pacific Northwest, loaded on ships, and carried to Japan, where they are unloaded, made into plywood, then reshipped for sale in this country.

Although New England has a large abundance and a replenishable supply of forests, it is often cheaper, using current wood energy technology and government subsidies to oil companies, to heat New England homes with gas or oil shipped from other regions of this country and the Mid-East. It is usually cheaper for New England builders to buy plywood from other parts of the country, since despite the availability of the raw materials in New England, the private financial sector has developed most of its plywood mills in other parts of the country.

While many parts of New England and the Mid-Atlantic states have appropriate climate and soil for growing wheat, it is usually cheaper to have wheat shipped in from other parts of the country. The West's preeminence as an agricultural region has much to do with the politics of water, the financing of water irrigation technology, and the increased use of chemical fertilizers. Much of the "rich" western land would have produced few edible crops without massive publicly financed irrigation programs and the extensive use of chemical fertilizers.

## The Short Life of Solar Energy

The development of regional energy systems was shaped not simply by what was most naturally available, but by what was useful to the large energy companies. The "new" solar energy systems of the 1970s actually began to be developed in California and Florida as early as the 1890s. But growing private energy companies, exploring for gas and oil in the 1900s, were able to nip that development in the bud.

The technology for present-day systems was patented in 1891 by Clarence Kemp, a Baltimore inventor who put four galvanized iron water tanks in an insulated pine box covered with glass. By the early 1900s thousands of solar water heater users in California were saving about 75 percent on their gas bills for heating water. By the 1910s at least 4,000 known solar water heaters had been manufactured, and uncounted others were being produced by local plumbers and tradespeople. By 1920 one small company was selling 1,000 units a year. Florida saw an even more impressive boom; by 1941, at least 60,000 solar water heaters had been installed in that state.

In the 1920s, the gas utilities expanded their energy role in California. As the companies made new discoveries, for a time they dropped prices drastically, helped finance the sale of gas units, installed them free, and sometimes even carried the loans on the gas heaters for a few years.[31] A similar kind of promotion was used by the electric utilities in Florida in the late 1940s and 1950s.

With the demise of solar development, the technology for gas and electric heaters improved. Electricity and gas became standard, solar energy an exotic, and increasingly nonexistent, alternative. As people became locked into the electric and gas system, the utilities could raise their prices. The effect of the energy company action was virtually to eliminate the development of solar energy, lock users into fossil-fuel systems, and accelerate our depletion of those fuels.

## Retarding Mass Transit

Transportation systems which might have fostered greater regional self-reliance and less energy consumption were systematically destroyed by large corporations. In the early 1900s, this country had extensive systems of electric trolley transit within cities, and similar, but usually larger, vehicles running between cities within regions. In 1920, for example, it was possible to travel on interurban streetcars from New York, stopping at cities and small towns, all the way to Massachusetts. In the East, the Midwest, and as far west as California these nonpolluting systems provided extensive and relatively fast transportation. Los Angeles, before becoming the pollution capital of the world, had a well-developed interurban system connecting it with surrounding cities and towns. Only forty years ago, the Los Angeles area had 3,000 electric interurban trains transporting 80 million people a year between fifty-six surrounding cities.

Had these systems remained, and had the technology

for them become more sophisticated, we would probably now have less congestion on our streets, less pollution in our air, and a well-developed system for people and goods transportation within many regions of the country. But between 1936 and 1949, the General Motors Company, according to a congressional study, working with Firestone Tire, Standard Oil of California, and two suppliers of bus-related products, bought out these privately owned lines throughout the country. They removed the tracks, sometimes replacing lines with buses, but often simply denying areas proper public transit, and inducing people to own cars.[32] After GM motorized the lines, they were typically sold back to local transit companies, under a contract prohibiting the local company from purchasing "any new equipment using any fuel or means of propulsion other than gas."[33]

In 1949, GM was convicted of criminally conspiring with other companies to monopolize bus sales. For their action, the corporation was fined $5,000; H. C. Grossman, who played a major role in GM's bus planning operations, was convicted and fined one dollar. The public, meanwhile, would spend hundreds of billions of dollars to build and use a less efficient means of transportation and thirty years later face the prospect of spending billions more to replicate a system which they once had. In 1973, Los Angeles, choking under the strain of its automobile dependency, contemplated the construction of a rail rapid-transit system. Building a system only a sixth the length of the one torn up not long before was estimated to cost $6.6 billion.[34]

## Profits from Dependence

As the American metropolis grew, it came to be more and more dependent on outside regions for food and other consumer products which it could neither produce nor manufacture itself. The existence within these metropolitan areas of enormous populations which had to be moved from place to place, which needed to be supplied with water and sewer systems, and which needed recreation facilities created enormous private financial opportunities for private investors, banks, and building companies.

Meanwhile, the bulk of jobs in the cities was shifting from production and factory work to marketing and servicing of goods which were being produced elsewhere. An economy of retail trade, real estate development, and public construction and service work developed. The city was producing less of what it needed to sustain itself, but was proliferating an elaborate array of techniques for marketing food, clothing, and housing—from small business people and owners of small apartment houses to chain stores, large banking institutions, and real estate developers.

In the early 1900s, there was still a large pool of blue-collar workers in the leftover industries of the big cities, and some industries, especially small shops and factories that required little capital to start and cheap labor to run, continued to grow into the thirties. But the new face of the big city was to become the center for financing and administering the expansion of the American economy. The big city was producing less and less; it was becoming a city of consumption, and becoming less able to bring in enough dollars to pay for that consumption.

The city's growing dependency upon outside resources, its clogged streets, its need to bring goods in to feed its inhabitants, created the need for vast privately financed, privately built, and publicly paid for improvement projects. Transportation was put underground in subways, as lines were extended out to help decongestion, while water supply and new sewers were built to safe-guard the public's health.

The public's problem of having to pay for its own infrastructure of dependence was already apparent by the 1920s. Streetcar lines and transit systems originally built by private developers (who often made more profit selling off the newly accessible land they owned next to their lines than in collecting fares) were turned over to city owner-ship as maintenance costs began to rise. Once the prof-itability had been milked from land speculation, the private companies had little reluctance to being "na-tionalized" by the cities—indeed business would often promote the takeovers themselves. The public would then find itself saddled with the expense of maintaining the old lines and building new ones.

The costs of public infrastructure such as streets and . subways, which the cities had gone into debt to finance, became overwhelming. "[F]or the first time in our his-tory," said historian Sam Warner, "public works drove our major cities toward bankruptcy. . . . When the depression struck in 1929, the capabilities of municipal finance had been so distended by street and subway construction that the cities could not meet the welfare obligations they had honored since the formation of the Republic."[35]

The pleas for federal help to finance the cities' state of dependence in the seventies are part of a cycle already apparent in the thirties. In 1932, the *New York Times* reported, "Half a million Chicagoans face starvation unless Federal aid is procured, a group of bankers told President Hoover by telephone today. . . ."[36] In New York City that year the situation was similar. New York's original fun-city mayor, Jimmy Walker, was attempting to get the banks to "roll over" the city transit debt—stretching short-term obligations into long-term ones. A bankers' committee instead called for higher transit fares and municipal workers' pay cuts. Walker, not unlike his 1970s successor, begged aid from Washington politicians and declared pay cuts for city employees.[37] Even today New Yorkers are still paying the debt on the subway system built earlier this century and big cities throughout the country are forced to refinance their old debts while taking on new ones.

A city or region's dependence on large amounts of imported products is bearable so long as these places continue to produce the kinds of products and services that can be exported and traded for dollars to buy imports. The cycle of dependence, however, begins its collapse whenever the national or international market for a region's products falls, or when large numbers of companies that produce these exports simply decide to leave it.

The modern American city or region being strategically abandoned by business is now on the horn of several dilemmas. It is dependent on a growing amount of imports, it is producing fewer exports to pay for these imports, and it is limited to the role of policeman-accomplice, unable to create a local economic planning process which it could directly control. In response to this problem, it is trying desperately to buy time by extending old debts and taking on new ones, in the future hope that by more aggressively entrepreneuring than other places in similar straits, it will eventually attain some form of solvency.

# 5
# THE ROOTS OF REGIONAL ROTATION

People don't want to work. It's as simple as that. . . .
Let you go hungry a few times, then you'll start
scratching around. . . . When I was going to school,
if I didn't work, I didn't eat.
> —Russell DeYoung, Chairman, Goodyear
> Tire and Rubber Company, explaining in
> the early 1970s why the company was
> moving to other states rather than
> expanding in Akron, Ohio.[1]

Whether or not workers move to where the jobs are, or
the jobs are moved to the workers, the conditions which
now make regional rotation possible are the same today as
they were more than 100 years ago—the existence of large
pools of unorganized low-paid or unemployed workers in
less economically developed regions. This technique to
reduce wages by shifting and threatening to shift jobs
from one group of workers to another was as much a part
of immigration practices as it is of today's migration of
industry. When Samuel Insull, the nineteenth-century
utility magnate, said, "the greatest aid of the efficiency of
labor is a long line of men waiting at the gate," he was

116

describing the attempt that has been adapted by business in various forms, at various times to keep workers from controlling their wages and job conditions.

The need for the "long line" of workers was not simply the policy of rapacious nineteenth-century industrialists, or a temporary aberration found during periods of economic recession and decline. From business's position, this line is a contemporary and permanent requirement to maintain a damper on workers' wages. In 1978, for example, *Business Week*'s editors openly called for maintaining unemployment rates higher than what it termed a "flash point," in order to keep workers from making excessive demands. ". . . [A] consensus among both liberal and conservative economists is beginning to emerge," said the magazine's editors, "that places the flash point somewhere between 5½% and 6% unemployment. To expand the economy beyond that point by (government's) stimulatory policies would intensify the shortages of qualified workers and heighten the pressure for wage increases."[2]

What is striking about the long-line philosophy as it developed over the past century is the similarity of the approach used by business during this period and the consistent effect it has had on the labor movement. While it's true that the labor movement has grown and become much more organized since the early 1900s, it is also true that it has become less radical and more sanitized. The periodic surges in militant labor organizing and the labor movement's growing power have been consistently countered by major organizing efforts by business to tear that movement apart.

The techniques for maintaining the long line have relied on maintaining ethnic, racial, and regional antagonisms between workers, on characterizing labor organizing as a particularly undemocratic and unpatriotic activity, and on capitalizing on the availability of large numbers of workers unable to find adequate jobs. The strategies of those who helped draft the Taft-Hartley Act, used since the late 1940s to purge union radicals, and which specifically helped shift jobs to less unionized areas, have their antecedents in the regional job shifts and the government red purges of the 1920s.

Today the techniques may be different, but the effects of low-paid, unorganized workers competing against each other are the same. When Jay Gould, the nineteenth-century railroad owner who used gunmen to keep his workers in line, boasted he could hire one-half the working class to kill the other half, he was describing industry's bald power to exploit economically desperate and unorganized workers.³ Today companies like Texas Instruments use industrial psychologists to develop techniques that keep their low-paid, unorganized workers in such fear of losing their jobs that they are willing to spy on each other's prounion tendencies.⁴

### Competing for Work

In the early forms of job shifting through immigration, newly arrived people in America, docile from hunger and desperate for wages, could be used by business to break strikes, help disrupt labor organizing, and destroy the chance for united action by the workers. In the early 1900s, the average wage for foreign-born and black workers was about half that of American-born whites.⁵ John R. Commons, a sociologist reporting on a visit to a Chicago meat packing plant in 1904, explained business's job-shifting techniques. On the day he arrived at the plant, he noticed only Swedes were being hired. "Last week," the employment agent told him, "we employed Slovaks. We change about among the different nationalities and languages. It prevents them from getting together." Explaining how other firms used this technique also, the agent said, "We have the thing systematized. We have a luncheon each week of the employment managers of the large firms of the Chicago district. . . . If agitators are coming or there is considerable unrest among the labor population, we raise the wages all around. . . . It is wonderful to watch the effect. The unrest stops and the agitators leave. Then when things quiet down we reduce the wages to where they were."[6]

In 1917, the managers of the Aluminum Ore Company in East St. Louis imported black workers to break a strike by the company's white workers. Their efforts were followed by a bloody race riot in that city.[7] Two years later, the violent scene of the massive steel workers' strike in Pittsburgh and the gray towns that dotted the Monongahela River to the north, provided the grim setting for the company policy of pitting workers against each other. The 300,000 workers striking against United States Steel were mostly Eastern Europeans and Italians. To break the strike, the steel company hired Italians to spread stories in Italian communities of Eastern Europeans going back to work, and at the same time hired Eastern Europeans to tell other Eastern Europeans that the Italians were returning. To cap their efforts and drive home the powerlessness of the strikers, the company then imported blacks to work in the mills.[8]

## Prelude to the 1950s

The dependency of the nation on its corporate powers was vastly increased by the approach of World War I. Business seized on the war effort as an opportunity to put to rest the tedious and unprofitable battles with labor, to discipline the nation against political deviance, and not in the least to expand profits in the new markets of military hardware.

It was Woodrow Wilson who was to perceive the same danger in business domination of a war effort that Dwight D. Eisenhower described some forty years later when he cautioned the nation against our "Military-Industrial Complex." "War means autocracy," said Wilson. "The people we have unhorsed will inevitably come into control of the country for we shall be dependent upon the steel, ore and financial magnates. They will run the nation."[9]

Decked in bright red, white, and blue bunting, business and public officials championed the national cause with new vigor. Those who refused to snap to at the patriotic call, those who threatened strikes or who might otherwise slow the military machinery were declared dangerous to the country; they were thrown in jail, they were deported, and in some cases they were to lose their lives in a wave of antired hysteria that swept the country.

As the war in Europe drew to a close in 1917, the war against radicalism at home was taken up with new energy. The national crusade for patriotic purity was mixed with the puritanical Victorianism of the prohibitionists. The nation was to become pure in both spirit and body; America's political leaders urged their flock to turn their ears and minds from foreign radical ideologies, while they passed a new law to regulate their liquor drinking. As it happened, they would be more successful in altering the nation's political consciousness than its drinking habits.

The war fervor, accompanied by sedition acts, no-strike pledges from the conservative AFL, and the wholesale arrests of radical organizers, severely limited labor organizing. The dismal economic conditions at the war's close, with prices rising and wages remaining low, brought a brief, but doomed resurgence of labor militancy. In

1919, there were 3,600 strikes involving 4 million workers in building trades, shipping, mining, public transportation, steel making, and a host of other industries. In Boston, for the first time in American history, an entire police force went out on strike.

The war and the repression of radicals left labor badly divided. Though millions of workers had been on strike that year, no union existed which could represent the interest of all workers in a concerted action against business. Most of the Wobbly leaders and many of the Socialists were in jail. For its part, the AFL refused to join with other than its craft union affiliates in disputes. Even in the Boston police strike, where the police were affiliated with an AFL local, other AFL unions refused the policemen's call for a general strike. Against the backdrop of factional bickering and decimated labor organizations, an evangelical United States Justice Department in the early 1920s moved against workers with all the legal and illegal apparatus at its command.

The Justice Department that year was headed by A. Mitchell Palmer; its General Intelligence Division was headed by a young and aggressive assistant, J. Edgar Hoover. Palmer's efforts to rid the country of "reds" and their sympathizers was perhaps the most infamous binge in crushing political freedom in America until Joseph McCarthy capitalized on the enthusiasm for such practices some thirty years later.

Palmer's favored tactics of intimidation against the radicals were court injunctions against striking workers, the disruption of workers' meetings, and the swift arrest and often deportation of suspected radicals. His injunctions against hundreds of thousands of striking workers in 1919 and his arrest of their leaders effectively disrupted an already wounded movement.

His most famous tactics, however, were mass raids and

deportations. In December, 1919, at Palmer's direction, 250 people considered to be radicals, guarded by another 250 soldiers, were placed on the military freighter *Buford* and shipped off on a journey that would eventually take them to Russia. The New York *Evening Mail*, waxing moralistic in the spirit that had gripped most of America's press, commented, "Just as the sailing of the Ark that Noah built was a pledge for the preservation of the human race, so the sailing of the Ark of the Soviet is a pledge for the preservation of America."[10] Emma Goldman, the radical labor organizer who was one of the prisoners on board the *Buford*, proclaimed defiantly, "I consider it an honor to be chosen as the first political agitator to be deported by the United States."[11]

The 1919 raids were a curtain raiser to the terror that followed. As the newspapers ballyhooed Palmer's "ark," calling for bigger ships and more deportations, and as Congress generally acquiesced, the attorney general confidently readied another salvo against the radicals.

During a cold winter night on the second day of the 1920 new year, Palmer initiated a series of simultaneous roundups in dozens of cities across America. In Palmer's dramatic nationwide dragnet to rid the country of the "menace" once and for all, meetings were disrupted and people taken from their homes in the middle of the night; they were crowded into jail cells or camped out, in government offices and corridors to await questioning. In all, somewhere between 6,000 and 10,000 suspected "reds" and sympathizers were arrested.[12]

Most of those rounded up were later released; some died in jail, while many remained there for long periods awaiting trials and deportations. Between 1919 and 1920 close to 600 people, whose political beliefs were considered dangerous to America, had been deported. They were people who, according to the attorney general of the

United States, were hardly human. "Out of the sly and crafty eyes of many of them," said the nation's chief judicial officer, "leap cupidity, cruelty, insanity, and crime; from their lopsided faces, sloping brows, and misshapen features may be recognized the unmistakable criminal type."[13]

## "The American Plan"

Aside from these actions of the Justice Department, business in the early twenties began an organized, national drive to administer a final blow to organized labor. Capitalizing on the patriotic hysteria in government and the media, corporate businessmen, through their national organizations like the National Association of Manufacturers, the Chamber of Commerce, and the National Metal Trades Association, prepared a new antiunion program. Wrapped in the patriotic motif of the day, they called their program "The American Plan."

The plan, according to John Edgerton, president of the National Association of Manufacturers, was a program to maintain the open shop. "I can't conceive of any principle," said Edgerton, "that is more purely American, that comes nearer representing the very essence of all those traditions and institutions that are dearest to us than the open shop principle."[14] The union or closed shop was characterized by the national business group as a subversive organization. "You can hardly conceive of a more un-American, a more anti-American institution," said Gus W. Dyers, a propagandist for the NAM, "than the closed shop. It is really very remarkable that it is allowed to exist. . . ."[15]

The American Plan was not, as its proponents claimed, a plan to give workers a choice of union or nonunion work, but in fact, an aggressive program to keep them from organizing. Those who belonged to labor organizations weren't hired, or if they attempted to organize, found themselves without a job. Workers were forced to sign "yellow dog contracts," pledging not to join a union in order to find work. "Company unions," organized by industries, were effectively used to block workers from organizing their own unions. The National Metal Trades Association, a major industrial organization of large firms, backed the American Plan, pooling the resources of member firms to provide strikebreaking services, police, spies, and workers' blacklists for any member facing the threat of labor organizing.

The effect of business's coordinated and well-organized effort behind the American Plan was devastating. In Detroit and Los Angeles, the gains thousands of workers had achieved during World War I were eliminated. In the labor stronghold of San Francisco, old unions either lost strength or were unable to organize new workers. Between 1920 and 1924, the powerful Machinists Union in Cincinnati lost over 75 percent of its membership after a strike was effectively destroyed with the help of the National Metal Trades Association.

The conservatives in the labor movement, fearing for the very existence of their organizations, soon took up business's cause against radicalism with a new enthusiasm. Communists and other radicals, who had once been among the AFL's most effective organizers, were driven from the union. The AFL's Philip Murray, who twenty-five years later would marshal a similar purge of the CIO, took the lead in attacking the labor radicals. "Having burned its witches and driven the communists out of its stockade into the wilderness," wrote Len DeCaux, a former Wobbly, "a purged, purified, sanctified AFL bundled up for a 12-year sleep."[16]

The radical purges and the somnambulance of the AFL decimated labor's prewar strength. During the booming economic decade of the twenties, the number of workers in the country grew by almost 4 million; during the same period, membership in the country's labor unions dropped by 1.7 million.[17]

## The Old "New South"

The American Plan of the 1920s parallels business's current "Right-to-Work" movement. The newer movement was boosted by the 1947 Taft-Hartley Act, which gave the states the right to have open shop legislation within their borders. Both movements were accompanied by the migration of industry to low-wage, unorganized sections of the country, especially in the South. The "runaway shop," far from being a new problem, has its roots in business strategies half a century old. Indeed, even the 1970s' phrase "New South" was one that was used in the twenties to describe the lure of cheap jobs and financial incentives offered by southern states to migrating northern industries. During the twenties, many southern states were already matching or outstripping the growth of industrial jobs in northern states. Had the national economy not tumbled so steeply after that fateful October in 1929, the dramatic effects of the shift would likely have been felt in the midwestern and northern industrial states long before the 1970s.

It was no mere coincidence that during the 1920s, the same John Edgerton, president of the National Association of Manufacturers, who so zealously promoted the American Plan, was also a southern textile mill executive espousing the virtue of southern labor as an alternative to northern unionism.[18] The southern worker, declared

Edgerton in a clumsy metaphor, "is a native soil in which exotic radicalism does not thrive." These workers, he said, had "a heritage of sturdy Americanism," making them "a dependable factor in industry."[19]

By 1929, the movement of industries escaping better working conditions in the North was already well under way. In North Carolina, furniture manufacturing began to rival Grand Rapids, Michigan. Thousands of workers in North Carolina were producing fiber cord for auto and truck tires, while many thousands more were manufacturing textiles for a variety of other uses. Cigar and cigarette manufacturing in the South during the twenties supplied over 40 percent of the country's total production. Sixty percent of the nation's fertilizer and almost all of its turpentine was produced in that region. Rubber factories were moving toward Alabama's cheap labor in the twenties, and Birmingham with its steel mills had already been dubbed the "Pittsburg of the South."

In the hills of the southern Piedmont, stretching through Virginia, the Carolinas, and Georgia, over seventy new manufacturing plants set up production in 1928 alone. Many of the new plants were textile mills built to compete with those of the North. By 1929, a third the value of the South's manufacturing was in cotton textiles. By that same year, more than half the textile spindles in the nation were in the South.[20] By the early 1930s, increasing amounts of coal were being dug and shipped from the nonunion fields of West Virginia, Kentucky, and the South.

Dollars traveling to America's southern mill towns in the twenties came from investors speaking a variety of languages and dialects, but all appreciating the advantages offered by the antiunion governments. Yankee capital from New England mill owners was invested in the new southern mills; the Lehmans of New York, the du

Ponts of Delaware were putting their money in rayon manufacture in Tennessee, as were German and Belgian industrialists, while English pounds were being exchanged for dollars to build plants in Virginia. "In the last few years," said Ethel Smith, of the National Women's Trade Union League (NWTUL), in 1929, sounding very much as if she were writing in the seventies, "the South and its rich resources have become the new 'boom' territory of American industry."[21]

While the specific conditions may be different, the campaign of selling this New South to prospective investors rings familiar. Local chambers of commerce, prodding local government officials, had undertaken a campaign of touting antilabor legislation, low pay, and government financial incentives. Advertisements to manufacturers by southern chambers of commerce in the twenties explained how "cheap and docile labor" was available for "$8 a week and up," how children over fourteen were allowed to work eleven hours a day, that favorable business legislation meant "no night laws for females over 16," that the sixty-hour work week was allowed "with no restrictions on the number of machines operated per worker," and "there are no labor unions."[22]

In Marion, North Carolina, where mill girls worked their first month with no pay, their next four months at five cents an hour, and after that at sixteen cents an hour, where the sixty-hour work week and child labor were standard, and where the housing and factory conditions were miserable, the local Kiwanis Club declared that "Marion is an ideal hometown, with a fairyland about it. . . ." The local worker, said the businessman's club, "is of a most intelligent, loyal and desirable kind."[23]

"Houston," said the city's chamber of commerce in the late twenties, "has available for textile mills over 7,000 native female workers ranging in age from 18 to 44. . . . Operators in the twelve Texas textile mills receive an average of $14.41 for a 55-hour week."[24] The comparable wage for Massachusetts textile workers was $16.47 for a forty-eight-hour week.

Textile workers in New England mills in the late 1920s were earning 50 percent more than their southern counterparts; in 1929, common laborers in basic steel earned 66 percent more in the Great Lakes region than in the South.[25]

In 1929, a southern field representative of the National Women's Trade Union League reported on the campaign of local business and government groups to attract capital. "I saw not long ago an advertisement from Texas," said Matilda Lindsay, "playing up the fact that there was practically no labor legislation, that native white labor would be content with low wages and a low standard of living, and that by building factories in their state, no heating plants need be installed because of the climate."

In Elizabethtown, in Tennessee's "Happy Valley," local government persuaded German manufacturers backed by New York money to build a number of rayon plants with the lure of free land and ten-year tax exemptions.[26] The Germans, according to Lindsay, unfamiliar with local practice, actually paid better wages than other businesses in the area, "[But] the Chambers of Commerce in adjoining cities," she said, "told them to reduce wages in order not to ruin the people. The same kind of thing happened in Virginia."[27]

The twenties, much like the fifties, sixties, and seventies, were landmark years for southern job growth. Even while white and black southerners were migrating to northern cities by the hundreds of thousands, southern jobs were expanding rapidly, in many cases as fast if not faster than those to the north.

During that heady period of the 1920s national economic growth, jobs in Alabama, South Carolina, Tennessee, and Mississippi were all growing about three times as fast as Massachusetts, and about as fast as Ohio. Both Oklahoma and Louisiana, with about 20 percent job growth, were expanding at about the same rate as Illinois; Arizona, North Carolina, and Texas all bettered New York State's 22 percent job growth.[28] Alabama, Arkansas, Arizona, California, Florida, Mississippi, North Carolina, South Carolina, Tennessee, Texas, Georgia, Oklahoma, Virginia, Louisiana, and New Mexico, with a total population of 37 million in 1930, had added 2.8 million jobs during the previous ten years while New York, New Jersey, Pennsylvania, Ohio, Massachusetts, and Illinois, with a 30 percent higher total population, added just 2.7 million jobs during the same period.

The 1920s job shift to the less developed South is even more pronounced than it first appears. Southern states during the 1920s had added only 700,000 people through migration, while the North had gained almost 2 million.[29] Indeed, many of the southern states that were adding substantial numbers of jobs, Alabama, Tennessee, South Carolina, Arkansas, Georgia, Mississippi, and Virginia, were doing so in spite of losing hundreds of thousands of people through migration. Those who stayed behind in the southern states were to find more jobs available than ever before, but under the harsh conditions of low pay and long hours, and with the constant threat of harassment, firing, and violence when they tried to organize.

## The Lintheads

The "lintheads," as the workers of the textile mills came to be known, fought a losing battle against a hometown police state. The mill owners owned the workers' homes, their stores, their schools, their hospitals, and often paid for the mayor and the local police force; in some cases they even paid when the National Guard was called out against strikers. Recalcitrant workers could be disciplined by withholding not only their paycheck and their job, but by withholding most of the necessities of life. Even the local church, often owned by the mill owner, could be used to discipline workers.[30]

Labor "justice" in the South was swift and deadly: The lynching of blacks in that part of the country is a painful part of American history; violence against white workers tends to be a more silent chapter. In the wave of unsuccessful strikes across the Piedmont mill towns in 1929, union organizers were kidnapped and beaten, workers lost their homes and jobs, were flogged, maimed, and killed. In Gastonia, North Carolina, Ella Mary Wiggins, a twenty-nine-year-old union organizer and mother of five, was killed when a gang of vigilantes opened fire on a truck filled with union people on their way to attend a murder trial against other union leaders. In nearby Marion, six workers were killed by a sheriff and his deputies for refusing to disperse their picket line; in Elizabethtown, Tennessee, where over a thousand workers were arrested in a single day, company guards sat atop mill buildings with machine guns and held striking workers at bay, while scabs took their places at the looms.

The concerted assault against the fledgling success of labor in the teens and twenties bore its fruit. Legal injunctions, red-baiting, open shop legislation, violent repression of organizers and workers, and the geographic shifting of industries successfully eroded the precarious position labor had fought to establish. By 1929, before the stock market collapsed, not only had the labor movement's radical claws been pulled, but even conservative unions were in disarray. From a post-World War I peak of 5 million, the country's union membership dropped to less than 3.5 million; over 85 percent of these workers who remained members now belonged to the pro-business AFL, whose own membership rolls had dropped by over a million.[31]

The economic depression of the thirties opened a new chapter in labor organizing, eventually providing the conditions for a spectacular resurgence in union growth. Faced with an economy in shreds and the growing popular organizing around alternatives like communism and socialism, liberal Congressional leaders moved quickly toward legal protection of the less radical trade union alternative. In the early 1930s, Congress passed a historic series of labor laws. Beginning with the Norris-LaGuardia Act in 1932, and culminating in the Wagner Act in 1935, labor gained an important legal foothold against industry.

The Wagner Act, which was belatedly supported by President Roosevelt, not only gave workers the legal right to organize and form unions, but created the National Labor Relations Board to oversee compliance. Drafted by Robert Wagner, a progressive New York senator, the new legislation also gave organized labor a critical key to their future power—the possibility of the union shop. The act provided that when a firm signed with a union, a majority of workers could vote to make union membership a condition for getting a job in that firm.

Aided by the continued deterioration of economic conditions, the aggressive work of union organizers and the legitimizing effect of the two labor acts, the union movement virtually exploded. Between 1933 and 1934 the International Ladies Garment Workers quadrupled membership, with the Amalgamated Clothing Workers gaining almost as much. The United Mine Workers, led by its fiery leader, John L. Lewis, won back West Virginia, an important source of its strength.[32]

By the late 1930s, before there had been any serious

recovery from the depression, nine million Americans had joined a union. From representing less than 12 percent of the labor force in 1930, the unions now represented nearly 30 percent of the nation's workers.[33] By 1947, after World War II had stoked economic recovery, there were 15 million union members.

This phenomenal growth was in large part the result of insurgent groups within the labor movement headed by John L. Lewis. Lewis, who was not a political radical himself, joined with socialist and communist union leaders and organizers to promote a new approach to labor organizing. Contrary to the "skilled trades" policy of the AFL, the insurgents moved to organize unskilled workers in the new mass production industries like steel, coal, and automobiles.

Lewis's group, renamed the Congress of Industrial Organizations in 1938, became a dominant political force over the next twenty years. By 1938, just two years after they had been expelled, the CIO already claimed over four million members. By the end of World War II, its membership climbed to six million, 40 percent of all organized workers in the country—more members than it would ever be able to claim for itself again.[34]

## Flag Waving Again

Faced with increased union activity in the thirties, business resorted to its traditional defenses—parading behind the flag and propagandizing against "unpatriotic" labor organizations. The National Association of Manufacturers published and distributed over two million copies of its book, "Join the CIO and Help Build a Soviet America."[35] This same powerful business organization also published the Mohawk Valley Formula, a set of tactics devised by James H. Rand, Jr., of the Remington Rand Company to combat striking workers. Thomas R. Brooks, a labor historian, wrote:

> The ingredients of the formula are relatively simple. The plan of attack calls for an employer-conducted strike ballot; the labeling of union leaders as "outside agitators," "communists," and "radicals;" economic pressure on the community by threats to move plants; the organization of a back-to-work movement to cover up the employment of strikebreakers; a show of police and "Citizens' Committee" force; and a grandstand opening of struck plants.[36]

The Mohawk Valley Formula was adapted by Tom M. Girdler, president of Republic Steel, who enthusiastically embraced red-baiting in battling workers' organizing. "Must Republic Steel and its men submit to the Communistic dictates and terrorism of the CIO?" asked Girdler. "If America is to remain a free country the answer is 'No.'"[37] In 1937, during the infamous Memorial Day Massacre, police killed ten striking workers in South Chicago; thirty others including three children were wounded. In Massilon, Ohio, another two Republic strikers were killed— Girdler's tactics had effectively blocked union success at his plants.

Government antired activity once again followed business's antilabor campaign. By the early 1940s, the House Committee on Un-American Activities (HUAC), directed by Congressman Martin Dies of Texas, had been set up to drive the reds from America. At the end of World War II anticommunist activity by the government increased. The Taft-Hartley Act in 1947 formally excluded communists from labor unions and at the same time created a mechanism for promoting regional rotation and sapping union strength. The infamous section 14-B of this act allowed the states to decide individually whether or not to outlaw the union shop. Since Taft-Hartley, twenty states, eleven in the South and nine elsewhere, have taken advantage of 14-B to discourage union organizing, to keep wages low, and to improve their competitive climate for attracting business.

Yet even the creation of antiunion laws in states around the country did not immediately threaten the unions' ability to deliver benefits to their workers. A growing national economy allowed business to meet labor's demands in those states where unions had already grown. American hegemony over world resources and world markets meant business could continue to both meet the rising demands of organized labor *and* increase its profits. The partnership-with-business spirit that George Meany's docile sector of the union movement had inherited from Samuel Gompers appeared secure.

The Korean War provided an opportunity to reassert the values of American patriotism against what was described as a growing problem of communism in that part of the world. The battles waged against the Wobblies in the 1910s, and against the radicals in the labor movement in the thirties and forties, had now been consolidated and seemed complete. Joseph McCarthy, who hoped to ride the wave of Americanism following the Korean War with his rantings as chairman of the Senate Subcommittee on Investigations, eventually became embarrassingly excessive in style. In the end he was removed from the scene by more level-headed liberals, who knew radicalism presented no challenge to the security of the world's most powerful economic and military apparatus.

It wasn't until the Vietnam War that a new form of radicalism was to reassert itself, and a new business and government campaign against this menace had to be mounted. It is no accident that the beginning of the Vietnam War and the accelerated shift of jobs from union-strong to union-weak parts of the country coincide. American business, faced with declining rates of profit, turned to a traditionally tested formula of stimulating the economy with war expenditures and the preservation of its access to materials, markets, and labor in an undeveloped part of the world. At the same time it would use regional rotation to develop a more profitable strategy at home.

George Meany's support of the same policies David Rockefeller and other business leaders were pressing in Indochina announced the desperation that traditional unionists felt in the lagging strength of their partnerships with business. If business could not succeed in its imperial strategies, then the gains of organized labor would have to be put on the block. Meany could see regional rotation and other antiunion strategies coming.

As Samuel Gompers did before him, when he supported business efforts to send troops to Europe in 1913, George Meany opted for the quick fix of war. Ironically, had business's strategy been successful in Vietnam, and indeed, had American military operations kept Vietnam open as a source of corporate penetration, American workers would have found themselves competing with yet one other place in the world where industry was exporting its capital to create nonunion, low-paid work forces.

In the 1910s, America, draped in the flag, had gone to war in Europe and faced radical resistance to the war at home. Fifty years later America marched off to Asia and again was confronted with radical opposition. The resistance in the 1960s did not grow from the labor movement, although more progressive unions would come to oppose American involvement. What was left of the labor movement after the purges of the forties and fifties had been effectively sanitized from radicalism and pacified by its share of American economic expansion over the previous twenty years.

The new radicals were those more removed from the day-to-day struggle for livelihood; they were people who did not see their futures tied to American world domination, but instead had tasted the fruits of this domination and had found them wanting. The new resistance grew from a complexity of factors—from moral opposition to war, from the resistance to a world of increased consumption, from a resistance to being killed in a war which could only continue those values that were being rejected at home. It was also a war opposed by civil rights activists who saw blacks and other minorities shipped off in disproportionate numbers to fight and die in a war against other people of color, while ghettos in this country were being destroyed by government-organized redevelopment programs.

The loss of Vietnam, and the huge expenditures and debt required to support the war took a disastrous economic toll. It meant a vastly increased national debt, which had to be paid for by higher taxes, more demands for wage increases to pay these taxes and less availability of supplies that were directed toward the war effort—all of which were to contribute to inflation.

To add to business's postwar economic problems, a new environmental movement began to gain political power. Well-organized lobbying by environmentalists on the state and national levels resulted in a raft of laws aimed at cutting industry's use of the air and water as a sewer for its wastes. New industrial expansion and in some cases existing facilities now required expensive equipment for their operations.

To counter the effects of inflation and other rising costs on profits, business was now forced to speed up its search for new ways to hold down wages and decrease its cost of environmental cleanup. The shift, and the threats to shift to hungrier regions, more antiunion regions, and to regions with more relaxed environmental standards, would now accelerate.

# 6
# THE JOYS OF CORPORATE COOPERATION: Who's Afraid of Free Enterprise?

> In the beginning, God was an entrepreneur: He qualified by creating something from nothing.
> —*New England Business* magazine.[1]

The growth of local government, our premier entrepreneur, taking risks and gambling with people's tax monies, with their environments, their wages and job conditions, has an ironic counterpart in the world of corporate business. As local government incentives for business escalate, business itself now moves toward even greater economic concentration and cooperative noncompetitive practices. Ever fewer companies are coming to control the major industries, with ever fewer of them holding the nation's private assets. Price fixing, supply control, and other noncompetitive behavior have become a recurrent theme of corporate practice.

A Byzantine pattern of business leaders, sitting on a multiplicity of corporate boards, is able to coordinate the buying and selling of each other's products and secure the available investment capital for each other's ventures. In short, as the public and its governments struggle with the most severe burdens of its free enterprise system, large corporate business has come to embrace the rewards of its own rather exclusive and cooperative enterprise system.

In spite of the creation of federal antitrust laws in the 1890s, the trend toward large corporate power has continued. Forty years ago, 1 percent of all United States corporations controlled 52 percent of all manufacturing assets; by 1974, slightly less than 1 percent of our corporations controlled almost 65 percent of our manufacturing assets. In 1935, 4 percent of all United States corporations controlled 84 percent of all net profits; by 1974 only 2 percent of all these corporations controlled almost 90 percent of all net profits.[2]

In most major industries the trend toward economic concentration has resulted in oligopolies in which relatively few companies virtually dominate the market for any given product. In autos, railroad equipment, batteries, building insulation, glass, turbines and generators, refrigerators, sewing machines, washing machines, typewriters, building wallboard, tires and cigarettes and other products, only four companies in each industry category now control at least 80 percent of the value of goods shipped. In many of these industries the four largest companies control over 90 percent of these goods.[3]

The concentration of capital resources and production in diminishing numbers of businesses is accompanied by the concentration of a limited number of business people who sit on the board of directors of a multiplicity of companies. A few noteworthy examples of these interlocking directorates are G. William Miller, chairman of the Federal Reserve Board, formerly director of the Textron Company and at the same time a director of the Allied Chemical Company, The American Research and Development Corporation, and the Federal Reserve Bank of Boston. President Carter's Secretary of Commerce, Juanita Kreps had been simultaneously a director of Eastman Kodak, J.C. Penney, and the Western Electric Company. And Melvin R. Laird, former President Richard Nixon's Secretary of Defense and Domestic Advisor, sits on the board of directors of Phillips Petroleum, Northwest Airlines, and the Metropolitan Life Insurance Company, in addition to *nine* other companies.

These interlocking directorates provide an environment in which companies, presumably in competition with one another, may be able to exchange information and coordinate prices and production. A 1978 Senate subcommittee study found that "companies at the top of corporate America were heavily concentrated through interlocking directorates," warning:

> Such interlocking directorates among the Nation's very largest corporations may provide mechanisms for stabilizing prices, controlling supply and restraining competition. They can have a profound effect on business attempts to influence Government policies. They can impact on corporate decisions as to the type and quality of products and services to be marketed in the United States and overseas. They can influence company policies with respect to the employee rights, compensation and job conditions. They can bear on corporate policies with respect to environmental and social issues and possibly, control the shape and direction of the Nation's economy.

Detailing a variety of cases where corporate directors from presumably competing companies could meet and coordinate policy, the subcommittee researchers pointed to one of the more extreme examples.

> The corporate board that provided the broadest opportunity for a summit discussion on energy was not a financial institution, but a heavy machinery manufacturer. Caterpillar Tractor's board included directors from Exxon, Mobil, Shell, Standard of California and Atlantic Richfield—five of the seven major energy companies in the analysis. Chemical New York—where four majors met—was also directly interlocked with Caterpillar. Similarly, A.T.&T., IBM and United States Steel were on the machinery manufacturer's board.

In addition to the interlocking between the companies themselves, there are a number of formal national corporate policy-making and research organizations at which these directors have the opportunity to coordinate and control business programs that effect consumers and workers. The three major organizations are the Business Roundtable, the Conference Board, and the Business Council. In these organizations, the firms represented form a list of most of the largest, most powerful corporations and banks in the world.

The forty-five members of the Business Roundtable, for example, include Reginald Jones, chairman of General Electric, Thomas Murphy, chairman of General Motors, David Rockefeller, chairman of the Chase Manhattan, Irving Shapiro, chairman of DuPont, Edgar Speer, chairman of United States Steel, Rawleigh Warner, Jr., chairman of Mobil Oil, Walter B. Wriston, chairman of Citibank, and John D. deButts, chairman of American Telephone and Telegraph. Many of these same men not only sit on other company boards, but are members of either the Conference Board, the Business Council, or both.[4]

With the enormous concentration and coordination of corporate power that is now possible, large American corporations would appear to have little problem maintaining their control over the United States economy. With their ability to set prices and limit supply, they would seem able to insure their profitable positions.

Superficially, the large American corporation is in fact stronger than ever; its size and its dominance over markets have insulated it from any serious threats from small upstarts. The long-run threat comes from outside America's corporate boardrooms: competition from other giant companies abroad; cost increases by other countries for their natural resources; competition by other countries for American markets; and the demands of consumers, environmentalists, and workers in this country.

The solutions proposed by business and government leaders appear contradictory. One theme is familiar: it's time to think about less, to lower our demands, to understand shortages, and to realize we've had a good thing going and that we could blow it all by assuming that our successful past can be maintained exactly in the future. At the same time our leaders speak about conservation and limits, they are looking for ways of expanding economic growth.

A few years ago Henry Ford II, discussing our energy problems, explained how he personally was learning to make do. "I'm conserving a lot of electricity at my house," he said earnestly. "More than I've ever done before I'm going around turning my own lights out."[5]

This homey confession by a man whose legendary wealth derives from massive energy consumption might ordinarily seem so much banal public relations. His message signals no sudden conversion of corporate leaders to ecological leadership, but it does suggest that they are feeling the effects of an economic crisis and the need to do something about it. At the same time Ford was expressing his concern about energy conservation, he and other business leaders were relaying their fears about the survival of our economic system, and proposing the sort of massive government intervention that might once have seemed blasphemous.

Many businesses are trying to improve their lagging economic performance by strategies such as regional rotation—moving to regions of this country and abroad where labor costs are lower, and where local governments are willing to entrepreneur for them with higher tax abatements and other subsidies. But some business leaders, like Henry Ford, are even more alarmed at private enterprise's future survival prospects, and are calling for more drastic new strategies, which would lead to even less risk by private companies and more by government. In this new strategy federal, rather than local, government is looked to as the public entrepreneur.

## Corporate-Government Planning

Faced with a declining economy in the future, there is a strong logic for companies to join to create an orderly program to insure stability, growth, even survival. But private agreements among companies to organize materials, supplies, and markets, to establish prices they will pay for materials, and to fix prices they will sell their products for might bring serious charges of collusion and monopoly.

But if instead of *private* agreements, the *government itself* became a partner to the agreement, the legal problems would disappear. What in flush times would be seen as a strange and incongruous position becomes the pragmatic path to survival in lean times. Recently, some of America's most important corporate leaders have openly called for a radical government-initiated strategy to increase economic growth—relying on techniques of massive federal financing, government guaranteed return on corporate investment, and federal planning for the entire United States economy.

In 1975, Robert Roosa, a former undersecretary of the Treasury and a partner in a large New York investment firm, joined a business-supported group to urge national economic planning. Lamenting America's "yearning idealization of laissez-faire," he warned, the "only hope for approximating the conditions of laissez-faire must be in planning ahead for the resource needs of the future." The role for his planning group, said Roosa, who simultaneously sits on the corporate boards of Texaco, Anaconda, Owens-Corning Fiberglas, American Express, and a number of other companies, was to help this process by converting planning "from a pejorative to an operative word in the vocabulary of the American public and government."[6]

Major business support for more direct federal involvement with business comes from Henry Ford II; Thornton Bradshaw, president of ARCO oil; Felix Rohatyn, a New York investment banker and one of the chief architects of New York City's new fiscal program; and a host of other high-echelon executives. Testifying before a congressional committee in 1974, Henry Ford suggested that government introduce national economic planning, specifically calling for a government agency modeled on one which had lent money to banks, railroads, and insurance companies during the thirties. Following the old Reconstruction Finance Corporation (RFC) format, the new agency, said Ford, could make "large amounts of capital available to industrial concerns, utilities, and banks."[7]

In 1978, Ford reiterated his call for government planning. He chided his conservative colleagues for calling him a "socialist," explaining that government incentives could be coupled with planning and that planning would give each business an opportunity to see what others were doing, and to join together with incentives to chart a profitable future. "We must know how each others' actions affect another," said Ford, "and be willing to change or eliminate those that are counter-productive." Government incentives should be provided to business, "to do what should be done because it is demonstrably in their (business') best interest to do so." "Even a donkey," said Ford, "will respond to a carrot as well as a stick."[8]

Felix Rohatyn, the New York investment banker and ITT director who became the celebrated force behind the various state committees of bankers and corporate leaders charting New York City's future finances during the city's fiscal crisis in the midseventies, carried this idea a step further. Like Henry Ford and other corporate leaders who favor more government involvement, Rohatyn, a corporate director of ITT, Owens-Illinois, Pfizer, and several other companies, is troubled by business's inability to generate enough capital for needed investments. "At every level," he says, "our institutions are burdened with debt. In the past ten years the debt-equity ratio of individual corporations has gone from 25 percent to 40 percent." Rohatyn would go beyond the 1930s' model, building a federal agency that could not only tide business over its short-term difficulties but, as he says, provide it with a "safety net" of a long-term, "large infusion of equity capital." When necessary, says Rohatyn, whose own talents helped ITT with numerous mergers in the sixties and Lockheed with its government financing in the seventies, Washington could put money into troubled companies.

Concerned that his proposal, which would start with $15 billion in government funds, might be seen as a step toward state planning, Rohatyn insists it would be something quite different. "What many will call state planning would, to the average family, be no more than prudent budgeting." The idea of corporate leaders and government officials dividing $15 billion in tax money among corporate recipients hardly matches the tableau of mom and pop setting about balancing the family check book. A more accurate representation would be a family forced to invest its money in companies whose policies it does not control, who can pollute its environment, relocate or eliminate its jobs, who can raise prices for its necessities, and who generally have more influence over that family' life than its elected political representatives.

One of the business community's most articulate spokesmen for national economic planning and national subsidies has been Thornton Bradshaw, president of the Atlantic Richfield Oil Company (ARCO) and a director of RCA and the Security Pacific Company. Bradshaw, a former member of Jimmy Carter's campaign task force on energy, explained to business leaders that the OPEC countries are unpredictable; they can neither be counted on to keep prices at appropriately profitable levels in the future, nor is there any assurance that OPEC's interests will necessarily coincide with those of the oil companies.

Especially worrisome, according to Bradshaw, would

be the vagaries of free market competition in the event of new energy discoveries. "Consider a bit of history," ARCO's president reminded business leaders in 1977. "For a brief period in the late 1920s the price of crude oil was set by a 'free market' on the Gulf Coast in the U.S.—at that time the world's principal oil field. Then, in 1930, the East Texas field was discovered. The price of oil declined from $1.10 to 10¢ a barrel. . . . First, voluntary restrictive action on production was tried. Then the government stepped in and, through the producing states, managed the flow of oil and the price to provide for an 'orderly market.'

"If there were a free market today (including OPEC oil)," he complained, "the newly posted price of crude would fall from $12.09 per barrel to $3 or $4." Through national economic planning, Bradshaw envisions the oil companies solving the problems of free market price fluctuations by simply being able to establish higher oil prices.

Besides the advantage of government involvement in price-fixing under national planning, Bradshaw points out other benefits for business—subsidies to explore and produce alternative energy sources, and strength against recalcitrant environmental groups.

To produce synthetic oil, for example, he envisions government "guaranteed loans to help build the first few plants, subsidies to compensate for high production costs, and contracts for the purchase of shale oil at a negotiated price." For other alternatives, such as solar and nuclear fusion, there would be further government subsidies. "Industry," said Bradshaw, "can hardly ask its stockholders to wait decades for a financial return while the research is proved out. The enterprise system simply doesn't allow for investment on such a scale and on so long a term." He does not, however, mention that while stockholders eventually profit from their investment, and own part of the company, taxpayers are being asked to make long-term investments without any hope of profit or ownership control.

In dealing with environmentalists, Bradshaw sees national planning helping energy companies short-circuit expensive controversies. Complaining of the time spent on the Alaskan pipeline, "the interminable lawsuits and legislative filibusters that have held up development of western coal, nuclear-plant construction, and offshore drilling," he sees promise in joining a national program. "[A] national energy plan," he says, "could mandate a more efficient means of coming to an acceptable trade-off between environmental protection and economic development."[9]

National economic planning as a program that could control what gets produced, which companies get the available supplies, and how much companies can charge for their products is by no means acceptable to a broad spectrum of business leaders. It is still extremely controversial and subject to intense debate within the upper echelon of the corporate community. Those industry leaders opposed to national planning have generally argued against losing control over corporate decision making to politicians and their planners. Herbert Stein, former chairman of Nixon's Council of Economic Advisors, has lamented the prospect of national goals created by uncontrolled "politicized experts."

In a paper widely circulated by the American Enterprise Institute for Public Policy, a conservative "think tank," Stein complained that the planning experts' national goals "would lead to policy in the direction of more government spending and more government controls."[10] Thomas A. Murphy, General Motors chairman, echoed this sentiment. In regulating railroads over the past ninety years, said Murphy, "the planners have imposed their own superseding view of the 'public interest' on national goals."[11]

Although business often publicly complains about government involvement in its affairs, difficult economic conditions could persuade even the more recalcitrant business leaders that further government involvement in their planning is desirable. If, through regional rotation, business could find itself with a supply of passive, less militant workers, and if at the same time, through national planning and federal investment help, the existing business oligopolies could be assured of a more predictable supply of investment money, a market and price for its products, a steady source of materials at favorable prices, and less necessity to compete, then national economic planning could become a more attractive alternative. Business leaders have only to examine the history of their enterprises to see how regulation was used for the benign policing and general promotion of industry.

During the depression of the 1930s, business leaders like Gerard Swope of General Electric and Henry I. Harriman of the national Chamber of Commerce called for suspending antitrust laws and increasing federal help to allow business collaboration.[12] The allegedly radical National Recovery Act provided few benefits to labor, and instead helped business consolidate its power. The NRA's director, General Hugh Johnson, called it "industrial self-government." "NRA," said Johnson, "is exactly what industry organized in trade associations makes it."[13]

The government regulatory agencies have a notorious reputation for stroking the industries they police; half of the 120 officials appointed to nine federal regulatory positions between 1970 and 1975 came from the same industries they were asked to regulate. As noted in Chapter 1, thirty-five of the forty states that created pollution control boards by 1970 had officials who were at the same time executives in the industries that were among the country's biggest polluters.[14]

The government planning of the nation's $56 billion Interstate Highway system is a good example of government-business cooperation. The planning committee, appointed by President Dwight D. Eisenhower, was headed by Lucius D. Clay, chairman of Continental Can, a company benefiting from the shipment of food; Stephen D. Bechtel, president of Bechtel Construction, a company which specialized in road building and large public works projects; William A. Roberts, president of Allis Chalmers, a company with special interests in road-building equipment; S. Sloan Colt, president of the Banker's Trust Company; and David Beck, president of the International Brotherhood of Teamsters, who incidentally was later convicted of tampering with union pension funds.

While bills for national planning may call for public hearings, past experience in centralized planning under our economic system suggests that the public's role will be severely restricted. The most significant influence in government planning has tended to come from those with the economic resources and time to study proposals and lobby the Congress, and from those with economic threats, like job layoffs, to wield.

When the highway program was established in the midfifties, it was not the communities affected by those highways who determined the nation's $56 billion commitment but the road-building lobby. Business, with its paid staffs of lawyers, technicians, and planners, rather than community groups with few resources, fit more "naturally" the needs of vast governmental agencies created to solve "social problems." National planning may be promoted as a way of cutting waste and distributing resources more fairly, but in our existing economic system, it tends, in fact, to centralize decision making in the hands of a few who are able to rationalize their interests with compendiums of statistics and long-term projections.

To understand why corporate leaders can at the same time support both more and less government involvement in private business affairs, one must understand that ideological labels do not fit modern business operations. Businesspeople can't afford to be conservative or liberal—they can only afford to be businesspeople, if they are to survive. Henry Ford has no ideological problem proposing that government require ordinary people pay their tax dollars to finance large business through a new Reconstruction Finance Corporation, though he balks at the suggestion that the government require that people drive fuel-conserving cars. "They're telling the consumers what they've got to have," Ford said. "If you make them pay more" for fuel, according to Ford, then consumers will conserve.[15]

Lobbying for a federal energy corporation to make $100 billion in government-backed funds available to energy companies to help develop more fuel supplies, Vice-President Nelson A. Rockefeller in 1976 also had an ideologically muddy rationale for shifting the economic risk of private energy enterprise onto government:

> Given the uncertainties that exist in this area, no one should blame private capital for not taking risks. . . . Neither should anyone be surprised to find that where actions are necessary, and private capital cannot take them, Government must step in . . . the Government will indeed be taking business risks, but one should not

equate risks with bad investments. Every businessman
takes risks. The hallmark of the successful businessman is that he took risks others would not take—and
they paid off.[16]

Rockefeller was saying that the hallmark of successful
businessmen is taking risks others would not, but when
they are unwilling, as in energy development, government
should step in and take the risks. As a precedent, he could
have added control of oil prices in the early 1900s, which
helped create his own family fortune. A more accurate
way of analyzing this confusing logic is that Rockefeller
was prescribing that government entrepreneur for business stockholders with taxpayers' money when business
finds it uneconomical to do so. If the risk pays off, the
energy companies will reap the reward in profits; if it fails,
the taxpayers—and not the companies—will bear the loss.
Meanwhile, the energy companies will maintain their
control over the facilities that produce the energy on
which the public depends. Basically, the public is asked to
entrepreneur its own state of energy dependence.

In the mid-1970s a number of political steps were
taken by business leaders, politicians and others to create
a more secure market through a structured partnership
between business and the federal government. The vehicle for this process was to be national economic planning.
In 1975, a group calling itself the Initiative Committee
for National Economic Planning, led by Nobel Prize
winning economist Wassily Leontief, suggested that a
team of hundreds of scientists and engineers develop
alternative fifteen-to-twenty-five-year plans for the president and Congress which would, after public hearings,
lead to the creation of a single master plan describing all

of the products and services to be produced in the country over a five-year period. The proposal was supported by Robert S. McNamara, president of the World Bank; Michael Blumenthal, then chairman and president of the Bendix Corporation and later secretary of the Treasury; William F. May, chairman of the American Can Company; J. Irwin Miller, president of the Cummins Engine Company; Henry Ford II; and a half-dozen senior bank executives.

At the beginning of 1977, a congressionally created advisory group of corporate leaders, economists, union officials, and politicians officially suggested creation of a federal commission to undertake national economic planning. "[M]uch of the Commission's work will be controversial," said the group, which included Roger S. Ahlbrandt, chairman of Allegheny-Ludlum Steel, Simon S. Straus, president of American Smelting and Refining, and Leonard Woodcock, former president of the UAW, so it should be given "some degree of political autonomy"; specifically, an initial eight-year life-span and a budget submitted annually to Congress, "without intervention from the Office of Management and the Budget." [17]

National economic planning provokes conflicting responses from big business. Some business leaders see a need for government to insure the survival of business and call for comprehensive schemes like national economic planning; others are fearful that an overall involvement of government might undermine their control.

The most likely result will be an ad hoc and piecemeal approach to government-business partnership. This partnership is likely to extend vastly existing financial support of corporate business stopping short of formal partnership in national economic planning. Government help in supporting the survival of business could translate into more liberal business tax credits to promote business expansion. Existing tax credits already help businesses migrate by allowing them to write off the cost of their moves, and the cost of new plants and equipment. A step-up in these credits, in addition to special federal financial incentives to urge business to move to "loser" regions, would help business rotate geographically and continue to keep their wage costs down.

The federal government is also likely to continue to support energy companies by providing direct investment money, allowing high energy prices, or creating more liberal tax deductions. The federal government could support and help coordinate the energy companies' search for new energy supplies whether nuclear, solar, oil, or other sources. The government is also likely to relax antitrust laws to allow a number of companies to form joint ventures in developing new resources, as for the Alaska pipeline; a consortium of companies using government financial support and aided by government planning might develop vast solar farms in the Southwest, build a solar satellite to orbit the earth, or develop projects for extracting oil from shale in the Northwest.

Government economic planning is no longer exclusively the technique of socialist countries. It is now promoted by corporate executives as a powerful tool to provide for people's needs, cut waste, and distribute resources efficiently. While planning can indeed help produce these results, it can also produce some very different ones; Henry Ford's and Thornton Bradshaw's brand of government planning could lead to more concentrated private power, just as government planning has helped create a monolithic, centralized, and unresponsive bureaucracy in the Soviet Union. To make good on the lofty promises that planning implies, we must first create an economic system which has more humane possibilities—one which learns both from the failures of our form of capitalism as well as from Russia's form of socialism.

# 7
# COLD AND WARM INVESTING: Big Macs and Other Choices

The Cinderella story of American capitalism is legendary: with 6 percent of the world's population we produce 25 percent of the world's steel, 40 percent of its aluminum, 33 percent of its electricity, 40 percent of its trucks, and 60 percent of its autos.

It is one of the great paradoxes of history that this success in producing is the American economy's most serious flaw. The problem is not how to produce more wealth, but how to produce a new kind of wealth. The problem is how to redirect the country's enormous productive capacity toward meeting people's real needs.

Our present economic system cannot do this. With its own very precise logic and incentives for investment it has given us the capacity to produce enormous quantities of virtually any kind of product or service, but few ways of directing production to any particular ones. It has given us the world's highest ownership of autos per capita, but also one of the highest incidences of cancer; we have the highest agricultural productivity of any country, but also the highest use of lethal chemicals for fertilizers and pest control; we have one of the highest standards of living, but we are depleting our resources and the world's resources at a faster rate than any other country.

To understand how dangerous our present system is and the need for change, we might begin by describing two opposing approaches a society can take toward investing in its future. The first, which characterizes our existing system, could be called a "cold" investment system. In this approach the society invests its material and human resources in building a productive capacity which may have some immediate useful results like providing food, buildings, and medical services, but which at the same time leads to diminishing future returns on the investment. Using pesticides in farming may immediately improve crop yield, but their continued use leads to the depletion of resources in order to produce the pesticides and to care for the human and environmental hazards, and to develop new pesticides to kill new strains of insects resistant to the older pesticides. Over time, cold investments not only tend to deplete material resources, they also generate high cleanup costs for pollution and often result in the waste of human energy in training for unnecessary or quickly obsolescent skills.

"Warm" investments characterize an alternative approach in which a society consciously attempts to use its human and material resources in ways that bring expanded or at least sustained return on the original investment. Social investments in renewable resources and in techniques of reducing consumption, for example, can create a productive system in which the more production increases, the more resources there are available and the more ability that society has to sustain itself in the future. A warm investing society would provide a maximum of opportunities to train people in skills which have long-

term use and which help produce necessary and replenishable products.

Our present productive system provides few incentives
for developing warm investments. The use of resources is
determined by clearly anticipated rates of profits, not by
the criteria of long-term social needs. As Nelson Rockefeller explained in 1976, when he proposed a $100 billion
government assistance program to help private companies
develop alternative energy sources, "Given the uncertain-
ties that exist in this area, no one should blame private
capital for not taking risks in the development of alternative energy sources."[1]

The search for certain, minimum-risk profit leads to
an undirected, anarchistic system of investment, in which
the society's resources flow toward a broad spectrum of
possible activities, with virtually any product or service
becoming a candidate for economic expansion. If, for
example, space exploration, nuclear technology, or insurance selling has more certain and higher profit possibilities than other activities, then more of the nation's
resources will be used for these enterprises than for
others.

In theory, the fact that investors search for high profits
presents no problems for the rest of society—indeed, it
presumably benefits them. In theory when there are
needs, private entrepreneurs will rush to beat each other
out in providing services or products to meet them. Those
entrepreneurs best able to meet those needs will presumably receive the most profits. To paraphrase an old adage,
investors and consumers will beat a path to the door of the
best mousetrap builder. In practice, however, the match
between people's needs and where resources are invested
is not accomplished so easily. Those who control capital
have a very wide range of opportunities to make profits

and these opportunities often have little to do with real needs.

Housing is a good example. With millions of dilapidated and substandard buildings throughout the country, there has long been a high demand for good housing. In theory, money should have moved toward housing production and the housing "crisis" should come closer to being solved. In practice, however, only certain kinds of housing units offer attractive investment opportunities— normally conventional housing for higher income people and, over the past ten years, condominiums for higher income people, and mobile homes for lower (but not the lowest) income people. For the rest, especially those with extremely low incomes and vast segments of the middle class, decent housing becomes more difficult to afford and government subsidies are increasingly necessary.

Profits can be gained by solving some needs for some people. Profits can also be made by manipulating demand rather than solving real needs or by investing outside the country altogether. Advertising and other persuasive techniques have become a firmly established technique for manipulating demand. In 1974, $24.6 billion was spent on corporate advertising in America—almost double what all of industry was spending on research and development and more than the total welfare costs under the public assistance programs of all federal, state, and local governments that year.[2]

Another staple technique for creating demand has been government contracts. Through a military-industrial complex, a highway and public works lobby, and other industrial lobbies, business has been able to find investments outside the normal workings of the private market. Its use of foreign and domestic tax credits and depletion allowances again indicates its ability to use its influence in government, rather than relying on the market to generate profits.

Business's flexible ways of stimulating demand and of finding new places for investment both in this country and abroad lead to a constantly expanding, but undirected economic system. The bottom line is a society which cannot rationally plan its resources for the future. This rudderless system results in creating jobs, extracting materials, and changing the environment, while the country's future risks shortages, higher costs, and serious health hazards.

In this cold investment system capital flows toward virtually any activity where profits can be maximized at the least risk. Many people live in slums or deteriorated housing, but if an investor can make more profit with less risk by putting money into developing a new hair shampoo, building nuclear reactors in Iran, highways in the U.S., gambling casinos in Atlantic City, condominiums in the Alps, or military hardware for Saudi Arabia—then these facilities will be developed. For example, the fact that fast-food restaurants are an attractive investment now, while building supplies are not, means that over the next five years, money will flow toward building almost two McDonald's hamburger franchises a day while investment in the development of building supplies will lag.[3]

## The Legacy of Cold Investing

In a cold investment system, where resources are opportunistically shifted to the highest profit ventures, the society accumulates two extremely destructive forms of social costs. First, it must forgo its current ability to build better capacity to provide for its future needs, progressively locking itself into paying higher costs later.

Second, it leads to the growth of unemployment and inflation, which also create high social costs.

Both the fast-food industry and the real estate selling (as opposed to building) industry, two of the few current growth industries of the United States economy, are graphic examples of this process in action. In fast foods as well as many other industries that grow from cold investment, the producer takes an already existing product or service, then reshapes and repackages it in a more profitable form. What the consumer receives is essentially the same product or service as before, but through a redefined delivery system. In selling Big Macs, the same amount of food is consumed (perhaps a different variety—or lack of it), but through a process that uses a different mode of producing, distributing, and marketing the product. New facilities are built to transport meat to franchises, and to cook, serve, and sell more hamburgers.

Over the short term, a society may actually benefit economically from the increased cold investment expansion of selling another billion Big Macs. More jobs may be created and more money may be available for hamburger workers to spend for their housing, education, food, and energy. In this way, demand can expand for products other than hamburgers, new jobs can be created in other areas like housing and energy, and the needs of more people be met. But the consequences of expanding Big Mac production do not remain so simple.

The more human and material resources are engaged in one investment area, such as fast food, the less available they are for other potentially more socially necessary areas. The cold investment of funds in Big Mac production is a missed opportunity cost which the entire society eventually has to bear. The building of franchises uses human and material resources to build outlets and production facilities, to blacktop parking lots, to make special clothing for hamburger cashiers, to run a McDonald's training program, and to operate networks and newspaper companies to tell the public "we do it all for you." The paper packaging of McDonald's foods, for example, now consumes an average of over 300 square miles of forests each year. The annual electricity the company uses could supply the total yearly needs of the combined cities of Boston, Washington, D.C., and San Francisco.[4]

What we as a society gain from this process is an enormous increase in the number of people who know how to cook hamburgers, punch cash registers, and make change. What we miss, however, is the opportunity to use those bricks and mortar, that blacktop, that clothing, the media facilities, and all the resources that go into Big Mac making and selling for other purposes. At the same time, the supply of money available for other investments is reduced, contributing to higher borrowing costs and inflation in other parts of the economy.

Perhaps an even more striking example of the effects of undirected and uncontrolled investment in "growth" industries has been in real estate. As a result of the high profits possible in buying and selling of buildings, large numbers of people have entered the field.

In contrast to people who actually build housing, real estate people add little value to what the consumer receives. Yet high profits in the buying and selling of buildings and in speculation result in more investment in this activity, and more people becoming part of the real estate work force. Between 1972 and 1977, the number of real estate agents and brokers in this private finance bureaucracy jumped by almost 45 percent; over the same period the number of people in the construction trades increased by only 8 percent.[5]

Real estate sales have become so lucrative that the

country's biggest retailer, Sears Roebuck, and its biggest stock brokerage house, Merrill Lynch, have recently set up their own subsidiaries to make commission sales in residential property. Between 1967 and 1977, gross real estate commissions jumped from $4 billion to $15 billion. In 1976 real estate commissions represented about three times all federal, state, and local government agencies spent for all of their housing and urban renewal programs that year.[6]

The real estate industry not only adds directly to the cost of housing through fees, but also contributes to added costs, through speculation in land and building. In the process of real estate trading, prices are bid up, and the consumer ultimately must pay higher rents for an apartment, a higher price for a home, or a higher price for a product or service from business, which pays more for its lease or building space.

The consequences of real estate industry growth are "cold" since it accelerates the use of our resources, without adding to our ability to survive. Each time the fee of a real estate broker or speculatively increased amount is added to the cost of producing a home, two results can occur— either the house price goes up to cover the added cost, or the price remains the same by reducing some other costs of building the house, such as reducing construction workers' salaries or using more automated equipment to replace these workers. In this struggle between workers and owners, the end result, as we will see, is unemployment or inflation, depending on who wins. Both problems in a cold investment economy can only be solved by more expansion in the economic system and more use of resources.

If as a result of increased real estate costs workers are forced to accept lower salaries in order to keep house prices down, then these workers are less able to buy products and services they need. This leads to unemployment in other sectors of the economy, since fewer jobs are now necessary to provide these products and services.

If producers successfully use automation to offset higher real estate costs, some workers will lose their jobs. While some of them will find new jobs, others will be forced to rely on unemployment or welfare. As a result, workers with jobs must now pay higher taxes for the public cost of supporting unemployed workers. The employed workers are then forced to ask for higher salaries, pushing up prices and increasing inflation.

If salaries don't go down and automation is not used to compensate for the added real estate costs, then house prices must go up and inflation is accelerated. The people who pay the higher prices for housing must now ask for higher salaries and this leads to still more inflation.

Another outcome of higher real estate costs is that builders are forced to take smaller profits in the sale of housing. But if this happens, builders and the investors who finance them will be discouraged from putting money into housing altogether. They may look toward foreign investment possibilities, energy development, municipal bonds, fast-food franchises, or whatever brings a higher return. The result is fewer jobs for construction workers, less housing available to consumers, and higher prices for the housing that is available.

The only way for the present economy to deal with the inflation and unemployment caused by the added burden of a cold investment industry like real estate is for other sectors of the economy to expand. Rising housing prices, for example, can be offset by expanding markets in other parts of the economy. This will mean a trickling down of investment returns to workers in the form of higher salaries and more available jobs. This in turn will mean more people able to buy housing and to pay higher prices for what they buy.

This kind of expansion, however, does not solve our problems; it delays them. It requires that more resources be used to sustain inflated prices and to keep people in jobs. This is expansion not for the sake of providing for real needs, but expansion for the sake of keeping up with inflation and lowering unemployment. The society has no control of the kind of resources being used in the expansion process; it cannot control whether or not expansion will involve renewable or nonrenewable resources or whether the jobs being created will lead to skills useful for replenishing the resources which are being used.

## Warm Investing

A warm investment approach would attempt to reverse the diminishing returns which accompany our current economic expansion. It would be geared consciously to planning and creating the kind of productive capacity that would allow us to produce for future needs at a continually *reducing* human and material cost. That is, investments would be made in production systems which used progressively *less* depletable resources and unnecessary human work and progressively *more* replenishable resources and purposeful human effort.

A simple example of this would be to use a renewable energy source like plant-derived fuels or the sun to heat greenhouses in colder climates in order to replace the massive concentration of food production in limited areas of the country. The result would be food production using less energy and human resources for transportation and the conservation of more water in the water-starved regions of the country. Another example would be the development of a technology to use wood and plant-based chemicals to replace oil derivatives in producting synthetic materials; still another could be the more rational organization of regional manufacturing production, to move goods and people fewer miles, with the result that fewer resources would be used for transportation activities and people would spend fewer hours in redundant or unnecessary work.

The investment of the same billion dollars, which is projected for McDonald's expansion over the next four years, in the creation of insulation production facilities or more efficient steel mills, more efficient canning technology, the development of alternate energy sources, and the training of people to research and build more energy-efficient systems, would create additional productive capacity, which in turn would lower consumption and produce greater self-reliance. A warm approach could, for example, channel investments in some northern states to build power plants that burned local renewable fuels like wood and plant-derived alcohol, and that used the heat generated in this process to grow vegetables in greenhouses for local consumption. What we would have created at the end of this warm investment process is not simply an alternative way to serve and cook hamburgers, but real wealth in the form of facilities and skills that quantitatively increase our ability to sustain ourselves with the use of fewer resources.

Warm investments are difficult if not nearly impossible to make in our present economy. Private investors making warm investments would place themselves in a dangerously unprofitable position by trying to make investments that do not have immediate paybacks. Nelson Rockefeller was correct when he explained why energy corporations must have government subsidies to develop more energy sources. They simply have no incentive to make long term investments, whether they are socially useful or not. A way of understanding this is to examine how our economic system deals with energy conservation.

In order for America's insulation industry to expand production significantly, investors would have to see a long-term, sustained market for their product. This expansion of capacity would require enormous investment. Borax, a mineral used in insulation, is in short supply. Alternatives would have to be researched and quickly developed; existing facilities would have to undergo major upgrading. To do this, it would be necessary to attract private investment capital, and unless insulation companies can show more lucrative prospects than, say, McDonald's or other investments, the insulation industry simply will not get the capital it needs to expand.

Defenders of this approach argue that the sum of individual decisions about what to buy or not buy adds up to the public good. What's more, they argue, this allows individuals the maximum freedom to determine their own economic activity—to have or not have insulation, to spend money on heat or keep the thermostat at 65°. But this "freedom" is illusory and individual decisions do not magically add up to public good.

The insulation market depends on the price of fuel; as fuel cost rises, it becomes increasingly "cost effective" for homeowners to insulate their buildings. As fuel prices go up, demand for insulation should increase; as a result, insulation companies will expand and new ones should presumably enter the market. Investment money for insulation companies at this point could become more attractive than fast-food chains.

But as yet, many homeowners still do not find it sufficiently "cost effective" to add insulation; they simply don't have the capital to invest, monthly payments may be too high, or they may be owners of rental property who can pass higher fuel costs on to tenants. This waiting for the market exacerbates our energy problems. The longer homeowners wait to insulate, the more energy will be wasted in heating, the less available energy will be in the future, the more that remaining energy will cost.

If one person fails to insulate because he is so wealthy he doesn't care about paying a higher heating bill, and a second person does the same because he is too poor to invest in proper insulating materials, these decisions impinge on everyone's freedom to have lower energy bills. If only some people conserve, then the demand for fuel remains high, and those same people will still be paying high costs for the fuel they do use, while the society will continue to deplete its fuel supplies and face future shortages. While some people may earnestly try to conserve, their decisions to do so can have no real impact unless they are part of a coordinated plan. In a world where every individual's actions affect his neighbors, there is no meaningful freedom involved in the individual decision to use insulation or not conserve energy. To be effective, energy conservation has to be part of a long-term public action.

Recognizing this inherent problem in the free enterprise market, the government may step in with a proposal to give a tax credit or other subsidy to people to insulate their homes. But if this happens and the market for insulation would suddenly expand, the price for insulation could skyrocket, potentially wiping out the benefits of the subsidy, and indeed, possibly costing homeowners even more than were there no subsidy. The fact that only three companies control virtually the entire national production of fiber glass insulation means few new companies will rush in to cut fiber glass prices as demand increases.

Faced with this problem, some politicians may propose that government give homeowners a subsidy and at the same time fix the prices insulation companies could charge for their products. But with this fixed price restriction, the incentive for expansion by insulation companies would be dampened, supplies would lag, and the purpose of the program be subverted.

In short there are no internal incentives under our present economic system to solve critical public needs except to raise profits to levels acceptable to the companies who control production. The investment choices of those who finance these companies are so broad that if people can't afford to pay what is asked for certain products, they will shift their investments to other products or services. The investment system they operate in is not one which guides dollars to the most socially useful production, but is instead determined by investment opportunism of the moment.

The increasingly critical need to make delicate and precise long-term decisions about the use of scarce resources is on a collision course with an economic system that thrives on unguided investment anarchy. Our constant step-ahead-of-inflation expansion may have been less destructive, or at least less noticeable to our environment and our economy when the scale of that expansion was smaller, when there were fewer countries competing with us for the world's resources and its markets, and when there were more resources available.

But private capital in America is now forced to rotate regions within this country and to travel the globe more aggressively to find more profitable investments. It is consuming resources more rapidly and generating less of its own capital for expansion.

Shadowing this frantic and uncoordinated expansion is unemployment and underemployment in abandoned cities and regions. This expansion is forcing ordinary people to entrepreneur with their wages, their taxes, and their environment to bolster business's declining profitability. The cornucopia of riches America seemed capable of producing into some long unmeasurable future is coming up against the hard limits of available resources, the capacity of the environment to be used as a sewer, and the capabilities of government to support financially the unprecedented abandonment of loser regions. The search for an alternative to this process is not a conjecture for the distant future but an imperative for tomorrow's politics.

# 8
# REGIONAL SOCIALISM:
## An American Alternative

The question of economic change in America is no longer whether we will have socialism, but rather whose socialism we will have. We already have a form of socialism where the nation's wealth, created by the work of ordinary people, is being distributed by government among our most powerful private businesses. It is a socialism of depreciation allowances and of government subsidies for private energy companies, of government military contracts to support an armaments industry, highway contracts to support a road building industry, and public financial help to underwrite faltering companies like Lockheed and the Penn Central Railroad.

The problem for a progressive movement is to develop a program and strategy for shifting the socialism we now have toward one that could benefit ordinary people. We face two fundamental problems. What vision do we have of a better society? And how do we move as quickly as possible to the point at which a sufficiently large constituency is willing to take the political actions necessary to create that society?

The vision of a better society is necessarily speculative and easily dismissed as "wishful," "unrealistic," and "utopian." Doctrinaire Marxists argue that only when the capitalist system is completely destroyed and socialism created are we free enough of the constraints of our bourgeois culture to envision more humane forms.

We have, however, more than enough evidence that different forms of socialism, all forged in the pain of revolution, have produced radically different social approaches. The overthrow of an existing order in Russia did not automatically introduce a benign and humanist social life. Any real change in people's attitudes—a shift from competitiveness to mutual help, an evolution from central decision making to local decision making, from male dominance to nonsexist attitudes—must be developed consciously. Ideas about what kind of society will be created have to be formed through processes of speculation, experience, and vigorous debate throughout the stages of change.

Not many years ago it would have been much more difficult to write about the possibility of a popular socialism in America. For generations of Americans bred on tales of the Russian red terror, socialism came to represent a monolithic, unresponsive, and undemocratic system. And the real experience in Russia, a country that laid claim to world socialist leadership, gave credibility to a hysterical legend in America.

A number of important events have made possible a new and potentially more hopeful dialogue. A partial thawing of the Cold War demonstrates that both the United States and Russia recognize that their mutual survival depends on respecting the hegemony of each other. And the new socialist countries have exhibited a broader spectrum of alternatives. These countries have provided visible evidence that socialism can be stretched to fit various cultural experiences. The development of western European Marxism has demonstrated the potential for socialist parties to adapt existing democratic techniques and to grow stronger as a political force within existing capitalist systems.

A factor in a new socialist dialogue has been the change in America. The declining rate of economic growth in this country has forced people to think about ideology through their pocketbooks. A radical alternative seems less radical when the existing system can't produce the jobs and the life-styles it had once seemed capable of.

America, perhaps more than any other country, provides a cultural and social background sympathetic to a democratic form of socialism. The industrial expansion of America was supported by massive human exploitation. But in this process of growth, and in the Revolution that gave this country its independence, a parallel ideal of local democratic processes and the protection of individual rights was also in a measure achieved.

The challenge for this country is that it should mesh its political ideology of "equality" with an economic system that can make good on that ideal. We have in effect a system only half right. Now in an economy which is likely to produce even less opportunity for economic movement than it has in the past, that precarious half-right system will afford even less protection for those without.

Political equality is no guarantee of economic justice, nor is economic equality any guarantee of political justice. If economic equality is a society's only goal, the political result can be grotesque. The Soviet Union is not a model of how socialism could work, any more than America is a model of how democracy could work. Russia demonstrates that a strong measure of economic equality is insufficient to bring about a humane society, while America shows that formal principles and processes of democracy and legal protections are also in themselves not enough to produce economic justice.

What follows, then, is an attempt to propose an approach to a more sane future. It is a speculative sketch, intended in the spirit of making explicit, rather than making exact; it is a path intended for criticism, debate, and development.

The proposal is based on a simple proposition—to combine the best cultural qualities of the American experience with the best economic and cultural features of a variety of socialist experiences. America's existing political and legal processes, its decentralization into states, both its experience and ideology of home rule and its identifiable regional cultures could provide a hospitable climate for a new system of what might be called regional socialism.

In this system, America would remain politically defined by the existing division of states, cities, and smaller local governments. Each state and in some cases regional groupings of numbers of states could be formed to develop their own government-owned and -operated forms of economic production. The goal would be self-reliance; regions would not be economically independent, but as much as possible they would develop an economy that relied less and less on massive imports of consumer goods, energy, and agricultural products—and more and more on an internal system of producing and consuming.

The economic shape of regional socialism would find the major enterprises, such as energy production, raw materials processing, and transportation systems, owned in common by all the people of a region. On another level, however, individuals or small groups could engage in independent production and could own limited amounts of property, say, not more than the number of acres an individual could reasonably farm or garden or the amount of buildings and land that are necessary for the actual production or sale of products. These individual or jointly owned enterprises would be possible as long as there were no economic distinctions between owners and employees—that is, one person could not buy the labor of another in order to make a profit. This would allow the possibility for individuals or combined groups of people to work in small-scale individually or cooperatively owned enterprises to produce goods for their own use or for sale.

While it's unlikely that the world's most highly developed industrial nation could ever be transformed into a country of individual and cooperatively owned farms or factories, this kind of enterprise is an attractive and culturally rooted alternative for large numbers of people. To the extent these enterprises did not draw off critical resources, they could make an important contribution to regional self-reliance. Individual gardens could reduce the need to import agricultural products, just as individual or jointly owned local repair operations could reduce the need to import new consumer goods.

In its eventual form, regional socialism would be a combination of individual enterprises, small cooperatives, and regional government-owned production facilities. Major facilities for energy production, basic materials like steel and chemicals, would be owned and run by government on a town, city, or state level. The particular level of government ownership would be determined by the scale of needs, the availability of resources, and the scale of technology needed to serve these needs. Basic steel and basic chemical production, for example, that involves scarce nonrenewable resources is more likely to require more government-organized production, while agricultural production that involves replenishable resources and smaller scale technology could in many cases be organized at the level of the individual or small group. A relatively extensive agricultural enterprise, involving production, canning, and distribution, could be organized efficiently at the town or subregional county level. Even within the existing capitalist production system, there are now a number of producers, canneries, and nonprofit distribution co-ops.

As tempting as it might be to develop a concrete hierarchy of productive activities, rated by their most appropriate level of ownership, it would be misleading. Agricultural production might be primarily organized on a town or county level, but this production might often be dependent on irrigation systems and energy systems organized at the level of state or several states ownership. The development of an American regional socialism, in contrast to socialism as it developed in Russia, should be predicated on building public ownership from the very bottom levels of government up. What can first be efficiently organized on the local level of town, city, or county, should be, and only those enterprises that require more centrally organized facilities for production should be managed by state or multistate organizations.

Instead of a concrete plan that predetermines all levels of ownership and management, a planning process would attempt to relate use to government level of management by the particular resources and needs of each region. Large states with proper soils for agriculture are likely to develop in the direction of smaller, town- or county-owned agricultural production. States with severely limited areas appropriate for agriculture are likely to need state ownership of farming in order to insure that all are provided for.

• • •

Although many federal government functions under regional socialism would have to be redefined, its formal structure would be similar to what it is now. The government would remain separated into the three branches of the Executive, the Legislative, and the Judicial. Washington would continue to tax all regions of the country, perhaps through state governments rather than through individuals. Washington would also continue to make foreign policy and plan for national defense. Because of the important role Washington would play in assisting the coordination of local economic planning, a representative national government would remain a critical part of this system.

The Congress and the president, in addition to coordinating the individual economic plans of different regions, would prepare a national plan. This plan would not be a single, centrally determined policy for national growth, but would reflect the development policies and political consensus of all regions. It would be developed over a long period of planning and revision, and would indicate how each region intends to use and replenish its resources over the intermediate and more distant future.

The national plan would grow from the bottom up. States or combinations of states would present proposals for their own regional self-reliance to a national planning group under the direction of the Congress. The regional plans would indicate the extent to which each region expects to achieve self-reliance, what steps they are taking toward that goal, and what role they would like to see other regions and the national government play in helping accomplish their particular plan. Local plans would cover a period of approximately five to ten years, and would show not only what outside assistance each region needs, but the probable surplus of resources and products each region could make available to others.

The national planning group would bring together all of the regions' plans and would help planners negotiate trades with one another. It would then develop a national plan to express the results of negotiating processes. The national plan would show what kind of, and how much, aid the federal government would provide to each region, and how much total revenue would be required to make this aid possible. It would indicate the resources the country would have to import, and what resources would be available for export.

Both the president's office and the Congress would work with the national planning group in the preparation of its proposals, and both would have to approve the final plan. Although the plan would project the country's five- to ten-year economic future, it would be in a constant process of being monitored and revised, as regions either met or failed to meet their initial expectations. An ongoing and vigorous debate could be expected in the Congress and through the president's office, as well as on the local level, to determine what goals the plan should contain, and which goals should take priority.

It would be blind optimism to expect easy consensus on either the goals of different regions or their ways of achieving them. There may be general agreement, for example, that pollution should be reduced and resources conserved. But there are likely to be wide differences about whether certain living patterns should be changed, and how soon, in the process of reducing pollution or conserving resources. Planning under regional socialism won't eliminate these debates. What it will do is allow the consequence of using our resources in certain ways to be seen and democratically decided, instead of being determined by the anarchy of private investment decisions. If this process did nothing else, it would at least make explicit the choices that were being made about the country's future.

Representative government under regional socialism would not only be maintained, but strengthened. Instead of Congress and local government playing their schizophrenic roles of policemen and accomplices to private business, constantly trying to provide both incentives and sanctions, political representatives would play a more positive and creative role. With local governments assuming increased economic power under regional socialism, politicians, democratically elected, would be faced with much more stringent measures of accountability.

Political leaders are now more likely to blame their failure to attract jobs or improve the local economy on private economic forces outside their control. Since politicians operating under regional socialism will be able to structure local economies directly, rather than simply act as the entrepreneurs of "hopeful anticipation," voters will be able to see the real results of their actions and make more meaningful choices about whom they should and should not keep in power.

Just as now, there would no doubt be hot political disputes in Congress under this new system about the amounts Washington should distribute to each region. Some regions will complain they are more underdeveloped than others and need more federal aid, while others will complain they are being financially drained to benefit less-developed regions. Situations might easily arise that would resemble what happened in 1975, when New York City was forced to ask Congress for money and representatives from other parts of the country resisted the request.

There is, however, a very important difference in the way federal aid would be used under regional socialism and the way it is used now. While federal aid under regional socialism would not eliminate the conflicting interests of different regions, it would provide a basis for consensus on distributing aid. The 1975 debate around federal aid to New York City and other debates about federal aid to "needy" cities or regions were debates about how many federal dollars should be used to provide welfare services to places unable to maintain themselves economically; they were debates about how much money Washington should spend to pacify people in the loser regions.

The federal redistribution of funds under a system of regional socialism would have a quite different function. It would not use funds to pacify people without jobs, but instead to eliminate *the conditions* that lead to joblessness. An industrial state like Ohio, for example, is now providing for decreasing amounts of its own need for food and energy. If, through federal aid, Ohio could move toward creating its own diversified and more self-reliant economy, in which the people of that state progressively produced more of what they consumed, then federal aid would be progressively less necessary. As a result, the state would gradually become less of a drain on other states, and regional socialism a less threatening alternative to the bottomless well of welfare.

## The Difficult Path Toward De-specializing Regions

America's unique material and human development provides a vast storehouse of resources that could contribute to building regional socialism. America is obviously not a developing country; it has the accumulated wealth of the existing form of its cities, suburbs, towns, and transportation systems, of its facilities to extract natural resources, and of the productive capacity of its factories, machinery, and farms. The country also has vast numbers of people who are skilled and capable of training others; it has some of the best-equipped educational facilities in the world, many of which, incidentally, are becoming more equitably distributed throughout the country.

The problem of moving toward regional socialism is not so much one of developing vast quantities of *new* productive capacity, but of distributing what we have more equitably. It is a problem of directing all of our existing capacity, determined by the cold investments of capitalism, toward warm ones which could be made possible by a socialist economic system.

Perhaps some of the most serious objections to regional socialism can be raised concerning the unequal distribution of natural resources and climatic conditions throughout the United States. Some areas have real advantages over others in providing their own energy, in growing their own crops, or in having raw materials to convert to consumer products. Some areas will have more developed production facilities, as do the steel and auto plants in the Midwest, while some areas with more attractive climates will have lower energy costs.

Regional socialism, however, is not meant to be a panacea for creating total regional economic independence. A regional socialist economy would involve significant economic exchange between regions. The goal is not necessarily to eliminate, but to substantially reduce the energy and resources used in transferring goods and services between regions, and to eliminate the opportunity for private capital to control and specialize a region's resources and jobs. It is more accurately a program for regional self-reliance than total regional independence.

But while some regions will have more "natural" advantages than others, all regions will be able to develop a much greater degree of self-reliance than might first seem possible. As Chapter 4 explains, the nature of our country's current regional specialization and dependence masks the real potential for regional self-reliance. What has come to appear natural or inevitable was not divinely ordained, but is the result of how natural endowments of regions were shaped technologically by the private finance community. The transfer of goods and services from one region to another provided the backbone of a profitable private economy of regional specialization and dependence.

To use the present "cheapness" of goods or crops being shipped between regions or the "natural" advantages of regions as reasons for continuing regional specialization, rationalizes the present into a more dismal future through the patterns of the past. It maintains a dependent, inflexible regional economy unable to adapt to new situations. A region now has no way to insure it will have the products it needs, if the businesses which now control these products decide to raise prices. And a plant producing millions of tons of polyvinyl products is of little use to a region that produces it when the international market for polyvinyl products collapses and when the region's need for polyvinyl is a fraction of what its factories produce. Had the same capital been used to develop the warm investments of diversified food production and processing, home-building equipment, and exploiting and producing local sources of energy, the region would begin to find itself in a much healthier position to control its own economic future.

Regional specialization is often justified as a cost-reducing technique. Those regions with abundant natural endowments, according to this argument, are more easily exploitable than others, and even the additional cost of processing and shipping its resources long distances still do not increase their costs beyond what a less-endowed region would have to pay for the same locally produced resources. But this approach more often only leads to short-term "cheapness," producing higher long-term costs for both the specialized and dependent regions.

The economies of regional specialization must be measured against the alternative of regional self-reliance. This comparison is obviously difficult since the self-reliant alternative doesn't exist. Still, we do know the current effects of specialization, and we can project the possible benefits of self-reliance.

Initially, a region with a natural advantage for growing crops or producing energy, for example, can undercut the costs of a less naturally endowed region. As a result, the less-endowed region progressively invests less and less in producing energy or in growing crops; these regions may then shift their economies from agriculture or energy production to industrial products or services. They tend to become the specialized regions of factories, office buildings, and industrial cities and towns. As a result, the farming or energy-producing capacity of these regions declines, and they progressively devote fewer physical and human resources for developing self-reliant economies. With cheaper agricultural products being shipped from the outside, for example, there is little incentive to develop new technologies for more efficient local agriculture.

Since the booming manufacturing region has few incentives to develop its agricultural or energy technology, it falls progressively farther behind the agricultural or energy-specialized regions in its ability to do so. It is trapped in its own production specialization in order to generate the dollars it needs to buy the food and other resources required for its survival.

It is now extremely uncertain that America's path

toward regional specialization can be continued, or if it could, that it would be effective even on its own terms. Our dependence on "cheap" specialized agricultural regions is coming home to roost. The western drought during 1976–77 demonstrated how vulnerable a food production system we have, despite an elaborately developed irrigation technology. The underdevelopment of energy resources in some regions has not only forced people in these regions to pay higher energy costs than do others, but has limited the total supply of energy, forcing all prices to rise. Our escalating need for more fertilizers which requires more energy and higher costs to produce is a result of our reliance on single-crop farming for large-scale markets.

Barry Commoner has estimated that it took five times the amount of fertilizer to produce the same crop in 1968 than it did twenty years earlier. Research at the University of Wisconsin demonstrates that ten calories of energy are now required to produce the same ounce of food that one calorie produced in 1910. Since more than half the food in the United States is processed for shipment we used 30 percent more fossil fuels in agriculture in 1970 than in 1964.[1]

Instead of accepting the conventional logic of the immediate cheapness of specialization, we have to ask ourselves what kind of sophisticated alternative technology would we *now* have if warm investment decisions had been made to increase regional self-reliance. We must ask, would we by now have developed "scrubbers," for the oxides of the burning process to allow wood, a renewable resource, to be burned cleanly in order to generate electricity in vast quantities. Would alternative policies to massive suburbanization around the big cities have kept fertile land available for farming, and would investment in the technologies of greenhouses, frost-retardant agri-culture, and canning have meant we would now have more regionally self-reliant food systems? If the capital for developing oil and nuclear power technology had been channeled toward more regionally independent, energy sources, would these alternatives now be more economically efficient?

It will obviously be expensive to unplan the plans that companies like General Motors have provided us. We would have to go beyond solutions that simply add public transit to an already irrational system of human settle-ment. A sane approach to using our resources would eventually involve warm investment in the complete re-orientation of our production· system to return more resources to a community at progressively lower costs. It would mean the building of a local food production network, the development of alternative energy systems to serve the entire community, and the design of new transportation and human settlement patterns.

A sane approach to using resources will mean not simply more rapid transit or better fuel-conserving cars, but a pattern of living, work, and recreation that requires less time and resources than are now consumed in the process of transportation. It requires reducing working time to real needs, so that energy resources and peoples' time are not simply expended in the process of generating profits; it requires the planning of work and shopping facilities to make them as close as possible to people who use them, and it requires a new food production approach to make supply as close as possible to consumers. It could mean, for example, that in East Coast states, most of which have the proper climate for growing wheat and many other foodstuffs, government would construct grain storage elevators and food processing plants to reduce the need to ship food over large distances.

•   •   •

At first the existing specialized production system, the product of years of regional colonialization, will make conversion to self-reliant production difficult. Plants will have to be retooled, existing agriculture diversified, new agriculture created, and new energy systems developed. This conversion could conceivably involve an entire industry of recycling construction materials within and between regions. In the most heavily industrialized and overbuilt areas, industrial buildings and elevated highways could be "mined"; structures could be dismantled and shipped to other regions that need these facilities. Alternatively, parts from these structures could be melted down to produce the raw materials necessary for new facilities. Eliminating the need for the existing private finance bureaucracy would make some office buildings available for conversion to housing or schools, and other useful purposes.

The prospect of this kind of "urban mining" may seem much less radical considering what we already do with our abandoned residential and industrial buildings. Many are simply left vacant for years, while people are without jobs or decent places to live. Parts of structures which are now melted down or recycled are usually used in building new facilities such as highways, office buildings, or factories to support the same economic system that requires further waste and abandonment to survive. The image of the Pruett-Igoe, an immense government housing project in St. Louis, being blown apart by demolition crews less than twenty years after it was built is a symbol of the vacuousness of our housing solutions and a graphic lesson that there must be better ways of reusing our existing structures.

## Socialism as a Condition for Warm Investment

An important difference between a self-reliant socialist approach and the system we now have is a possibility for long-term cost savings. In our existing economy, business tries to reduce its production costs and improve its profits by moving to cheaper places to operate. By contrast, the politicians of a new regional socialist government would not be able to assume that the region's economic fortunes would improve by the government's leaving. Forced to shape a fixed-place economy, planners and politicians would have to take maximum advantage of the region's own resources, and plan for their long-term use and restoration.

In our present footloose private economy, housing can be built by private developers, profitably operated, resold many times over, and then easily abandoned. While the private real estate investor is allowed tax losses on the property, the public not only absorbs the tax loss, but it also pays for the housing inspectors, building department officials, the firemen, the sanitation workers, and social workers who are all part of the abandonment process. Fostered by the regional shifting of business, the average American family now moves every six years. The shifting process provides work for real estate agents, bankers, and related financial workers, who collect more fees and interest as ownership changes hands. Meanwhile, the rest of the national economy has to expand to create additional wealth to take care of the fees and interest payments.

In a regional socialist society the collection of factories, homes, farms, and offices which the society has already built becomes in effect a resource bank, which once in place allows the society to look toward meeting people's other needs. It allows us to get off the endless inflationary treadmill of repaying what has already been paid for.

Since the housing and production apparatus a regional socialist society builds is less easily abandoned, there is a strong incentive to build well and for long-term use. Systems that would seem too expensive in a private investment economy, because they have to be capitalized over short periods to be profitable, would now become available.

Widespread use of well-insulated buildings, for example, becomes a more available possibility in this new economy. In America, real estate developers now tend to calculate a six- to ten-year payback period on their investment in rental housing. In an individually owned home, the owner will calculate a longer or shorter payback period depending on the amount of money he can afford to invest in his home. An owner in this situation has little incentive to invest in the added cost of insulation unless the payback on his investment in insulation is greater than paying the added cost of fuel over that period. Owners of rental housing who don't pay for the fuel costs of their tenants have even less incentive to conserve. The only real incentive that persuades people to provide insulation in our present economic system is increasing fuel costs or publicly subsidizing insulation installation.

Under our existing economic system, the outcome of energy conservation in housing or automobiles is that energy companies can raise their rates without consumers feeling the pain as much. At the same time, conservation means more energy is then available for use in manufacturing or operating other new products, like electric knives, amphibious recreation vehicles, or military hardware. A democratically organized socialist society, on the other hand, can collectively decide where it will use the money it saves in heating homes or running cars; it may not use the energy at all, or it may make it available to heat more homes, to build and operate more schools and hospitals, or, indeed, to make more electric carving knives and military hardware.

Today, in effect, we have no mechanism for publicly determining how to use the nation's resources; capital flows to the most profitable activities. The availability of more energy under our present system will tend to breed more uncontrolled cold investments in whatever activities can be shaped by business to yield the best financial return on the money it invests.

The critical edge of a regional approach to self-reliance is how the region's economic decisions are made. Politicians often talk of creating more local political power and reducing larger forms of government bureaucracy. But in reality that kind of local self-reliance is possible only when local government has real power to deliver the community's needs. If local government is permanently cast as entrepreneur for business's regionally specialized activities, then this government and its people will be permanently limited to planning by "hopeful anticipation."

A new structure based on noncompetitive economics, and democratic forms of governance would allow government to make decisions based on internal regional needs rather than those of the corporate marketplace. The word "allow" is central because socialism, regional or otherwise, is no panacea for the problem of imperialism or the personal hunger for power or deeply rooted cultural differences. The recent conflict between China and Vietnam bears tragic witness to this unfortunate condition. Socialism does not create a better existence, it makes it possible. Presently, Americans can be humane and noncompetitive, of course, but only by struggling against economic conditions that pose every incentive to do otherwise.

## A Hindsight Approach to Regional Socialism

In this country, socialism is often equated with losing individual freedom, with an inability to own one's own home or business, and with bureaucratic, inefficient government. A wide variety of socialist countries throughout the world presents a much more varied picture of socialist possibilities. The elements of these can be useful in clarifying old misconceptions and in shaping a new form of American socialism. The socialism of China was not the socialism of Russia; Mao Tse-tung, in contrast to Joseph Stalin, stressed social equality and cultural change, not simply economic equality. He called not simply for economic progress, but a politically more difficult continuous "cultural revolution" in China that would stress social values. Mozambique's socialism is not the socialism of East Germany or other Russian satellites; the Frelimo party's active education programs against male dominance and the sharing of what was considered female work indicate a commitment to breaking down cultural forms of dominance outside the direct economic system.

The searches for democratic institutions by socialists and communists in Europe all attest to a much broader, more democratic strain in many new socialist approaches. It is not at all clear at this point what form (or forms) of socialism will emerge from the European situation—what does seem important is that the forms of political control, from decentralization to centralization, are being openly argued. These debates have expanded beyond the simple Marxist view of economic "structure" of production determining the "superstructure" of cultural values.

The exploding varieties of experiences in socialist countries like Russia, Cuba, China, and Yugoslavia, in partially socialist countries like Italy, France, and England, and indeed partial socialist institutions in this country can be examined for their failures and successes, providing us with the hindsight of history in framing our own nondogmatic approach. Our own cultural emphasis on homeownership and small business could, for example, be adapted to the Chinese approach, where people do, in fact, own their own homes and businesses. They can also own plots of land to grow crops and raise livestock, and they can sell their products at market. The restriction in China is not against individual ownership, but against the kind of ownership that allows one person to profit from another's work. Individual ownership is permitted, as long as products come from the labor of those who work the land or own the business, and as long as the amount of land owned is reasonable for individual use.

Housing production in Cuba could be a useful model that might be adapted to our own cultural ideology of local initiative and community self-help. In Cuba, local factory workers have organized construction teams, called "microbrigades" to build housing for other members of their factory. About 5 percent of a factory's work force, usually those with some construction experience, are relieved of their normal jobs to work on the housing microbrigades. To make up for the lost factory time of microbrigade workers, the remaining factory workers increase their own production effort at the factory.

Other pieces of different socialist systems should be considered and accepted or rejected as part of a nondogmatic approach to socialism. China's form of decentralized democratic community decision making, organized as "street committees" on an even smaller scale than the New England town meeting, or the neighborhood justice system that used nonprofessional local committees to judge minor crimes in Chile before the coup, are possible methods.

## Some American Models

The idea of individual states developing their own government-run production enterprises is not new to the country. In July, 1934, during the depression, Ohio began to operate shutdown factories using federal money to lease them from private owners. In its brief existence, the program, the "Ohio Plan," employed close to 900 people in twelve factories. The factories' products were based on the critical needs of families on relief—seven produced clothing, two made furniture, one stoves, one dishes, and another blankets. By early 1935, only six months after operations began, the factories were coming close to turning a surplus for the state. In March of that year, the state-operated factories, which were providing residents with jobs and necessities, cost the state less than $900.

But the Roosevelt Administration, eyeing the political implications of the possible success of this and similar socialist approaches developing in other parts of the country, was not enthusiastic. At about the same time the Ohio Plan was gaining momentum, Upton Sinclair, a socialist, had been campaigning in the Democratic primary in California as a candidate for governor. His platform called for state-run production enterprises, specifically recommending programs like the Ohio Plan. Sinclair, while attempting to gain support from the President, strongly differed with him. "I personally made no secret of my disapproval of parts of the New Deal," said Sinclair, ". . . the destruction of food, the limitation of production, the turning of the NRA into a price-fixing machine for big business."[2]

At the urging of Democrats opposed to Sinclair's approach, and faced with the specter of its possible success, the Roosevelt Administration withdrew federal aid for the Ohio experiment. In May, 1935, less than a year after they began production, Ohio's state-run factories closed their doors.[3] Meanwhile, Sinclair, who went on to win California's Democratic primary by gaining more votes than all of his seven opponents combined, was never able to carry out his plan for state production. Although he received almost a million votes in the final election, he was defeated by his Republican opponent after Roosevelt refused to lend him support, and after almost all of the state's major newspapers denounced him as a godless radical who would bring Bolshevism to America.[4]

In spite of such historic opposition there are some surprising examples of what might be called quasi-regional socialist enterprises existing in this country. Contrary to business-promoted stereotypes, many publicly owned ventures demonstrate public enterprise can be even more efficient, better managed, and less costly than private ones. Some of the more interesting examples of public enterprise are found in the nation's conservative heartland. The state of South Dakota runs a concrete production company in competition with other firms, while neighboring North Dakota operates a flour company, the largest agricultural business in that state. Sold under the trade name "Dakota Maid" throughout the Midwest, North Dakota successfully competes with companies like General Mills and Pillsbury.

North Dakota also has the nation's only state-owned and -operated bank. Created in 1919 as part of the antibusiness movement led by socialists and populists, the Bank of North Dakota refutes the theory of public inefficiency. The bank's return on assets in the midseventies was double the rate of the best showing by any of the hundred largest private banks in the country.

Herbert Thorndal, the state bank's president, attributes higher profit rates to low overhead and dealing in large-volume business, such as state and local government deposits. "We have only four tellers," says Thorndal, "no advertising budget and we don't give away alarm clocks." "Even the most optimistic boosters of the idea of a state bank," he told a New York State banking committee, "would be surprised by the magnitude of its success today."

A state-owned bank and flour company do not mean socialism has come to North Dakota. The bank, for example, does only a limited amount of lending in competition with other private banks in the state; with few exceptions, it is prohibited from making private and commercial loans. And while 75 percent of state funds are deposited in the bank, only 30 percent of the local governments do so. Yet to the extent the Bank of North Dakota has been able to carry out progressive social policies, and to the extent profits from both the bank and flour enterprises are used to help reduce the burden of taxpayers, they represent an important model of the potential benefits of regional socialism.

Profits from the state bank and mill, which would normally have gone to private companies, often in distant cities, were projected to provide 5 percent of North Dakota's total revenues in 1976 and 1977. "[T]hat's tax money," North Dakota Governor Arthur Link boasted, "people don't have to pay." The benefits of this kind of alternative, as against those of tax-reduction schemes like Proposition 13, are considerable. On the most fundamental level, state-run enterprises not only create the potential for lower taxes, but in contrast to Proposition 13, these enterprises can mean high levels of public services, like schools, health facilities, and fire protection.

In addition to reducing state taxes, the Bank of North Dakota also plays a leading role in advancing innovative social programs. The bank was the state's first lending institution to accept federally subsidized housing programs and it was the first bank in the country to issue federally insured student loans; it currently ranks eighth nationally in the volume of these loans, no small accomplishment coming from one of the country's smallest states, and from a bank with assets only a fraction that of most larger private banks.

The North Dakota bank also helps keep interest rates down for local community borrowing by underwriting a city or town's bond issues, or by lending money to some communities whose issues are so small they would ordinarily be forced to pay higher interest rates to attract any private bidders. It also lends low-interest money at low rates to various state agencies. "Without us," said the bank's president, "the State Treasurer would probably have accounts in Minneapolis, Chicago and New York. We help keep money in the state and provide real financial leadership for the economy."[5]

Another visible example of successful local public ownership in America are the thousands of government-owned energy companies. These energy companies, usually owned by a city or town, now serve about 15 percent of the American people. Ranging in size from over a million consumers in Los Angeles, to sixty in Reynolds, Nebraska, these systems, according to the Department of Energy, average 36 percent lower rates than privately owned companies. Aside from these impressive economies, their record of less expensive management (about three-quarters the cost of private companies) should help dispel the myth about the necessary inefficiency of publicly run enterprises.[6]

The insurance industry provides another glimpse of what could happen under regional socialism. In Wisconsin, a state-run life insurance company begun in the early 1900s continues to provide state residents with the cheapest premium rates in the country. In Canada, three provinces, British Columbia, Saskatchewan, and Manitoba, offer citizens this alternative. These programs, initiated by the socialist New Democratic Party (NDP), have had the effect of not only reducing insurance costs by as much as 20 percent or more over private companies, but according to a survey by the *Toronto Star,* have also returned more to people on their insurance claims than private companies normally do. In addition, state-run insurance has helped reduce local taxes by using premium "profits" to help build schools and hospitals.[7]

In Canada, insurance became an especially hot political issue because most of the private premium money was being exported to American insurance firms. A similar political issue might be developed in this country around the need for state-owned insurance companies. The premiums collected by private firms within a state, whether or not the company is located in that state, are now invested where they will bring the most profitable returns. A private insurance company might invest in the same state in which it receives its premium monies, but it has no obligation to do so. The irony is that people paying their insurance premiums tend to accelerate unemployment, welfare, and job abandonment problems where they live. People in Ohio could be paying premiums to an insurance company that invests in Taiwanese steel mills and contribute to worsening Ohio's problems since the state faces the abandonment of its own steel mill towns.

In addition to its state auto-insurance companies, Canada also has a number of community-owned sports teams. These teams are potentially a very important public ownership model, considering the dilemma now faced by American sports fans and taxpayers who support local sports team owners. Escalating ticket prices, the unresponsiveness of monopoly owners to team fans, and the cost of subsidizing teams by local taxpayers in this country have all contributed to strong antiowner feelings.

Five of the nine-team Canadian Football League are now community-owned. The teams have tended to use profits to improve stadium facilities rather than support team owners, and generally have less of a salary differential between ordinary players and "stars" than the privately owned teams. In spite of the significantly lower assets, incidentally, the community-owned teams appeared to be relatively evenly matched with privately owned ones on the playing field. The public teams won eleven of the past twenty-four playoff games against the private teams.

Community-owned Canadian teams also tend to have more nonseason tickets available, making events more accessible to lower income people. The community-owned Winnipeg Blue Bombers team is required, in the event the team dissolves, to use all money from the sale of its assets for local athletic programs. A somewhat different prospect awaits cities in the United States when their teams are sold by private owners.

## Shifting from What We Have to Where We Could Be

The change from America's existing cold investments system to the warm one possible through regional socialism poses a number of difficult problems. Under capitalism the need for economic expansion creates the twin traumas of unemployment and inflation. Although social-ism can eliminate the unemployment side of this problem (by distributing work equitably and by matching jobs to people's needs), a socialist-run economy faces a problem similar to capitalism's inflation. A socialist government can control inflation by simply announcing a limit on prices. But if that government can't produce the materials, products, and services its people need, then low prices have no meaning. If a socialist government decides to use a significant amount of its material and human resources in a crash program to insulate buildings, this could lead to fewer resources being available in other areas like trans-portation or food production.

An underdeveloped country, whether socialist or not, cannot always afford warm investments as it begins its economic expansion. A country with few resources or a small industrial capacity, whose people are under-nourished or dying of disease, must solve its immediate problems at once. An underdeveloped country may at first require enormous economic expansion in cold, non-recoverable investment in order to provide for people's most immediately pressing needs; money must be quickly pumped into education systems, factories, road building, health skills and hospitals, agricultural training and farm equipment. Investing in conservation industries like in-sulation, for example, requires enormous start-up capital, which may mean diverting capital and human resources from other activities that a country may need for its sheer survival. A delicate and often difficult choice must be made in those countries between cold, immediate-result investments and warm investments that bring improved and sustained long-term results.

America has an obvious advantage in a socialist trans-formation. Its capacity to produce for immediate needs is highly developed and in some areas, as we painfully know, it is enormously overdeveloped and wasteful. Our production and skill capacity is potent; the problem is to retool these capacities, to mine our existing wealth of cold investment resources, and to extract those resources most useful in designing an investment system for regional self-reliance.

Yet, even with the advantage of its existing capacity, the transfer to warm investments will not be an easy one. While this problem shouldn't be minimized, it should also be seen in historic perspective. If the transfer of this country's resources to warm investments is difficult under socialism, capitalism has proved it has no mechanism to make this transfer possible, except by maintaining enormous public subsidies to business.

The list of work needed to create regionally self-reliant economies is long; there is no lack of potential jobs, only the lack of an investment approach that would create them. There are the problems of redesigning food systems, irrigation, fertilizers, consumer-products systems, and transportation systems for more local use. In addition to building a conservation industry which could produce new building insulation techniques, more thermodynamically efficient heating and cooling systems, and the retrofitting of existing buildings, we have the problem of developing entirely new energy systems.

To produce the initial energy necessary to build alternative energy systems we must solve the problem of metering our nonrenewable resources. Energy self-reliance cannot be based on a single solution. It will depend on the adaptation of new energy systems to regional environments. We might expect a combination of wind and solar in most regions, wood-burning and wood alcohol systems in forested and agricultural areas, energy from shifting tides in coastal areas, hydropower in river valleys and the highlands, peat in the Great Lakes region, and geothermal power in the South and West.

We first have the problem of learning how to use oil, coal, and gas resources as "starters" to seed renewable energy systems; we also must learn to use the technology for these systems in less environmentally destructive ways. There are hundreds of thousands of jobs for engineers designing better pollution control systems, safer ways to mine coal, and for construction workers to remodel old systems and build new ones.

The transfer of old skills is, of course, a serious problem. A real estate salesman or a McDonald's foods processing engineer can't be shifted directly to designing solar collectors, methane digestors, or regional food systems. The solution to these problems will be difficult and they may require changes in people's attitudes toward what work they consider useful. But such problems are hardly worse than contemplating how to end enormous unemployment; it is hardly more difficult to face these problems of conversion and retraining than to find solutions within a system in which an enormous number of people must sit idle while others are employed at jobs that will generate more future unemployment.

## What Is Warm? Toward Ecology *and* Economic Health

In choosing approaches to warm investments we may find ourselves making quite different choices from those currently considered progressive. In environmental planning, new investments could require more extensive harvesting of forests in some regions, more water diversion for irrigated farming, more dams and man-made development in others. Instead of simple "environmental preservation," the critical criterion for investment should be: does the action contribute to both regional self-reliance and an ecologically sound approach?

An irrigated water distribution system designed to provide a region with greater food self-reliance, and technically designed so that it doesn't deplete the water resources of other regions, contributes to a national program of reducing the use of energy and resources for all regions. It can result in less energy and material needed to store, refrigerate, and transport goods from one region to another, and it can also mean that currently specialized regions, like the West, will also be able to diversify, leaving more people, land, and water resources available for its own regional production.

"Preservation" is an idea born of fear of loss. "Ecology" is a result of understanding nature's role in the process of human survival; preservation is appeasement that allows the continuation of cold investment. A society that uses its natural resources for real needs, that has a technology designed to maintain and replenish these resources, does not need to fear nature's devastation. Husbanding nature through warm investment encourages a consciousness of interdependence. Nature is not simply isolated vacations and retreats, refuges from the city. Nature is the world around us, urban and rural, which we can use to the extent that we have developed an investment system which allows replenishment.

In making warm investments a region may find itself using more forest products in order to diminish its dependence on synthetics made from nonrenewable fossil sources. These investments might involve major harvesting of currently "unspoiled" forests, but they would also contribute to a healthier long-term use of resources through a production system based on using renewable resources, such as synthetic products derived from wood. The warm approach does not mean we must deplete our forests more rapidly; simply that we consider them as usable, replenishable resources rather than simply as conservation areas.

Our present cold investment economy has transformed forests into an endangered species, constantly threatened by corporate need for economic expansion. A warm investment approach, which could deliver on the goal of longevity of resources, eliminates the threat. A society with real power to plan for its future, rather than simply "hopeful anticipation" of business decisions, can be a society in which people's consciousness about the use of nature can change. In an environmentally secure society, people may still wish to preserve some redwood forests in their natural state, but the simplistic concept of preservation, or nature as a zoo, would give way to the very different ecological approach.

## Toward Self Reliance

A new approach to sane economic productivity must enable a region or a country to eliminate cold investment expansion with its accompanying unemployment and inflation and "deliver the goods" at reasonable cost. An essential ingredient is self-reliance. A socialist system can plan to have all the socially progressive economic expansion it pleases, and it can even attempt to eliminate inflation by fixing prices and wages and by eliminating speculation and fixing interest charges. But all of these efforts will fail if local government cannot create a more self-reliant economy.

Prices may be officially fixed (controlled). But if the

region is highly dependent on imports, the government must subsidize the difference between the fixed price and what it actually has to pay to import the products. Moreover, the more a country imports, the more it is forced to produce the kind of products that are determined not by what it needs, but by what it can sell outside to make money to pay for imports. That is, if a country primarily produces agricultural products for export, and also has to import most of its manufactured goods, then it will tend to remain agriculturally specialized in order to be able to continue to buy the goods it needs. And if this country can't produce enough income from its specialized exports, then it can't buy these imported goods and shortages result. The country's inability to obtain imported necessities will often lead to a black market for the available goods, or what might be called inflation through the back door.

The most fundamental way for a country or region to control inflation or shortages is to be able, on its own, to produce more of what its people need. Superficially, it might seem that the 1973 oil crisis moved America toward more national self-reliance. Since that time, business leaders and politicians have championed the increased exploration and development of our national energy resources. But developing more energy resources in itself doesn't lead to self-reliance; it simply means we're accelerating the depletion of our natural resources, that we have more energy available to produce and consume in the same wasteful ways we have in the past, and that we will have more energy available for energy companies to export.

Business leaders and politicians told the American public in the early seventies that the Alaska pipeline was desperately needed to supply America's own energy needs, to shift it from foreign dependence, and to insure our economic survival. In 1978, however, after the pipeline had been built, many of those leaders were promoting the sale of oil from this "lifeline" of survival to Japan.

The kind of national self-reliance being promoted by business is now leading us toward further regional specialization. Instead of developing new renewable energy systems appropriate for use within regions, new investment is flowing toward extracting what available non-renewable fuel we still have, as fast as possible. When the Atlantic Coast states speed up off-shore oil development, or the Northern Plains states allow accelerated strip coal mining, these states are not becoming more self-reliant, they are simply shifting their economies toward specialized production, tying themselves more closely to the economy of cold investment expansion. They are allowing their wealth to be rapidly siphoned off, while they pay for infrastructure of docks and transportation facilities needed by the energy companies; they pay for the long-term social problems caused by rapid boom town development, and for the long-term welfare problem when the economy shifts downward and reduces the demand for the specialized product they produce.

The problem of specialized economies is not only covering ugly scars of strip-mined land or mopping up the inevitable oil spills in the ocean. The essential problem is the use of a region's current human and material resources to make that region even more dependent in the future than it is today. It is the problem of *missing the opportunity* to use those current human and material resources to build an economy better able to insure the region's future.

Regional socialism requires a balanced and sustained agricultural and industrial production system, in order that the region may consume what it needs without relying on vast amounts of imports, and without having to deplete its resources. This kind of self-reliance must be carefully planned and constructed, using both existing technologies and new ones. How to combine the approach to technology with an approach to politics is not simple. It is, however, critical to the failure or success of regional socialism and worth a trip down the worn path of an old debate.

# 9

# THE LESSONS OF LITTLE ORPHAN ANNIE IN CREATING A TECHNOLOGY FOR REGIONAL SOCIALISM

Technology is our schizophrenia—cause and cure, accused because it underpins the centralized power of business, enshrined for creating better health care and social benefits. As mass production techniques and complex industrial machinery are blamed for social alienation, new agricultural technologies are praised for abundant harvests. Is there an approach, within these debates, to the use of technology which could help create and sustain regional socialism?

There is a growing movement toward "alternative," "humane," or "small is beautiful" technology to foster a safe, ecologically sound, and socially decentralized future. It seems at first an attractive idea. No matter what our scientific background, community-sized or roof-top solar collectors have an intuitive feel of being conducive to local self-reliance rather than a reliance on nuclear power. On a most fundamental level, transporting, storing, and using radioactive materials are activities quite different from running hot water through pipes.

Alternative technology may be safer to use and could

provide important benefits to a regional socialist system, but it would be a political mistake to invest these technologies with more power to transform society than they have. The search for technical strategies for a regional socialism should go beyond the intuitive good feel of these approaches to look at their political and economic implications more thoroughly. If technology leads to dangerous health hazards, there is sufficient reason to demand alternatives. But it is a misreading to draw the conclusion, as some advocates have, that the use of safer, smaller, less complex technical approaches, by themselves, can lead benignly to decentralization.

A "small is beautiful" technology can be easily absorbed into a regressive political system, just as a technology which is large, complex, and difficult to manage can be progressively harnessed by a more humane system. There are ways to make these choices. Technology itself has no independent power to change political and social systems. It is absorbed by those who control the existing systems and shaped by them to reach their goals.

A long succession of social movements have promoted new inventions and scientific techniques to improve social relations between people. This idea engaged the nineteenth-century French social utopians such as Fourier and Saint-Simon, the new communities inspired by progressive English factory owner Robert Owen, and a variety of social reform movements during the 1930s. Today's alternative technology movement is one response to our deeply rooted political and economic crisis. It is a response to our inability to sustain profitable expansion without degrading the environment, exhausting resources, and creating high levels of unemployment and inflation.

When America faced an economic and political crisis

in the 1930s, technology was also raised as a cure. A Technocracy movement emerged which promised economic recovery and stable politics through the use of new industrial inventions and scientific management techniques in business and government. The Technocracy advocates, led by engineers and industrialists, called for an end to political ideologies, the creation of a society governed by principles of efficiency, and the building of inventions to solve material needs.

A Little Orphan Annie cartoon appeared during this time, reflecting the movement's most hopeful fantasies. Daddy Warbucks, Annie's guardian and a benevolent capitalist, had teamed up with Eli Eon, an irascible old inventor, to market Eon's discovery of "eonite." Eonite was a substance that would never wear out; it could be used to build houses, clothes, factories, and battleships which would last forever. "In a few years," said Warbucks, "all shacks and slums will be eliminated—living costs will fall—national wealth will increase tremendously—those with the least will live better than the rich today." Nothing seemed beyond the capacity of this new discovery. "The nation," proclaimed Warbucks, "is on the eve of its greatest advance in history. And *this* time there'll be no Crash at the other end."

In answer to those who forecasted that eonite would do away with business and jobs, Warbucks smilingly replied, "The world will require eonite—we alone can supply it—then this nation will control world trade—our people will be the happiest and most prosperous on earth."

But the fate of eonite and the country was not to be left to Warbucks' benevolence and wisdom. First, a group of big-toothed, black-bearded labor organizers try to organize Warbucks' workers against him, but his loyal workers won't listen. Next Warbucks' archrival "Slugg," an unscrupulous businessman, hires Claude Claptrap, a political demagogue, to organize non-Warbucks workers to sabotage Warbucks' operation. "Eonite is ours," shouts Claptrap to the mob. "Shall one man thwart us in seizing what is ours?" The mob storms the plant, burns it to the ground, and destroys Eli Eon and his plans. "Kill the Cossacks," yell the workers, as they battle the militia.

Annie, upset at events, breaks down and cries on Warbucks' shoulder, her faithful dog Sandy sadly looking on. "He was such a swell guy," she says of the dead inventor. "Yes, he was kindness and generosity itself," says Warbucks, his arm around Annie's shoulders, "what a shame his life was wasted by mad fools incited by shallow knaves and wind-bags." And so ends the story. If not for the madness of labor organizers, demagogues, and their mindless followers, America, led by its more enlightened scientists and businessmen, might have solved its economic crisis.

The Orphan Annie story, a piece of outrageous antilabor propaganda, was a timely bit of melodrama. For newspaper readers of the thirties, who often found their front pages filled with tales of yet another new economic crisis, the cartoon conveyed a soothing message. There could be a simple technological solution to the intractable problems of the collapsed economy; technology harnessed and directed by the right leaders could overcome poverty and unemployment. In a society where a budding collection of technological hardware had suddenly become impotent, it was a message that wanted to be heard.

Today "small is beautiful," and alternative technology is also a message that wants to be heard. Unfortunately, some of its most prominent leaders often present it as the kind of social panacea that eonite was to be. Amory Lovins, for example, has made a well-publicized case for the use of what he calls the "soft" energy path of solar energy as opposed to the "hard" one of nuclear. He has made an important contribution to a saner energy policy by technically demonstrating the enormously higher cost for nuclear power and the serious safety hazards of the nuclear approach. But when he begins to make claims for the political and economic benefits of solar energy he begins to sound like Daddy Warbucks. Says Lovins:

> . . . it helps to avoid conflict between constituencies by offering advantages to all of them: jobs for the unemployed, capital for businesspeople, environmental protection for conservationists, increased national security for the military, opportunities for small business to innovate and for big business to recycle itself, savings for consumers, world order and equity for globalists, energy independence for isolationists, exciting technologies for the secular, a rebirth of spiritual values for the religious, radical reforms for the young, traditional virtues for the old, civil rights for liberals and states' rights for conservatives.[1]

## Appropriate Technology, Inappropriate Politics

The theoretical underpinning for Amory Lovins's benign view of how political and economic transformations will result from solar energy were set forth by the late E. F. Schumacher, in *Small Is Beautiful.* "Although man shapes technology," said Schumacher, "once he has shaped it, technology tends to shape him. It shapes him, his pattern of settlements, his life style, and it also as it were determines the 'essence' of his political system. That is to say, the 'shape' of technology has become the dominant formative agent, and without changing technology nothing important can be changed." Schumacher elaborates this view, describing how the size, cost, and nature of technology shaped our cities and countryside.

> When technology develops in such a way that large, complex, highly capital costly production units appear to be the most "economical" (from the point of view of the unit's cost accounting), it is virtually inevitable that industrial development will be confined to major towns and cities. . . . Technologies for mass production by highly complex methods at a high level of capital intensity can do nothing to create jobs outside the already existing great concentrations of people and wealth. To promote work in the rural areas, technologies are needed which are suitable for *efficient* small-scale production, without undue complexity, and with modest capital requirements.[2]

But the experience of this country shows a different picture of technological location. The migration of business to the countryside, which is now accelerating, has taken place in both capital-intensive and labor-intensive industries, and in both small- and large-scale industries. Large automated factories, nuclear power generators, auto assembly plants, aluminum production facilities have been decentralized. General Motors has located in rural Louisiana, Volkswagen in rural Pennsylvania, Michelin in rural South Carolina, and Reynolds Aluminum in rural Arkansas. Even in early periods of history large, automated plants had decentralized: Ford Motor moving to the (at the time) rural Dearborn, steel mills locating in (at that time) rural Indiana and Ohio.

Although any generalization that relates the location of industry to its degree of technological complexity is likely to be incorrect, a case could be made for the opposite of Schumacher's analysis. New York, the largest manufacturing city in the United States, has always been a haven for small-scale, labor-intensive industrial production. Its typical industry employs less than twenty workers in labor-intensive work such as garment making, metal work, and small equipment manufacturing. The same is true of Boston, Philadelphia, and many other big cities.

Indeed, probably the smallest, most labor-intensive industry this country has seen was incubated in the big cities. Historian Sam Warner's description of New York's homegrown garment industry in the late 1800s should put to rest any serious doubt that "small" technology is a guarantee against exploitation or leads to a benign lifestyle.

> They moved artisans, unskilled immigrants, women and children into their own shops where they could watch over them. . . . They might be housed in a floor or two of an ancient narrow building belonging to a merchant, in a basement, in a rear yard structure of one or two stories that resemble a barn, or perhaps some trades like the making of cigars or clothing in the tenement room of the worker himself.[3]

On the other hand, the most capital-intensive, large-scale operations were frequently located in the countryside. Textile mills, for example, which were this country's first large-scale mechanized industries, began in the New England countryside, then moved southward to Pennsylvania, and eventually to the small hill towns of the southern Piedmont. The "smallness" or "largeness" of the technology has been less relevant to most industries than the nature of the work force. The attraction for business has been and continues to be the level of wages, the degree of workers' organizing, and the political malleability of local government.

A small dress company may be located in a small town, it may have small, simple, easily understood and maintained equipment, it may employ small numbers of people working together at labor-intensive jobs, and it may require relatively little capital to maintain it. Yet in spite of the smallness and humbleness of the technology and the setting, it may not be so very beautiful; a dress shop that pays its workers low wages, and allows them little power to bargain collectively is still a sweatshop. We might shift from nuclear to solar, build millions of solar collectors in backyards and on rooftops all over the country, and still find ourselves with very little social improvement; in fact, it might actually make some things worse.

## The Control of Technology

Let us imagine, for a moment, that our energy system is suddenly transformed so that each of us has an extremely efficient solar or wind fuel cell at home which generates power to run our car and household appliances. Who, we must now ask, will provide the materials and equipment for our fuel cell? Who provides us with the autos, trucks, and appliances that will be powered by those cells? Who determines what kind of jobs will develop as the result of the new technology, what kinds of new products or services will be generated as the result of the cheap, clean new ways of delivering energy? Our immediate energy production system may be decentralized and small but the purpose of work, what work gets done, and how we use our natural resources, our steel, our copper, our magnesium, will still be controlled through centralized corporate decision making.

Contrary to making us self-sufficient, our backyard generators make us potentially more vulnerable to increased resource consumption. Even in the most optimistic case of passing the cost savings of new energy systems to the consumer, cheap energy in the private economy market allows for easier and greater consumption. "The sun," said one enthusiastic engineer testifying before a congressional committee, "is a bottomless oil well."

A cheap and bottomless oil well could mean that instead of one toaster, consumers can be persuaded to buy two or three, each with special features, each in a different color, each for different rooms in the house, and so on. Cheap energy without a political mechanism for sane consumption means the reflowering of the two-car-plus family, more speedboats for lakes, more electric knives, more garbage to dispose of. New consumption creates more use of other resources, copper and iron for appliances and autos, land and asphalt for more highways, and building supplies for more second homes. An era of "cheap, nonpolluting" energy with small, beautiful technology could be an environmental nightmare.

The only mechanism that can trigger ecologically sound business decisions under capitalism is increased profit. The paradox of this system may mean that the path to preserving the environment becomes the path to destroying it. The search for a more humane political system which simply awaits the creation of "appropriate," "small," "soft" alternatives will be futile. Until the alternative energy advocates join those with a political strategy for change they will find those very alternatives absorbed by the present system.

Private capital's hold over the use of new technical innovations is pervasive. Private capital is not being perverse; it doesn't want dirty air or the depletion of resources. It has no alternative but to use our resources and environment in certain ways, if it hopes to survive.

The dilemma and danger that our present economic system poses to all of us, capitalist managers and citizens, are seen vividly in two examples of environmental innovations being absorbed by this system—the uses of recycling and environmental cleanup.

Much of the paper that is recycled in this country is used by the automobile and building industries. The auto companies use it for linings in glove compartments, panels in trunks, and in packages for parts; the building industry uses recycled paper for producing plasterboard. In the early seventies, recycled paper brought about $45 a ton. During the economic depression of 1974 and 1975, with home sales and car buying down, the price for a ton of recycled paper dropped to $3, if there was a buyer. As recycling yards turned away used paper sellers, paper was gotten rid of in the traditional ways of dumping and burning.

There are severe limits to the way materials can be recycled in a capitalist economy. When the economy is expanding, the need for recycled materials increases; when the economy declines, there is little use for these wastes. To recycle more means to consume more.

Cleaning up the environment under capitalism presents similar problems. To make environmental cleanup acceptable, companies must be able to expand production to pay for the cleanup. What happened to several companies in the steel industry is a case in point. In the 1950s, two large firms, Armco and Republic, formed a joint company to extract low-grade iron ore from a location in northeastern Minnesota on the shore of Lake Superior.

As the extraction process went on, people noticed

asbestoslike particles in the air. At the same time particles from the dumped waste were escaping into the water and affecting the local fishing industry. Local people, environmentalists, and some state officials were becoming alarmed at cancer hazards. In 1973, the National Water Control Laboratory declared that the waste particles were widely dispersed in the lake that many cities were using for their water supply.

In the negotiations between the state and the companies, a controversy developed about who would pay for pollution control. After 1974, when the price of iron ore had doubled, the companies appeared more willing to consider pollution equipment. By 1977, the profitability of steel declined and steel plants began to close. In 1978, Minnesota gave Armco and Republic a two-and-a-half-year delay in using pollution control and agreed to finance a substantial part of the cost.[4] In Pennsylvania that year, politicians also offered steel companies delays in pollution control to keep them from closing.

Economic growth, which must take place to sustain and improve profit, leaves in its wake a strange kind of environmentalism; recycling and environmental cleanup occur when enough profit can be made in using more materials and consuming more. In this endless cycle—the more we consume, the more we are able to clean up and recycle—we *must first* become more and more dirty to become clean.

## The Different Political Paths of Solar

Today's environmental movement to clean the air, conserve resources, reduce the chance of nuclear disaster and cancer is extremely important. But this effort, without a strong political movement to change our economic system, can only treat symptoms. Unless we are able to change the economic *incentives* which produce these problems structurally, we will face ever more resource depletion and environmental hazards. To understand how technology might be approached differently, we can look at a "new" system like solar energy, and project how it might be developed under regional socialism.

Solar energy proceeds in two directions. One is a sophisticated and often highly imaginative form of "tinkerism," where systems are developed by individuals and relatively small companies. The second direction is being developed by large corporations and utility monopolies. The technology that will emerge from both could range from individual home heating units to enormous solar farms built in some parts of the country, as well as orbiting satellites that beam energy back to earth.

If present political trends continue providing corporations with large government subsidies to develop solar energy, we can discount the impact of "tinkerism" and expect that solar energy will be controlled by large manufacturers and large private utilities. The utilities will lease solar units to its customers or generate electric power through larger solar systems and will sell that electricity to its customers much as it does now.

Contrary to some opinion, our big energy companies are very interested in developing solar power. Since 1960, two-thirds of all the solar energy patents were claimed by large corporations. GE, Westinghouse, and Mobil Oil are a few of the big companies heavily involved in research or planning for production. The strategy of the companies is to control production by buying patents and thereby having a ready path if they should be forced by public pressure to produce solar energy systems.[5]

In 1978, a number of the country's major industrial

firms, including Rockwell International, Boeing, and Grumman, formed an organization called the SUNSTAT Energy Council to promote the development of satellites that would orbit the earth and transmit energy from the sun. Congress has already allocated $8 million to study the concept, called Solar Power Satellite (SPS), and that same year a congressional bill was introduced to provide another $25 million for more studies. Other possibilities for corporate development include construction of massive "solar farms" in the sun-intensive regions of the country, such as Arizona, Florida, and southern California, and transmission of solar-generated electricity to other parts of the country, either over power lines or by transporting storage units like photovoltaic cells.

In the development of individual home heating or cooling units, large manufacturers will make and sell entire home systems or the major components of these systems. The firms will either install the systems themselves through local outlets, franchise the installations through local businesses, or sell the systems directly to homeowners. Energy companies like Exxon have already established subsidiaries to develop these systems.

With large energy companies and utilities controlling alternative power we can expect little economic change from the present. A glimpse of this path can be seen in the alternative energy development approach of southern California's monopoly gas supplier, the Southern Gas Company.

The company recently initiated plans both for expanded gas supply and for a solar heating experiment. The experiment, "Project Sunflower," calls for installation of 315 experimental solar systems in homes, shops, and factories. To pay for this $11 million experiment, the company asked for increased rates; the average solar system would cost $40,000, about five to ten times what one of the world's largest solar manufacturing firms, located in southern California, charges for installing similar systems.[6] At the same time that Southern Gas initiated this solar experiment, it contracted with the military government of Indonesia and energy companies in Alaska for a $20 billion twenty-year supply of liquefied natural gas (LNG).

The danger of using this energy source is enormous. Transporting and storing LNG involves condensing the gas to one six-hundredth its original volume by chilling it to 260 degrees below zero Fahrenheit. Potential LNG accidents have been predicted to be as dangerous as those in nuclear reactors. A break in the storage tank would let the gas vaporize, and if ignited, it would explode in an enormous fire cloud. A study for the Federal Power Commission concluded that an LNG harbor spill near a high density population could kill hundreds of thousands of people.[7]

Though the gas company publicizes its interest in solar power through "Sunflower," its real commitment is obviously to LNG for the immediate future. It is unlikely that after investing in more than a dozen supertankers and millions of dollars' worth of additional Alaskan pipeline and terminal facilities it will dump these investments and turn to solar energy.

Solar becomes the reserve fuel, to be used when existing sources are exhausted or too expensive. In the meantime, research on solar is funded by rate increases and government grants, and prices for solar-produced energy are pegged at the same rates as existing fuels to insure the use and revenue of existing systems.

A technology to support regional socialism would be based on the goal of making reasonable and efficient use of the society's available resources. Because it does not have continually to expand its economy, this society can choose technological options which extend the long-term use of its existing resources, bringing forward new technologies like solar energy *before* the old ones are exhausted.

The size and design of the solar energy unit would be determined by a planning process which would gauge overall efficiency. Each energy system would have efficiency characteristics based on purposes to which it would be put. Neither small nor large is beautiful in the abstract. A single large solar farm installation might under certain conditions be a more efficient way of converting solar energy to usable energy than a combination of small units. In the aggregate it may require less material and less person-hours to build, less to maintain, and involve less conversion loss from solar to electrical modes.

If it were necessary to provide energy for a community of 10,000 people, the size of the facilities would have to be determined by the costs and benefits of several possibilities: building 10,000 individual units; building 100 units to each serve 100 people; or building one unit to service all 10,000 people. The decision would be made in a collective political forum, where the overall thermodynamic efficiencies of the technical process and the political consequences would be examined for each alternative. The conditions to be considered would include:

- the total amount of raw materials, energy, and human resources needed to produce each alternative
- the long-term costs of servicing different alternatives
- the conversion efficiency of different sized units; e.g., in the case of solar to electric conversion, how much energy is lost in the conversion process by different sized units?
- the most effective size for politically subdividing control

that would make possible real democratic decisions about how energy and resources are to be used
• the job conditions for workers producing the energy hardware and running the systems

The use of energy and resources to build and power cars, toasters, and TV sets would be a collective political decision rather than a market one; it would depend upon where the society placed its priorities—on housing or cars, motor boats or environmental reclamation. This is not to say that regional socialism automatically makes sane decisions. Public education and discussion about the dangers of conventional technology and the need for safer, non-polluting energy systems will be critical. The real advantage of regional socialism is that it would make these alternatives explicit through a process of democratic planning, and that it would not rely exclusively on profit and economic expansion as the major criteria. Under capitalism, technological alternatives can occur only where they contribute to at least as much profit and expansion as existed. Southern Gas has no ideological problem with solar energy. It will not shift from its gas investments, however, until solar can bring it as much return.

## Political Struggle and New Technology

Although technological invention is politically neutral it can be used to develop a political strategy for social change. The process of introducing a new technology or phasing out an old one provides an important vehicle for political organizing. The growing public concern about the safety of nuclear power and the disposal of nuclear wastes provides not only an opportunity to produce a safer energy system, but a political forum to argue the advantages of new forms of energy, ownership, and control.

The introduction of solar and other alternative energy sources, which are likely to involve billions in public research and development dollars, is a chance to lobby for returning the fruits of publicly paid research and development to the public through public ownership by state and city governments. Broad political coalitions of unions, community organizations, and environmental groups can be organized around the potent issue of providing a predictable and steady regional source of clean, renewable energy and the creation of useful jobs.

In recent years there has been a growing movement at a national level toward breaking up control of the oil companies. Worried about the possible effectiveness of this campaign, the companies have responded with lobbying and public campaigns aimed at improving their image. Political organizers in a number of states and cities, including Vermont, Massachusetts, and California, have developed active campaigns for reducing utility rates and for creating public power agencies. The emerging interest in public control of energy is likely to grow as energy costs rise.

Under growing pressure from many consumer, environmental, and some union groups, schemes for government support of solar production are also emerging. While many of these schemes could simply result in helping large energy companies and higher income people, the existence of pro-solar political pressure can provide an opening wedge for more progressive ideas.

The best-publicized of current ideas is for providing state and federal tax credits to homeowners who install solar equipment. This is obviously not a strategy aimed at public control. Tax incentives that encourage higher income homeowners to switch to solar and become more self-reliant will not reduce the cost of fuel to the majority. As people with collectors use less private utility power, utilities will charge more for the decreased total amount of power they supply in order to maintain their profit margins. Lower income people with no collectors will find themselves with higher bills. Homeowners with solar collectors will pay more for the power they use to run their appliances or to heat their water and homes during cloudy periods.

New coalitions will be fragile ones if the disenfranchised are ignored. There are already indications that low-income people will not sit by idly and watch tax concessions for solar power be given to higher income homeowners. In San Francisco, blacks and other community groups fought a city proposal to allow property tax abatements on solar installations on the grounds that they would help only higher income people.

A publicly owned alternative energy system that provided benefits for homeowners, renters, and small and large businesses, on a sliding scale, depending on the income of those served, could be a firmer basis for building a broad coalition for change. People who preferred to install their own systems would be free to do so, but without the benefits of tax incentives for a system they can afford, and which will obviously benefit them directly.

Hoping for decentralization through the back door of technological appropriateness is a thin political strategy. It leads to justifying political beliefs on the basis of the latest technical study of how cost effective a particular sized technology can be. Very soon another technical study will show the first was wrong. The argument turns on itself, and big government or big corporations become the logical manager of that technology.

In moving toward regional socialism a wide spectrum of *safe* technologies must be considered. They can be large or small, complex or simple, sit on our rooftops or occupy hundreds of acres of land. Their size and complexity are not nearly so important as the economic system and the political process which allow people to decide how they will be used.

# 10
# MONEY, MUZAK, AND THE SETTING FOR CHANGE

The man who marketed Muzak understood the secret of his success. It was, he said, the kind of music you only hear when it's turned off. The myth of American free enterprise, entrepreneurship, and competition has been humming in our ears for years. Only now, as that system is faltering, may people actually be ready to listen to the words.

Even today, as the hope of entrepreneurship is available to fewer and fewer, the residual culture of bygone days insists on the virtues of individual enterprise. Corporate-owned and franchised "convenience" stores now outdo the mom and pop stores. Less than 7 percent of the working population now owns a business (about half the percentage of 1960), and the number of people working for wages continues to grow. Today, according to the chairman of the United States Chamber of Commerce, three out of four small businesses can be expected to fail in the first year. By the early 1970s there were more people in America on welfare than owned businesses.[1]

In one sense it doesn't matter to most of us what

economic system we have, or is being advertised, as long as it produces the goods—a big enough paycheck so the good, or at least acceptable life can be had. If these goods can be delivered without those controlling the production system intruding too directly on our personal lives, the system, whatever it is, can survive. This doesn't mean most people believe in "the system"; it simply means not many people are about to take to the streets over the issue of the death of free enterprise, or the need for socialism, when they know that whatever system we have produces a standard of living to which they've become agreeably accustomed.

Movements for radical change have historically followed from a *desperate* economic need for change, not from ideological commitment. The attacks on the evils of capitalism notwithstanding, it is only economic collapse that would set the conditions for change. When the economic system can't deliver the goods, it becomes really visible. Like Muzak, when the sound stops, we hear it.

A potential radicalizing silence is now being produced by a series of familiar and growing economic problems—scarcities, inflation, unemployment, decline in corporate profitability. Business's method of dealing with these problems is accelerating them. Winner and loser regions which result from regional rotation create the need for more economic expansion at a time when our economic system is increasingly unable to sustain expansion. As business is forced to rely on such techniques, it creates the conditions for a breach in its own power. Under the right set of historical circumstances, that breach can be widened, a new national political consciousness can be created, and a movement toward regional socialism set in motion.

That movement must ultimately be sustained by a mass political organization. The most optimistic scenario is the creation of a national political party with a base of support from among a broad spectrum of workers, environmentalists, consumers, students, and other groups. The country is some distance from having anything resembling a strong national party on the left.

There are, however, many ways to begin a process of change now. Mini-cataclysms, which have already occurred in the loser regions and which will continue through regional rotation, the increased reliance on unsafe energy, the loss of hundreds of thousands of jobs, and the forcing down of wages, public services, and environmental conditions in these regions, provide the context.

No corner of America is free from the effects of business's current struggle for survival. People are being given the message that business has the option to move and will use it; they're being told that there's less fat in our productive system, wars like Vietnam are no longer easy options for consolidating power, we don't control cheap energy the way we used to, and investment funds are more difficult to come by. Maintaining profit and even reduced government services means resorting to fewer wage increases, move government subsidies for business, and reducing environmental controls. Business doesn't have to raise its voice much. The example of New York and other cities hangs ominously and conveniently in the background.

As business is forced to move its capital, it must directly attack the benefits won by organized labor in the abandoned regions. Unions, which could once see themselves attached to the rising fortunes of corporate America, must now confront the fact that class differences are real, not easily erased by recently acquired power which allowed the more privileged of the working class a larger share. The potential reaction of labor unions and others threatened by business's strategy could begin an important series of events. That reaction would have to go beyond traditional demands and techniques, such as strikes, to find more effective tools for change.

Instead of the single, traditional approach of denying labor to industry through strikes, two simultaneous strategies are needed. One must begin by recognizing that there are distinct conditions and opportunities for organizing depending on whether a region is a winner or loser. Conditions for change are very different in Ohio, where unions are strong and where industry is leaving, than in North Carolina, where the opposites are true. In North Carolina, more traditional union organizing could still be effective; in Ohio, an approach which involved more direct participation of government in industry will be necessary.

### Strategies in the "Winners"

Winner regions may now have low levels of union membership, and as the state promotional agencies proudly proclaim, little worker militancy. But historically the boom growth that typifies these regions leads to a rise in expectations and demands. For a time these regions offer attractive job opportunities for ex-farm workers, subsistence farmers, and other people with little industrial experience. For many people in these regions even minimum government wage standards translate into a better weekly salary than they have ever seen.

But as job opportunities and incomes increase, people who were once resigned to the conditions of a marginal economy begin to taste the possibility of moving beyond their rural shanties and urban slums. As more industries move to an area, the conditions of what might have been a marginal or subsistence economy shift. More people move to the community, and more schools, roads, and public services are needed. The community becomes more vulnerable to changes in national economic cycles, with more unemployment and welfare services necessary during dips in the economy. As the number of jobs expands and as more people relocate in these regions, competition for the available housing becomes intense, driving up the price of the existing housing stock, land, and new homes.

As incomes increase, people begin to expect better cars, better homes, better medical services, better education. Between 1972 and the end of 1978, the cost of living in most of the country's winner regions was rising more rapidly than that of its losers. "[W]ithin a few years," said a study by the Southern Growth Policies Board, "costs of living differentials between the regions will be virtually non-existent."[2]

Whether or not the differentials will disappear altogether, the fact remains that expectations of families in the winner regions are likely to increase more rapidly than those in other parts of the country. Coupled with the new need to provide more public services in these areas, and the costs of inflation in the overall economy, workers in winner regions will be forced to demand higher wages.

But in order to maintain their profitable position, businesses in these regions are, in turn, forced to resist. Companies may successfully resist at first by simply refusing to grant demands or by firing those who persist. When companies are forced to use such repressive tactics, workers have historically turned to the labor union, with its ability to induce business to comply through techniques like strikes. There is little reason to expect that future conditions in the winners will not follow the same pattern.

Even in North Carolina, the nation's premier antilabor stronghold, the availability of jobs and an inflated economy are already beginning to produce more success in labor organizing. By 1978 organizing drives by labor unions had begun to "soften," as *Business Week* described it. In that year less than 7 percent of the state's eligible workers belonged to a union, compared with a national average of over 26 percent; workers in North Carolina also received less average wages than those in any other state in the country.

But that same year unions in the state won more than 35 elections, unionizing the equivalent of about 12 percent of the jobs added to the state—almost double the existing rate of unionization. In the Piedmont region, unions won elections in Eden, Thomasville, Greensboro, and Lexington; the local Teamsters, with an especially aggressive style of organizing, won nine of the eleven elections, in the hill towns of this traditionally paternalistic and vehemently antiunion region.[3]

But the rising militancy and modest gains organized labor is likely to attain in North Carolina and other winner states, could be seriously jeopardized when the national economy slows, or when business is able to loosen the job market by rotating jobs to low-wage workers in other regions. "When the job market gets tight," said North Carolina AFL-CIO President Wilbur Hobby, "the workers aren't scared somebody is outside waiting to take their jobs, and they're more willing to join the union."[4]

In winner regions like North Carolina, increased organizing around the traditional issue of striking or threatening to strike for job security, higher wages, and better working conditions could be an effective way of winning demands and developing more organized labor strength. This technique, however, will work *only to the extent* that a new strategy is *simultaneously* developed in loser regions effectively to block business's ability to rotate regions. Strikes can only be effective in the winner regions, if business can't make good on a threat to move back to a hungrier labor market and cheaper conditions in the loser regions.

## Strategies in the "Losers"

Given a company's room to maneuver, unions in loser regions are hard-pressed to make good the claim that belonging to a union helps a worker maintain a decent job. The unions in loser regions may be able to keep management from the most blatant forms of oppression, but business still holds the trump card when it can strike against labor with its capital by taking its wages to a more hospitable home. If simply maintaining a job is a worker's first concern, not belonging to a union allows workers more easily to lower their own wages. In some industries, union members are finding it necessary to put their union cards "in their shoes," as the expression goes, when they apply for work at nonunion or open-shop firms.

In 1970, the American Builders and Contractors (ABC), representing open-shop construction businesses, had only 3,400 members in less than half the states. In 1977, it had more than 11,500 members in all fifty states. An even more disturbing implication for union workers is the fact that most of the open-shop strength is in small cities and rural areas, the fastest growing sections of the country. While most central city, high-rise construction is still dominated by union labor, a 1977 report by the Department of Housing and Urban Development noted that large firms, even in metropolitan areas, "confirm that they (can) no longer compete with non-union firms outside of major commercial and industrial projects."[5]

To develop an effective strategy in loser regions, labor

must have the kind of leverage with business which has real teeth. An essential direction would be a shift of government involvement from a limited role as policeman-accomplice of business to a more active advocacy of working people's interests. If government were able to help create jobs for those threatened with abandonment by business, the threat of abandonment would become less potent. Workers who knew they had alternatives, that their livelihood was not on the line when they opposed company policies, could develop more militant and effective positions.

## The Role of Labor

The recent dramatic decline in the percentage of workers belonging to unions in many loser states attests to business's ability to sap union strength by moving. Business, operating under the iron constraint of profitability, has no alternative strategy to reduce this threat to workers; it can't simply remain in an area, accede to union demands, and watch its level of profit fall. Whether or not unions move to embrace a direct form of socialism, or socialism by another name, the need for some mechanism for government control over what and where investments take place and how the benefits of those investments are distributed, is likely to become much more apparent to workers and their unions as regional rotation continues.

Many major unions, lulled by their successes in wage and job security over the past forty years, tend to remember the militancy of the 1930s more as nostalgia than as a model for action today. The record of many unions is layered with compromise and the outright purging of radicals; some union leadership has had ties with organized crime and has illegally tampered with their members' pension funds. Yet for all the justifiable criticism that can be leveled against some of America's unions, this movement remains the only consistent force in the country which has been able to support and protect workers against the more blatant abuses of business. As an institution, it can be refocused toward an even more progressive role.

Optimism about the union movement as a vanguard for change rests not on the record of its past leadership, but with present economic conditions and recent actions by its current leaders and rank-and-file members. As the growing economic crisis forces business to hold the line against cost increases, union leaders can't hope to deliver on their members' needs with the same "partnership with business" approach possible during the robust periods of economic expansion during and after World War II. Business's demonstrated ability to undercut labor's demands makes the inherent conflict between itself and labor more stark and more real. In this context, radical strategies can move from the theories of a fringe to becoming a necessity of the majority.

One of the most hopeful signs of change in American labor strategies is the emergence of insurgent rank-and-file groups within mainstream unions. Their growth, often in the face of serious personal danger, has moved some unions toward more militant positions against business and more democratic representation of rank-and-file members in union affairs. The strength shown by insurgents in the election campaigns of the United Steel Workers and the United Mine Workers, although they did not change official union leaders on a national level, indicates important support within unions for more progressive approaches.

The traditionally crime-connected Teamsters Union, whose $160,000-a-year president earns two to three times that of most of his counterparts, now finds itself the scene of growing reform movements from inside. One group called PROD, representing 6,000 members, grew from a Ralph Nader conference on truck safety, while a 2,000-member Teamsters for a Democratic Union (TDU) was created with the help of the International Socialists organization. Both groups have called for democratic elections, better working conditions, lower salaries for union officials, and less racial and sexual discrimination against members. In 1978, members of both groups won a number of important offices in local union elections.

Faced with the continued erosion of liberal political support for the labor movement over the recent past, labor leaders have been forced to search for new strategies. While this shift signals no immediate emergence of strong socialist positions, it nevertheless represents an important historic juncture which could move the country, or at least parts of it, in that direction.

During the 1970s, organized labor received a stunning series of setbacks at the hands of business and political leaders. Not since the Taft-Hartley Act became law some thirty years earlier had the movement been so seriously shaken. Business's faltering profitability over the past decade forced firms to step up their open-shop drives and migration to less unionized regions. The Democratic party, for its part, has attempted to help solve business's crisis by diluting labor demands on the legislative front.

Fighting against the freedom to move firms to anti-union regions, the AFL-CIO mounted a major campaign in the seventies to rewrite parts of the Taft-Hartley Act. The cornerstone of its strategy was to remove the infamous Section 14-B of the Act which allowed individual states to outlaw exclusive union shops and establish themselves as "Right-to-Work" states. Not only did a

Democratic Congress beat back this attempt, but it also defeated an effort to legislate common situs picketing, which would have allowed unions not directly involved in a strike to picket a company in sympathy with those who were striking.

Following in rapid order on the heels of these defeats, a Democratic Congress and president failed to pass the Labor Reform Act, with its rather mild rules for enforcing the provisions of earlier labor laws. Labor spent more money on its effort to pass that act than for any previous law. In the late 1970s, the same Congress and president presided over the redesign and emasculation of the Humphrey-Hawkins Full Employment Act; in its final form the Act guaranteed labor neither the creation of a single job, nor the reduction of the unemployment rate. And to cap these actions, the same Democratic president and Congress presented the country with tax cuts for business and natural gas deregulation, which most labor unions had staunchly opposed.

Buffeted by these setbacks, union leaders have been forced to search for new strategies. Democratic party support which could be counted on during times of rising national prosperity was now evaporating. Lifting itself from the years of its comfortable partnership with business and Democratic politicians, labor leaders have begun to cast about for new allies.

From conservative labor leaders like George Meany within the AFL-CIO hierarchy, to more left-leaning union presidents, a major movement has been formed around building coalitions with other interest groups like environmentalists, women's organizations, minorities, and consumers. In part, this new effort simply represents a jockeying among union leaders for the future leadership of the country's labor movement, now occupied by an aging Meany. But beyond this, and even more important, the maneuvering toward new coalitions represents an explicit recognition of labor's continuing weakness in union organizing, and its lack of support among outside groups. Even Meany's AFL-CIO, which has steadfastly supported the development of nuclear power plants, shifted gears in the late seventies to support environmentalists' efforts to develop solar power (while not abandoning nuclear) in return for environmental support of the Labor Reform Act.

The two most important attempts at aligning labor with outside liberal and leftist groups have been spearheaded by William Wimpisinger, president of the 900,000 member International Association of Machinists (IAM), and Douglas Fraser, president of the 1.6 million member United Automobile Workers (UAW). The efforts of both men toward more grass-roots organizing follow their frustrated attempts at change within established political forums.

In the summer of 1978, Fraser, reacting to business's successful alliance with a Democratic Congress to defeat the labor reform bill, declared business was waging "one-sided class war." Amid great fanfare, he resigned from the Labor-Management Group, a high-level organization of business and labor leaders established by the president to work out business-labor problems informally away from the bargaining table. A few months after his resignation Fraser brought together several hundred representatives of major unions, environmental, minority, and community groups in Detroit to create formally a national coalition aimed ambiguously both at reforms within the Democratic party and at searching for "new alternatives." Included in this group of over one hundred organizations and thirty labor organizations is the National Organization for Women, Friends of the Earth, the Oil Chemical and Atomic Workers, AFSCME, the New American Movement, and the Democratic Socialist Organizing Committee.

Just a few months before the formation of Fraser's coalition, William Wimpisinger, of the Machinists, put together his own "Citizens/Labor Energy Coalition," comprised of some sixty organizations, many of which were later represented in the Fraser group. Claiming the Carter Administration is incapable of taking on the oil monopoly, he suggested the only solution was to force oil producers to divest themselves of refining, distributing, and marketing subsidiaries, their holdings in other energy sources like coal, gas, and uranium, and to establish a national effort to develop alternative forms of energy.

Wimpisinger, although not explicit as to how this change would occur, called for "mobilizing grass-roots support." "In the tradition of Debs and Thomas," said Wimpisinger, who espouses socialist views, "we are going to raise enough hell that sooner or later the American people are going to wake up." At the 1978 Democratic convention Wimpisinger called for pressures to move the party leftward, and if this isn't possible, he said, "I'd say 'yeah' to a third party."[6]

The coalition-building now underway by labor leaders, environmentalists, consumers, minorities, and other groups is an extremely important event. Not because it is likely to produce many dramatic immediate improvements, but because it is setting a process in motion, which could lead to more progressive future changes.

The present strategy of coalition leaders appears aimed at strengthening the liberal wing of the Democratic party. Douglas Fraser has quite explicitly stated he is not interested in creating a third party, but rather in supporting liberal Democrats under attack by conservatives. The program for the future according to the UAW president should be to force the Democrats to make good on their political platforms of the past.[7]

But the difficulty of relying on this kind of strategy is that the Democratic party has proved it cannot deliver for labor, and if anything the party is moving rapidly toward an even more conservative stance. The decline of business profitability and rampant inflation are forcing both Democratic and Republican politicians to cut back social welfare programs, to control wage increases, to ease regulations protecting workers' safety, to use unemployment to dampen inflation, and to fight labor reforms that would impede business profitability.

These new positions are not easily taken by Democrats. They are being forced on them by the limits of the existing economic system. There is simply no way to expand social programs and protect workers' wages if the economy itself does not expand. Faced with declining expansion and declining revenues for public spending, more Democrats have taken political refuge by becoming "fiscal conservatives." The specter of Proposition 13-type reforms and the loss of political office now throw a long shadow across any future federal or local government programs for expanding public service or creating costly labor reforms.

As liberal programs of the Democratic party continue to slide, labor and other progressive interest groups will find themselves with fewer ways to protect their interests through traditional politics. When Fraser, head of one of the country's biggest unions, now talks of "class warfare" being waged by business against labor, and the lack of alternatives within both major parties, he is voicing the frustration labor feels as traditional political approaches are being closed out. The withdrawal of these options could set the stage for creating new forms of struggle.

## Coalitions and Strategies

Many labor leaders, including Fraser and Wimpisinger, have called for "new alternatives." It is not exactly clear what kinds of strategies Fraser will press after proclaiming the UAW will "reforge the links" with the labor militancy of the 1930s and the civil rights movement of the 1960s, or what Wimpisinger will do when he says, "we are going to raise enough hell." What is clear is that the simple formation of coalitions to issue demands to government leaders has much less clout when these same government leaders believe their tenure in office means shifting toward more conservative policies. To make political leaders and, more importantly, business leaders take note of demands means posing further serious threats to their sources of power.

For political leaders the most potent political threat is the loss of votes. The strategy for keeping the Democrats from the right, and for developing more progressive political strength would be the creation of an alternative leftist political party. With the Democrats the only current leftist contender, Democratic politicians now have a wide margin of conservative space to move into before losing significant power. The real current threat to the Democrats is not that progressive voters will move to a different party, but that they simply won't vote at all. With the emergence of a strong left-wing party organized by labor and other progressive groups, the Democrats could be forced to run joint candidates with this party, or at least pose its own progressive programs to compete with it for votes.

The most serious threats that can be posed against business leaders are the loss of profitability or, even worse, the loss of a business itself. Workers can pose this threat most potently where they work. The major gains that labor made historically were through organizing the work place and by making demands of their employers at the work place. By posing demands through well-organized unions rather than as isolated individuals and by using forceful strikes rather than idle threats, employers were forced to negotiate or watch their investments decline.

In the abandoned "loser" regions the kind of militant "sit-down" strikes Fraser alludes to could be an especially important alternative for making future demands. In the sit-down strike pioneered by the UAW in the 1930s, workers refused to leave their factories, often for a few days, sometimes for months, until owners met their demands. The use of this kind of strike today would pose serious problems for a company that attempted to abandon a community—most fundamentally it could pose the possibility, as has happened in Europe recently, that workers might actually remain in the work place for long periods, continue production, and even sell their own products.

Aided by the sit-downs in the 1930s, automotive workers' salaries increased substantially, UAW membership during the sit-downs increased from 30,000 to 500,000 in a single year.[8] Not only did labor organizing rise rapidly as a result of its increased militancy, but the new strike technique implied the potential for even more drastic action against industry. "We learned we can take the plant," said one General Motors worker during a sit-down. "We already know how to run them. If General Motors isn't careful, we'll put two and two together."[9]

In the two years following the first sit-down strike at a Goodyear tire plant in Akron, there had been 900 similar actions. The technique was effectively adapted by the civil rights movement in the 1960s when blacks sat in at segregated lunch counters and public facilities. It was later translated by the anti-Vietnam War protestors into sit-ins at campus and government offices.

Sit-down strikes and takeovers must obviously face the potential of repressive reaction of business and government. In the 1930s, police threw tear gas into factories and attempted to starve workers out by preventing food supplies from entering plants. Under pressure from business, the sit-down strike was officially declared illegal. In the more recent European plant takeovers, workers had to confront similar tactics by militia called out to protect private property.

In creating an effective strategy against this repression, labor must be able to develop local and national political support for the principle that worker or public takeovers are necessary to protect the jobs and livelihoods of workers. It must develop the political support which will allow government to help finance worker- or government-owned facilities, whether taken over in strikes or in negotiations with private owners. In many European countries, increased militancy by workers over the past ten years has resulted in reluctant, but increased government sanctions and financial support for worker takeovers. The possibility of takeover is often a sufficient threat in some countries to prevent or at least severely delay a company from moving.

In France there has been a virtual stampede of worker occupations. By late 1978, workers faced with rising unemployment were reportedly staging between fifty to two hundred occupations a month. Some lasted only a day or two to publicize a union's demands, while others have gone on for months or sometimes even years.[10] The publicity and at least partial success of many of these occupations have established a formidable national precedent and a threat to owners who contemplate moving, layoffs, wage cutbacks, and other antilabor actions.

The Lip watch factory in Besançon—the most famous worker plant occupation in France—was taken over in 1973 when workers learned of the company's plans to abandon operations. Since then a large number of workers have continued to occupy and manage the plant and produce and sell watches. Most recently the Lip workers presented the owners with a plan to take over operations permanently as a worker-owned cooperative, using financial help offered by the local socialist government to buy the buildings and land.

During the same year French workers began the Lip occupation, workers in Meriden, England, occupied the Triumph Motorcycle Works. After negotiating with the company and the British government for a year and a half during their occupation, the government agreed to help form a workers' cooperative and provided them with grants and loans to buy out the owners. The company faced stiff competition from Japanese motorcycle manufacturers both before and after their occupation. As a cooperative, however, the company continued to operate on a more modest scale, becoming the only British motorcycle company to survive. Since 1975, conditions have improved, and the cooperative has been slowly able to add more members. The members receive yearly incomes comparable to other vehicle industry workers, and have voted themselves better benefits, including free life insurance and twenty-six weeks' paid sick leave.[11]

In this country, support for worker takeover and protection of workers against plant migration will be more difficult than in Europe, where leftist parties provide important political support both inside and outside government. Recently, however, increased worker and union efforts here have resulted in a number of limited but important steps toward protecting workers.

At a national level, two bills are being considered in Congress which would require business to give workers longer term notification of abandonment plans and higher severance pay. In one case, two years' notice would be required, and the federal government would have the power to decide if the closing was economically justified. If the government declared the closing unjustified, it could terminate all federal financial help to the company, including tax credits, while at the same time providing severance payments to the workers. In the other bill, a minimum of a year's notice would be required, with payments to the workers coming from the companies themselves.

On a state level, with the exception of Wisconsin, which requires sixty days' notice of abandonment, and Maine, which requires companies to make a severance payment of one week's pay for each year worked, there is virtually no protection for workers. There is, however, a growing movement, supported by the unions, to change this situation. In Ohio, the Ohio Public Interest Campaign, a coalition of local union and community organizations, is backing legislation to require that companies give two years' notice of any plans to leave the state, and to indemnify workers and their communities when they do leave. The Coalition to Save Jobs, another labor-community group in Massachusetts, has a similar plan, with a one-year advance notice requirement. In Michigan, one proposed law would require companies to make severance payments to workers, while another would allow the state to investigate the possibility of worker-ownership of abandoned facilities. Still other plant-closing proposals are now being framed by labor-community groups in Illinois.

Some of these strategies, though an important indication of organizing against abandonment, still have serious drawbacks. Notification of abandonment is important; it will tell workers what is happening to them and give them time to organize. It is, however, no substitute for the real power to affect their future. Requiring severance pay from the company may temporarily delay a move, but it cannot keep the company from moving, if it can make the severance payments and *still* make higher profits elsewhere.

The federal proposal to withdraw tax credits and other government benefits from companies engaging in unjustified plant closings may again also help to delay such closings. But those who decide whether or not a corporate decision to close its doors is justified would be required by the law to use the argument of "economic viability"; that is, did the corporation make a sound economic decision in moving in terms of its own existence? One person's notion of reasonable corporate profit will not be another's. And regional rotation does indeed make enormous economic sense in terms of corporate viability—in fact, from the corporate point of view it can be a necessity.

In addition to these problems, the payment of severance to individuals can help set workers against each other. These kinds of benefits can tend to atomize protest against plant closings. A community united by the threat of a plant closing could be a strong force in a plant takeover, or in negotiations for cooperatively or publicly owned plants. Individuals because of their personal circumstances may have very different needs; some younger people with fewer community ties may be more physically mobile, while some older people may be looking forward to early retirement. Faced with the promise of early retirement benefits or generous severance pay, some workers may not be willing to join with others in demanding better long-term community alternatives.

Legislation against abandonment in individual states, while an important beginning, can only protect workers when it is also accompanied by a program for creating jobs. Public financial help for cooperative or publicly owned facilities could be a critical part of this strategy. Making a corporation pay heavier penalties in one state may simply make it even harder for that state to attract new jobs. But if these states also have strategies to develop productive jobs to replace those they may lose when companies are discouraged from locating there, the threat of private abandonment would lose its teeth.

There are a few recent cases where workers threatened with industrial abandonment have used government financial help successfully to buy out their companies. Since the financially ailing Chicago and Western Railroad became worker-owned in 1972, for example, it has produced, with the exception of the 1975 recession year, a steady series of annual profits. By 1978, the railroad's stock value jumped twelve times what it was when the workers took over ownership six years before. Between 1973 and 1976 several more companies were transferred to either worker, or a combination of worker and community ownership.

When Herkimer, New York, faced the closing of a Sperry-Rand furniture factory with a $3.5 million yearly payroll and $1 million in revenue loss to loggers, community groups rallied to put together a plan for worker and community ownership. In its first year of operation, the 250-worker Mohawk Valley Community Corporation which replaced Sperry-Rand earned a 17 percent profit after taxes—after setting aside $250,000 for a worker stock ownership plan. In Saratoga Springs, New York, a 120-worker-owned Saratoga Knitting Mill taken over in the early seventies has operated profitably, and like the worker-owned furniture plant, has done so after contributing substantially to an employee stock ownership plan.

In Lowell, Vermont, stock in an asbestos mine that was worth $50 a share when it was transferred employee ownership in 1974, was worth over $2,000 a share only four years later. The former GAF mine was sold to the company's 200 miners and to other community people after the company threatened to close, and the state of Vermont agreed to guarantee a $2 million loan to help the new owners. Had the mine, now called the Vermont Asbestos Group, closed, workers would not only have lost their jobs, but the town would have lost half its taxable income.

Still other examples of recent worker buy-outs are the 400-worker South Bend Lathe Company in Indiana, the Jamestown Metal Products Company, with over 100 workers, in Jamestown, New York, the Okanite Company with 1,800 workers, mostly in New Jersey, and a number of other companies throughout the country. In all, there are now some three to four hundred companies in the United States that are owned by their workers. More recently and more ambitiously, over 4,000 steel workers in Ohio's Mahoning Valley, faced with abandonment, are attempting with the help of community groups, church organizations, and unions to raise hundreds of millions of dollars, primarily in federal help, to buy their steel mills.[12]

The products produced by these worker-owned companies have remained the same and they are still principally governed by the goal of immediate profitability. In the absence of relating worker-owned enterprise to a broader program for social change, it is entirely conceivable that these and other financially successful worker-owned ventures might simply be returned to the ownership of large corporations or wealthy individuals in the future. In the case of the Vermont Asbestos Group, for example, an upswing in the international price of asbestos helped make the company so successful that in 1978, many workers considered selling their shares to one of the area's wealthiest businessmen.

To insure more democratic governance of the local economy, the choice of how the new enterprises are owned and managed is crucial. Since "worker ownership" (or even what's sometimes called "community ownership") often conveys control according to how much stock a worker or a resident can afford to buy, it's possible for some local people to own and control a much larger share of a company than others. Democratic decision making should be based on the principal of one person, one vote. To eliminate the possibilities for wealthier groups of workers or investors controlling an enterprise, government financial help could be coupled with the kind of single voting shares for workers and local community people which is often used in consumer and worker cooperatives. It could also require prohibitions against the future sale of public financed enterprises to individuals and small groups of investors.[13]

Government and government-assisted takeovers have to be approached cautiously and discriminately. Simply taking over any operation that plans to move out of town, and continuing to produce the same products under the same conditions as when it was privately-run, could lead to serious problems. Many times companies move because it is impossible for them to remain economically viable where they are. Without an understanding of what are both socially and economically useful forms of investment, the public or a group of workers could find itself saddled with the most unproductive and unprofitable ventures.

The result must not be for a state or cooperative to simply step into the shoes of the departing company, and continue socially unproductive operations abandoned by private investors. The local government should develop plans to transform operations once they are taken over. A chemical pesticide plant that was being considered for abandonment could become an opportunity for converting the plant's operation to producing a less harmful fertilizer. If the plant's physical conditions were inappropriate, then the government would not be encouraged to help buy out the plant, but to develop new facilities for producing safe fertilizers.

The intercession by government and concessions by business will not happen without militant organizing by a broad coalition of labor and other groups. In the past, business has been extremely effective in splitting the common interests of its antagonists by portraying the benefits for one group as the liabilities of another. It has tried to gain worker support for environmentally unsound ways of doing business by warning about lowered production and layoffs. "Corporate America has painted everyone into a classic dilemma," explained Anthony Mazzochi, the legislative director of the Oil, Chemical and Atomic Workers Union. "Now it's job versus the environment. The worker has a choice between his livelihood and dying of cancer."[14]

While some unions have fought environment cleanup, or shifts to safer fuels, others like the Oil, Chemical and Atomic Workers Union have fought for safer environments both inside and outside of the work place. Over twenty-five years ago, much before the growth of the environmental movement, Michigan's United Automobile Workers became one of the country's first groups to oppose nuclear power plants.

## Growing Mutual Support

The fact that corporate migration simultaneously puts pressure on workers at their work place and at home means the interests of unions, community organizations, and environmental groups are becoming closer. As regional rotation progresses, local governments will attempt to bid away their environments, their constituents' taxes, and local workers' job conditions in their entrepreneurial battles against one another. The degradation of the environment, the rising burden of inflation on consumers, and the effects of joblessness and abandonment on urban and rural communities are all issues that are contributing to the creation of a broad coalition of interest groups directed toward anticorporate programs.

In what might seem an uncharacteristic stand by organized labor, William Wimpisinger's Citizens/Labor Energy Coalition has opposed special breaks for industrial energy users. "A national policy," said the Coalition, "which would discontinue lower rates for higher users of gas and electricity would encourage conservation by industry." It also called for a shift from dependence on foreign energy sources controlled by noncompetitive industries to the development of domestic alternative energy sources and for uniform energy rates across the country in order to limit local government's ability to compete against each other. "By applying the standards nationally," it explained, "there would be less temptation for industry to leave the states with the fairest rate structures and move to states where consumers subsidize industrial rates."[15]

Another encouraging signal of the potential for more

unified organizing efforts between labor and other organizations is a growing mutual help and sensitivity. In California the Campaign for Economic Democracy, a left-wing Democratic political organization, was careful to couple their program for promoting solar development with a detailed analysis of how solar development would help create new jobs and improve the state's economy.

In 1978, environmentalists, including William Futrel, president of the Sierra Club, and David Brower, president of Friends of the Earth, supported the United Mine Workers in their strike against the coal companies.[16] Several years before, environmentalists supported the Oil, Chemical and Atomic Workers in their strike against Shell Oil to improve the safety conditions of Shell workers.

In New England, the Clamshell Alliance, an environmental organization which organized thousands of demonstrators at a number of sit-ins at the Seabrook, New Hampshire, nuclear reactor site, has worked with unions to support the 1977 Labor Reform Act. Friends of the Earth and other environmental groups have also lobbied for the bill, which was defeated after a massive business-supported effort.

These tentative beginnings are some distance from mass movement for change. What coalitions represent is a coalescing of an explicitly anticorporate attitude by a number of important social movements; they indicate that the conservative leadership in unions, environmental, and community organizations can no longer claim as strong a voice as they did; and third, they represent a recognition by these movements of a declining national economy which makes a unified front essential.

## Current Issues

Political pressure against regional rotation can be built through a variety of strategies, from plant sit-downs to electoral politics; there are also steps to be taken to improve conditions now while moving toward regional socialism. Coalition groups could capitalize on a popular antagonism toward private energy companies and the effort to develop alternative energy systems; they could work for publicly owned renewable systems to replace privately owned fossil-energy systems. As energy costs continue to rise, the efficiency and lower user charges of the hundreds of existing publicly owned utilities throughout the country could be used as a strong argument in a campaign for local public ownership.

Popular enthusiasm for a publicly owned utility was tapped in Mayor Dennis Kucinich's aggressive political campaign against Cleveland's bankers in late 1978 and early 1979. When the bankers threatened the city with default unless it sold its public electric company to private owners, the mayor refused. When the city then defaulted, Kucinich took the issue directly to the electorate through two referendum questions: one asked if the people wanted to sell their utility; the second, if they would agree to raise their taxes one-half of 1 percent to keep the city solvent. In a landslide 2 to 1 vote, Clevelanders told their government to keep the utility and that they would pay the tax increase.

Owning its electric company and having some more tax money in its public coffers may give Cleveland temporary respite from its financial crisis. Over the longer future the city will need strong control over the local economy and its jobs to achieve real fiscal stability. The Cleveland campaign, whether or not it moves in the direction of more public control, still remains an important landmark. It forcefully demonstrates that when given the option, citizens may indeed choose public control of what are traditionally defined as private enterprise facilities. The options presented in Cleveland were in sharp contrast to the service cuts New Yorkers were faced with during their fiscal crisis, or the options Californians faced during the Proposition 13 campaign.

The Cleveland campaign raises the very important political prospect, that when faced with the option of public ownership of productive, cost-saving ventures (and not simply the maintenance of public housekeeping services, or the maintenance of a public bureaucracy), many people will take the public ownership direction. The untapped reservoir of political support for local public ownership could become even more visible and vocal as people are given more opportunities to use public ownership as a way of saving productive jobs, lowering taxes, maintaining good public services, and wresting control of the local economy from corporations and banks.

The opening wedge to develop public, locally owned enterprises will depend on the specifics of the local situation. The threatened closing of a factory raises the possibility of a publicly owned work place to save jobs, the lack of alternative energy development by a private utility raises the possibility of publicly developed and publicly owned alternative energy companies, while private banks refusing to lend a local government money or charging the public high rates of interest raises the possibility of a publicly owned bank.

The privately owned sports team, a monopoly business enterprise, is an especially visible example of lack of popular local control, and could in some parts of the country present an interesting way of gaining support for public ownership. Regional sports affect millions of people through their attendance at events, and through radio, TV, and other media coverage. There are no other public events in the country to which hundreds of thousands of people, all over the country, will travel day after day. The high cost of seats, the limited numbers of nonseason tickets, the growing costs of public subsidies for team owners, and the unresponsiveness of owners to fans create a strong climate for change in many cities. The public cost of actually taking ownership of their teams could be relatively small. For about a tenth the cost of what New York City paid to remodel Yankee Stadium or less than the cost of one of its poorly used parking garages, the city could have bought the team when it was sold in the early 1970s. For the cost of its Superdome, Louisiana could probably have bought all sixteen major league baseball teams and still have some money left over.

Public ownership of a sports team would give fans more control over its major policy decisions and would insure that the "home team" would remain at home. The operation of the team could be made more democratic; it would not mean the public would decide the starting lineup, but it could vote on decisions such as when to televise the games or what percentage of seats should be held by season ticket holders.

Wherever possible, the financing for government takeovers of private enterprise should be accomplished without new taxes. In many cases it may be possible to shift funds from existing revenue sources or to create new sources. The creation of state-run banks, like the one in North Dakota, to which people could shift their savings and unions could shift their pension funds is a possible source of capital. The legislatures of New York, Massachusetts, New Jersey, the District of Columbia, and a number of other states have begun to consider seriously government-owned banks.

The bitter experiences of New York City and other cities and states where private banks profit from having billions of dollars in government deposits that they can invest outside these cities or states or outside the country, can create popular support for publicly owned banks. In 1977, the Chemical Bank in New York boasted "only" 70 percent of its equity invested outside the city. Other major banks had more; Citibank, one of the city's biggest banking institutions, had 85 percent outside investment.[17] Aided by tax credits allowed by the federal government, assets of American banks outside the country have grown rapidly. Between 1965 and 1976 these assets jumped from $8.9 billion to $229 billion.[18]

The shifting of funds from existing government programs into new public or worker cooperative ventures can create warmer investments and more permanent jobs without costing taxpayers more. New production facilities and jobs could be created by using some of the welfare funds governments now use to maintain people who are able to work but unable to find jobs; by shifting housing and urban development subsidies for private real estate developers and construction contractors; and by shifting the money now used to subsidize research and development for private corporations. Connecticut inched in this direction in 1972 by requiring that companies receiving public aid for research and development pay royalties to the state.

The use of royalties could be developed into a system for generating new capital for government-organized enterprise. Not only can governments require royalties on their research and development subsidies, but on the extraction of natural resources. Rather than putting their royalties into a general tax fund, they could be put in a fund specifically linked to the creation of government-organized enterprise. There could be a forceful logic in states which now have extremely specialized production like coal, lumber, or limited-crop agriculture, for linking the income of these current cold investment activities to the creation of warm ones. A state that relies heavily on its income from coal could use part of its current revenue from coal production in an effort to plan and create more diversified local economic activities.

Linking existing government revenue to the creation of more government-organized ventures has a broad range of possibilities. Perhaps one of the more controversial might be the idea of linking state lotteries and gambling to the creation of other state-organized operations. While public gambling can hardly be considered a traditional path to socialism, it might be useful to at least consider it as a step.

The shift toward more state-run lotteries and off-track betting operations is a sign of the current crisis of local government in the wake of regional rotation. State lotteries and state off-track betting parlors, which in 1977 brought in a total public income of close to $1.6 billion, have been used for the most part in those states where economic abandonment has been most deeply felt.[19] The two states that now have off-track betting are Connecticut and New York, while eleven of the fourteen states with public lotteries are states with relatively low rates of job gain.

Socialism, like gambling, has also been taboo in America. The fact that many states have been forced by desperate economic circumstances into operations considered sinful and immoral indicates the power of economic imperatives over long and firmly held ideological beliefs. It is an important lesson for those who believe socialism to be an inherently alien ideology and unrootable in American soil.

Those who favor state-run gambling have insisted that public ownership opens such operations to public view and control and protects citizens against the unsavory element in the private world of gambling. They have also argued that state profits from gambling help pay for useful public services such as hospitals and housing for the elderly, reducing the need for higher taxes. Variations of this argument are used all the way from state government lotteries down to the neighborhood association "Beano" games. A similar argument could of course be made for public ownership of manufacturing or energy companies. Public ownership would again open operations to public view and, as with gambling, protect the public from the unsavory side of corporate business: in this case, price fixing, bribery, unsafe products, and influence peddling in government.

Gambling is a regressive enterprise since most of the people who play lotteries or use off-track betting parlors are, according to a number of economists, those least able to afford it.[20] The problem is not getting more states to run regressive gambling operations but how to refocus existing gambling enterprise to create more progressive forms of socialism. A regional socialist movement could use the precedent of government gambling operations to demonstrate that public ownership is no longer a radical departure. The movement might attempt to have states use some of these revenues to help seed other more progressive and potentially useful state-run production enterprises. There might be popular and appealing logic in a loser state like Ohio, which already has a state lottery, and where private steel mills are being abandoned, to use part of the state's gambling income for public takeover, remodeling, and operation of abandoned mills. As an extension of this idea, the state might be required to set aside a special fund from its gambling income and, in those states which run liquor stores, liquor income to help start other productive public ventures.

A basic technique that governments can use in shifting capital to government-organized enterprise is through their own purchasing power. Local and state governments now spend billions in purchasing goods and services from private sources. Each year, for example, local governments spend enormous amounts for public school and office supplies and for fuel to heat and cool public buildings. A state-assisted venture in building office furniture or in alternative energy research and development would have a ready-made market through public use. By shifting government contracts to state-run ventures or workers' cooperatives, these new enterprises could begin with sufficient guaranteed income which they can then use as leverage in borrowing money from government banks or private sources. The borrowed money could then be used to buy existing businesses or to create new ones, without having to raise additional taxes.

In the loser regions, the prospect of losing markets or investment money, as opposed to the threat of traditional strikes by unions, becomes a threat to business. The coming together of several loser states in regional coalition to bargain with their combined purchasing power or their combined debt-financing programs, could be an effective technique for improving their joint economic health. The coalition of Northeast and Midwest states, which was recently formed to lobby for a more equitable return of federal tax dollars, would have potentially more effect in improving economic conditions for its citizens if it were to focus its combined power on private business and on creating its own productive enterprise, rather than fighting with other regions over the distribution of federal dollars. The power of a state government, or especially a coalition of these governments, both to withhold markets and to engage in their own economic ventures could turn the strategy of regional rotation on its head, transforming business's threats to leave into the occasion for building an alternative economic system.

## Possibilities for a New Approach

Business's ability to move jobs to other places in this country or to foreign soil has pitted community against community, worker against worker; those with common needs have entered into fierce competition. Those concerned with maintaining the integrity of the environment and people's health battle with people who are trying to save their jobs. People trying to attract business and revenue to their communities fight those who are trying to save their communities from the ravages of commercial development.

As business is aloof from this fratricidal warfare, it has reserved for itself the right of peace, cooperation, and government subsidies. It forms joint trade associations to fight labor organizing, it comes together to lobby the government treasuries for tax credits, protection from foreign competition, grants for modernization of plants, publicly supported industrial revenue bonds, and research and development money. It cooperates in giant industries where little or no competition exists and where the creation of new competitors is virtually impossible.

As the day of business entrepreneurship passes, the public inherits its worst defects. As business transcends competition, the public is on a treadmill of competition. Whether or not the public will remain in its present dilemma, it is clear that the historic conditions which generally force people to probe their problems are becoming more apparent.

The reaction is manifesting itself in many ways: in taxpayer revolts such as Proposition 13, and in the growing activism and alliances between labor and other groups. The reaction could lead to cutbacks in public social service spending and to lowering wage standards, or alternatively it could help forge a movement toward a more useful economic system.

In our declining economic system, traditional liberal approaches such as increasing welfare, health care, unemployment payments, will find less political support. Faced with increasingly shrill calls for tax relief, politicians of all stripes will be loath to support higher costs for unproductive government programs.

In this political environment, movements toward a particularly American style of socialism may be neither so radical nor so difficult to create. Regional socialism offers a strong alternative to welfarism; it provides an understandable and direct method of creating socially useful jobs, of preserving resources, and of developing more rational energy systems. And it offers these possibilities within a particularly American cultural and political context: the commitment to individual rights and local democratic governance, while maintaining reasonable levels of individual property ownership.

In the face of the restructuring of our economic system which must be undertaken by business for its own survival, these goals become less utopian. Business is forced to limit competition, to attack worker benefits, and to create a much stronger partnership with government in order to insure continued subsidies to underwrite profits.

To people paying the cost of maintaining vast loser regions of the country and to workers forced to give back wage gains, job condition improvements, and other social benefits won over the past forty years, regional socialism could be seen as a practical path to realizing an old American promise of local self-governance.

# NOTES

INTRODUCTION:
Against Their Better Interests

1. United States Chamber of Commerce figures; see *New York Times,* April 22, 1976.


1 PACKAGING THE PEOPLE:
The Public Entrepreneurs

1. *Greensburg Tribune-Review,* October 6, 1976.
2. Information on subsidies from personal interview with Norval Reece, Secretary of Commerce Department, Pennsylvania, February 1, 1978, and material provided by his office. Additional information from *New York Times, Wall Street Journal, Industry Week, Business Week,* and Ron Chernow, "The Rabbit That Ate Pennsylvania," *Mother Jones,* January, 1978.
3. *Greensburg Tribune-Review,* September 16, 1976.
4. *Wall Street Journal,* April 22, 1976.

5. *New York Times,* May 28, 1976.

6. *Wall Street Journal,* April 22, 1976.

7. Ibid., March 1, 1976.

8. *Business Week,* February 16, 1976.

9. *Wall Street Journal,* April 4, 1976.

10. Ibid., August 13, 1978.

11. See Robert Goodman, *After the Planners* (New York: Simon and Schuster, 1972).

12. *Detroit Free Press,* June 7, 1978, cited in Edward Kelly, "State and Local Taxes in Economic Development," Ohio Public Interest Campaign (mimeo, n.d.).

13. *Business Week,* February 6, 1978.

14. Personal interview with Norval Reece, Secretary of Commerce Department, Pennsylvania, February 1, 1978.

15. *Wall Street Journal,* June 30, 1978.

16. Peter J. Bearse, "Government as Innovator: A Paradigm for State Economic Development Policy," *New England Journal of Business and Economics,* Spring, 1976.

17. Report of the Select Committee on the State's Economy, Albany, N.Y., 1974, cited in L. Falk, "Industrial Inducements: Analysis of the Effect of the Pennsylvania Loan Program on New Jersey," Seventh Annual Report of the New Jersey Economic Policy Council and Office of Economic Policy, Trenton, N.J., 1974.

18. *Business Week,* June 21, 1976.

19. Ibid.

20. Ibid.

21. "The New Hampshire Story," New Hampshire Department of Resources and Economic Development, Concord, New Hampshire.

22. *Report,* Kansas Department of Economic Development, May, 1977, Topeka, Kansas.

23. "Bet on Nevada for Industry," Department of Economic Development.

24. *New York Times,* February 23, 1978.

25. Advertisement, *Barron's,* March 6, 1978.

26. *Akron Beacon Journal,* February 29, 1976, cited in Ed-

ward Kelly, *Industrial Exodus*, Conference on Alternative State and Local Public Policies, October, 1977, Washington, D.C.

27. Edward Kelly, *Industrial Exodus*.

28. *New York Times*, March 2, 1976.

29. Ibid.; see, for example, advertisements, *New York Times*, January 17, 1978, and *Barron's*, March 6, 1978.

30. *Wall Street Journal*, June 30, 1978.

31. *Industrial Development*, November-December, 1976.

32. *Wall Street Journal*, June 30, 1978.

33. Ibid.

34. New York City Industrial Development Agency pamphlet (n.d., received January, 1979).

35. See F.A.N.S. (Fight to Advance the Nation's Sports) newsletter, *Left Field*, January, 1978, Washington, D.C.

36. *Sports Illustrated*, July 17, 1978.

37. Dan Kowet, *The Rich Who Own Sports* (New York: Random House, 1977).

38. *Left Field*, March, 1978.

39. *New York Times*, March 19, 1978.

40. Kowet, *The Rich Who Own Sports*.

41. *New York Times*, January 13, 1978.

42. Ibid., May 30, 1978.

43. Statistics for states and metropolitan areas: A preprint from *County and City Data Book*, 1977, United States Department of Commerce (Washington, D.C.: United States Government Printing Office, 1977); see also *New York Times*, January 13, 1978, for information on Superdome.

44. On the Yankee Stadium, see Kowet, *The Rich Who Own Sports; New York Times*, March 19, 1978; *New York Magazine*, October 24, 1977.

45. S.P. Sethi, *Up Against the Corporate Wall* (Englewood Cliffs, N.J.: Prentice-Hall, 1971).

46. *New York Times*, October 30, 1977.

47. See the *Fantus Company, Economic Development Corporation, New York*. Prepared for the Foundation Committee for Economic Development. New York City, April, 1977, New York-Chicago.

48. Ibid.

49. Ibid.; see also *Special Report:* "Alabama Ranked Second Nationally for Good Business Climate," Alabama Chamber of Commerce, April, 1976.

50. Ibid.

51. Executive memo, Illinois Manufacturers' Association, November 4, 1975, Chicago, Illinois.

52. *New York Times,* October 1, 1975.

53. Ibid., December 7, 1970.

54. *Statistical Abstract of the United States,* 1974, United States Department of Commerce, Bureau of the Census (Washington, D.C.: United States Government Printing Office, 1974) (hereafter referred to as SA).

55. James O'Toole, *The Reserve Army of the Underemployed,* United States Department of Health, Education, and Welfare (Washington, D.C.: United States Government Printing Office, 1977).

56. SA, 1976.

57. *New York Times,* March 4, 1976 (advertisement).

58. *Texas Facts: The Book on Profitable Plant Locations,* Texas Industrial Development Commission, Austin, Texas, September, 1976; "Get on Board the ProfiTrain in Texas," Texas Industrial Development Commission, Austin, Texas; "Tennessee Industrial Training Service," Tennessee Department of Education, Nashville, Tennessee.

59. "Keeping the South Down; Economic Civil War; An Interview with Governor David Boren," *Property Journal,* Oklahoma City, Oklahoma, Winter, 1978.

60. "Manpower, a Powerful Plus," New Bedford Industrial Development Commission.

61. *Texas Facts . . .*

62. "Manufacturing Investment Opportunities in Alabama," Alabama Development Office, Montgomery, Alabama.

63. "Workers" (promotional package), Minnesota Department of Economic Development, St. Paul, Minnesota.

64. *Texas Facts . . .*

65. Celia Dugger, "Peddling the Promised Land," *The Texas Observer,* October 10, 1978.

## 2   WHERE THE JOBS HAVE GONE:
The Corporate Geography

1. *Corporate Financing*, March-April, 1971.

2. "Profitable Oklahoma," Department of Industrial Development, Oklahoma City, Oklahoma.

3. "South Dakota Welcomes You with Open Lands," South Dakota Department of Economic and Tourism Development, Pierre, South Dakota.

4. *Texas Facts: The Book on Profitable Plant Location*, Texas Industrial Development Commission, Austin, Texas.

5. "Virginia Facts and Figures 1977," Governor's Office, Division of Industrial Development, Richmond, Virginia.

6. "Utah!" Utah Industrial Development Commission, Salt Lake City, Utah.

7. "Florida Economic Development," Florida Department of Commerce, Tallahassee, Florida.

8. "Colorado: A Regional Approach," Colorado Division of Commerce and Development, Denver, Colorado.

9. Emil Malizia et al., "The Earnings of North Carolinians," June, 1975, Monograph, Occasional Papers Series, Department of City and Regional Planning, University of North Carolina, Chapel Hill, North Carolina.

10. "Right-to-Work Law in North Carolina," North Carolina Department of Natural and Economic Resources, Raleigh, North Carolina.

11. "Why Would a Manufacturer Want to Locate in Michigan?" Michigan Department of Commerce, Lansing, Michigan.

12. "Oregon: The Solid State," Department of Economic Development, Portland, Oregon.

13. "Our Great Adventure Now Is Growth," New Bedford Industrial Development Commission, New Bedford, Massachusetts.

14. "Manpower Is a Powerful Plus," New Bedford Industrial Development Commission, New Bedford, Massachusetts.

15. "Illinois Facts: A Corporate Location Guide," Illinois

Department of Business and Economic Development, Springfield, Illinois.

16. "It's a Good Move," Corpus Christi Industrial Commission, Corpus Christi, Texas.

17. "Arizona: An Economic Profile," Office of the Governor, February, 1977, Phoenix, Arizona.

18. "International Twin State Concept," New Mexico Department of Development, Santa Fe, New Mexico.

19. *New York Times,* April 22, 1976.

20. Personal interview, May 24, 1978.

21. Data from Bureau of Labor Statistics, Boston Regional Office.

22. *Annual Survey of Manufacturers (1974, 1975, 1976). Fuels and Electric Energy Consumed,* United States Department of Commerce, Bureau of Labor Statistics, Washington, D.C.; SA, 1978.

23. United States Department of Labor, *Rural Oriented Research and Development Projects: A Review and Synthesis* (Washington, D.C.: United States Government Printing Office, 1977).

24. *Southern Exposure,* vol. 4, no. 1–2 (Spring, 1976); *Time,* September 27, 1976, p. 76.

25. *Industry Wage Survey: Textiles 1971,* United States Department of Labor, BLS (Washington, D.C.: United States Government Printing Office, 1974).

26. *Industrial Development,* November-December, 1976; From the State Capital's Industrial Development Report no. 10, Bethune Jones, Asbury Park, New Jersey, Oct. 1, 1976.

27. Calvin Beale, "A Further Look at Nonmetropolitan Growth Since 1970," *American Journal of Agricultural Economics,* vol. 58, no. 5 (December, 1976); press release, United States Department of Agriculture, 258–77.

28. Calvin Beale, "Current Status of the Shift of U.S. Population to Smaller Communities," paper presented to the Population Association of America, April 21, 1977, St. Louis, Missouri (mimeo).

29. Brian D. Dittenhafter, "The Growth of Southern Cities

in the Sixties," *Monthly Review,* April, 1974, Federal Reserve Bank of Atlanta, Georgia, pp. 42–49.

30. Testimony by Paul R. Porter, 94th Congress, 2nd Session, Hearings, Committee on Banking and Currency and Housing, House of Representatives, *The Rebirth of an American City,* pt. 1, September 20–24, 1976 (Washington, D.C.: United States Government Printing Office, 1976).

31. Richard E. Lonsdale and Clyde E. Browning, "Rural-Urban Location Preferences of Southern Manufacturers," *Annals of the Association of American Geographers,* March, 1971.

32. Tennessee Valley Authority, Annual Report 1969 (Washington, D.C.: United States Government Printing Office, 1969), p. 9, cited in Lonsdale and Browning (1971), "Rural-Urban Location . . ."; McGuire et al., "Land Has to Be Kept Ready for Site-Seeking Industry," *Industrial Development,* May-June, 1977.

33. *Across the Board,* March, 1977, The Conference Board, New York.

34. *The New Englander,* January, 1978, Dublin, New Hampshire.

35. *Report on National Growth and Development,* The Committee on Community Development, The Domestic Council, Department of H.U.D. (Washington, D.C.: United States Government Printing Office, December, 1974).

36. Ibid.

37. *New York Times,* September 29, 1976.

38. Ibid., July 17, 1977.

39. *Report on National Growth and Development.*

40. *New York Times,* April 16, 1977.

41. SA, 1978.

42. *New York Times,* May 22, 1977.

3   REGIONAL ROTATION:
Harvest of the Losers and Winners

1. *New York Times,* December 17, 1977.

2. Ibid., December 20, 1978.

3. Ibid., November 7, 1977.

4. Paul D. Spreiregen for the American Institute of Architects, *Urban Design: The Architecture of Cities and Towns* (New York: McGraw-Hill, 1965). For more on this approach see Robert Goodman, *After the Planners* (New York: Simon and Schuster, 1972).

5. Anthony Downs, "Using the Lessons of Experience to Allocate Resources in the Community Development Program," Real Estate Research Corporation, Chicago, Illinois (n.d., received 1976).

6. Testimony by David Rockefeller, *Hearings*, Committee on Government Operations, United States Senate 89th Congress, 2nd Session, November 29, 30, 1966 (Washington, D.C.: United States Government Printing Office, 1967).

7. Daniel P. Moynihan, "Who Gets into the Army," *New Republic*, November 5, 1966.

8. Edward Banfield, *The Unheavenly City* (Boston: Little, Brown & Co., 1968).

9. *New York Times*, July 24, 1977.

10. SA, 1978.

11. *New York Times*, February 12, 1976.

12. Comments made at the White House Conference on Balanced National Growth and Economic Development, Washington, D.C., January 31, 1978.

13. Millers Falls information from *Boston Globe*, December 18, 1977; see also *Wall Street Journal*, January 9, 1978; and "More of the Same: Millers Falls Tool Threatens to Run Away" (pamphlet), Greenfield Popular Union, Box 251, Turners Falls, Massachusetts.

14. *Corporate Financing*, March-April, 1971.

15. Information from Bureau of Labor Statistics, Boston Regional Office and Amalgamated Clothing and Textile Workers Union, New England Regional Office. March 22, 1979.

16. *Boston Globe*, May 3, 1977.

17. *New York Times*, July 4, 1977, May 9, 1977.

18. Ibid., November 11, 1977.

19. *Business Week*, October 30, 1978.

20. *New York Times*, National Economic Survey, January 7, 1979.

21. Ibid.

22. *New York Times,* March 25, 1969.

23. Advertisement by New York State Department of Commerce, *Barron's,* March, 1978.

24. *New York Times,* National Economic Survey, January 7, 1979.

25. See *Wall Street Journal* Oct. 13, 1978, Oct. 20, 1978, and Oct. 23, 1978; *Facts on File,* Oct. 27, 1978.

26. Robert H. Frank, Richard T. Freeman, *Multinational Corporations and Domestic Employment* (Ithaca, New York: Cornell University Press, 1976).

27. See *NACLA's Latin America and Empire Report,* April, 1977, North American Congress on Latin America, New York, N.Y.; David Ciscel, Tom Collins, "The Memphis Runaway Blues," *Southern Exposure,* vol. 4, no. 1–2, Institute for Southern Studies, Chapel Hill, North Carolina, 1976; see also Edward Kelly, *Industrial Exodus,* Conference on Alternative State and Local Public Policies, Washington, D.C., October, 1977.

28. Brookings Institution, *Round Table Discussion on Urban Development Banking,* March 21, 1977, transcript, Washington, D.C.

29. Anthony Downs, "Using the Lessons . . ."

30. *Business Week,* May 8, 1978.

31. Gurney Breckenfeld, "How Cities Can Cope with Shrinkage," in *How Cities Can Grow Old Gracefully,* Committee on Banking, Finance and Urban Affairs, House of Representatives, 95th Congress (Washington, D.C.: United States Government Printing Office, 1977).

32. Brookings Institution, *Round Table Discussion . . .*

33. Joint Hearing, *Financing Municipal Needs,* Joint Economic Committee of the United States 95th Congress, July 25, 1977 (Washington, D.C.: United States Government Printing Office, 1977).

34. *New York Times,* editorial, November 25, 1977.

35. *Wall Street Journal,* January 9, 1978.

36. *Boston Globe,* December 18, 1977.

4   THE PUBLIC ENTREPRENEUR AS POLICEMAN
     AND ACCOMPLICE:
     Dilemma of the Living Losers

1. *New York Times*, January 25, 1970.

2. Ibid., October 28, 1977.

3. *Dollars and Sense*, October, 1975. Somerville, Mass.

4. *New York Times*, October 18, 1975.

5. Ibid., September 19, 1977.

6. Data cited in T.D. Allman, "The Urban Crisis Leaves Town," *Harpers*, December, 1978.

7. Testimony by Thomas Muller, Senior Research Associate, The Urban Institute, Washington, D.C. See "Service Costs in Declining Cities," 95th Congress, First Session, Subcommittee on the City, Committee on Banking, Finance, and Urban Affairs, House of Representatives, *How Cities Can Grow Old Gracefully* (Washington, D.C.: United States Government Printing Office, 1977).

8. SA, 1978.

9. Ibid.

10. *Business Week*, October 17, 1977.

11. Felix G. Rohatyn, "A New R.F.C. Proposed for Business," *New York Times*, December 1, 1974; Roger Alcaly, "Capitalism, Crises and the Current Economic Situation," in *Radical Perspectives on the Economic Crisis of Monopoly Capital* (New York: Union for Radical Political Economy, 1975).

12. Richard W. Kopcke, "The Decline in Corporate Profitability," *New England Economic Review*, May-June 1978, Federal Reserve Bank of Boston.

13. *Wall Street Journal*, October 23, 1978.

14. *New York Times*, December 6, 1978.

15. Report by Solomon Brothers, investment banking firm, New York City. Reported in *New York Times*, September 18, 1977.

16. James O'Connor, *The Fiscal Crisis of the State* (New York: St. Martin's Press, 1973).

17. *Business Week,* February 2, 1976.

18. The Business Roundtable, Statement of Position, "The Business Community and the Problems of the Cities," New York, September, 1976.

19. James O'Toole, *The Reserve Army of the Underemployed* (Washington, D.C.: United States Government Printing Office, 1977).

20. *New York Times,* December 28, 1978.

21. See state promotional advertisements, *Business Week,* March 15, 1976; *Fortune,* March-June, 1976.

22. *Wall Street Journal,* January 9, 1978.

23. *Corporate Financing,* November-December, 1970, March-April, 1971.

24. Information supplied by local planning agencies in A. J. Gobar and C. B. Coman, "Reserving Too Much Land for Industry Restricts Prospects for Broad Based Development," *Industrial Development,* May-June, 1977.

25. M. McGuire, C. Kanal, and P. Lovett, "Land Has to Be Kept Ready for Site-Seeking Industry," *Industrial Development,* May-June, 1977.

26. See, for example, *Industrial Development,* March-April, 1976.

27. Sam B. Warner, *The Urban Wilderness* (New York: Harper and Row, 1972). Warner also cites Philip Nichols, Jr., "The Meaning of Public Use in the Law of Eminent Domain," *Boston University Law Review* 20 (November, 1940).

28. Ralph Nader, Mark Green, and Joel Seligman, *Taming the Giant Corporation* (New York: W. W. Norton, 1976).

29. Stuart Chase, "Coals to Newcastle," in *Planning the Fourth Migration,* Carl Sussman, ed. (Cambridge, Mass.: MIT Press, 1977).

30. SA, 1978.

31. Ken Butti and John Perlin, "Solar Water Heaters in California, 1891–1930," *The Co-Evolution Quarterly,* Fall, 1977.

32. "American Ground Transport," Hearings, Subcommittee on Antitrust and Monopoly, Committee on the Judiciary,

United States Senate, 93rd Congress, Pt. 4a, Washington, D.C., 1974.

33. *United States* v. *National City Lines*, 1951 Trade Cases, para 62, 757 at 64–237 cited in "American Ground Transport."

34. Southern California Rapid Transit District, Rapid Transit for Los Angeles. Summary Report of Consultants Recommendations, July, 1973, cited in "American Ground Transport."

35. Sam B. Warner, *The Urban Wilderness.*

36. *New York Times*, June 3, 1932.

37. Ibid., January 12, 1932.

## 5  THE ROOTS OF REGIONAL ROTATION

1. *Forbes*, August 1, 1972.

2. *Business Week*, June 5, 1978.

3. Richard O. Boyer and Herbert M. Morais, *Labor's Untold Story* (New York: United Electrical, Radio and Machine Workers of America, 1955).

4. See *Wall Street Journal*, July 28, 1978.

5. Ibid., cites *U.S. Immigration Abstract of the Report of Immigrants in Cities, 1911.*

6. Thomas R. Brooks, *Toil and Trouble* (New York: Dell, Delta, 1964, 1971).

7. Henry Pelling, *American Labor* (Chicago: University of Chicago Press, 1960).

8. Brooks, *Toil and Trouble.*

9. Robert K. Murray, *Red Scare* (New York: McGraw-Hill, 1964).

10. Ibid.

11. Ibid.

12. Boyer and Morais, *Labor's Untold Story.*

13. Murray, *Red Scare.*

14. Brooks, *Toil and Trouble;* also cited in Irving Bernstein, *The Lean Years* (Boston: Houghton Mifflin, 1960).

15. Bernstein, *The Lean Years.*

16. Len DeCaux, *Labor Radical* (Boston: Beacon Press, 1970).

17. *Historical Statistics of the United States, Colonial Times to 1970*, United States Bureau of the Census, Department of Commerce (Washington, D.C.: United States Government Printing Office, 1975).

18. Bernstein, *The Lean Years.*

19. Ibid.

20. Pelling, *American Labor,* refers to cheap labor and favorable tax statutes.

21. Ethel Smith, *Life and Liberty Bulletin,* National Women's Trade Union League (NWTUL), Chicago, December, 1929.

22. Smith, *Life and Liberty Bulletin.*

23. Bernstein, *The Lean Years.*

24. Gladys Boone, *The Women's Trade Union Leagues in Great Britain and the United States of America* (New York: Columbia University Press, 1942).

25. Brooks, *Toil and Trouble.*

26. Bernstein, *The Lean Years.*

27. Corabel Stillman, NWTUL Convention Proceedings, May, 1929, Washington, D.C.

28. *Historical Statistics. . . .*

29. Ibid.

30. See for example the statement by Reverend William P. Stofford in *Life and Labor Bulletin,* NWTUL, December, 1929; and discussion in Bernstein, *The Lean Years.*

31. *Historical Statistics. . . .*

32. Pelling, *American Labor.*

33. *Historical Statistics. . . .*

34. Pelling, *American Labor;* Brooks, *Toil and Trouble.*

35. Boyer and Morais, *Labor's Untold Story.*

36. Brooks, *Toil and Trouble.*

37. Boyer and Morais, *Labor's Untold Story.*

## 6   THE JOYS OF CORPORATE COOPERATION: Who's Afraid of Free Enterprise?

1. *New England Business,* February 1, 1979.

2. 95th Congress, 2nd Session, Report of the Subcommittee on Antitrust, Consumers, and Employment, Committee on Small Business, House of Representatives, *Future of Small Business in America* (Washington, D.C.: United States Government Printing Office, 1978).

3. *Future of Small Business in America.*

4. 95th Congress, 2nd Session, Staff Study by the Subcommittee on Reports, Accounting and Management, Committee on Governmental Affairs, United States Senate, *Interlocking Directorates Among the Major U.S. Corporations,* January, 1978 (Washington, D.C.; United States Government Printing Office, 1978).

5. *New York Times,* February 17, 1975.

6. Press release, February 27, 1975, Initiative Committee for National Economic Planning, White Plains, N.Y.

7. *New York Times,* December 12, 1974.

8. News release; speech by Henry Ford II, *White House Conference on Balanced Economic Growth and Economic Development,* Washington, D.C., January 30, 1978.

9. *Fortune,* February, 1977.

10. *New York Times,* September 21, 1975.

11. Ibid., December 21, 1975.

12. Barton J. Bernstein, "The New Deal: The Conservative Achievements of Liberal Reform" in *Towards a New Past,* Barton J. Bernstein, ed. (New York: Vintage, 1969).

13. Ibid.

14. *New York Times,* December 7, 1970.

15. Ibid., February 17, 1975.

16. Nelson A. Rockefeller, "Towards Energy Independence," *New York Times,* February 24, 1976.

17. Report of the Advisory Committee on National Growth and Development in *Challenge,* January-February, 1977.

## 7 COLD AND WARM INVESTING:
Big Macs and Other Choices

1. Nelson A. Rockefeller, "Towards Energy Independence," *New York Times,* February 24, 1976.
2. SA, 1978.
3. *Business Week,* July 11, 1977.
4. *Dollars and Sense,* no. 29, September, 1977, Somerville, Mass.
5. SA, 1978.
6. Real estate fee data, *Forbes,* September 4, 1978; housing and urban renewal data from SA, 1978.

## 8 REGIONAL SOCIALISM:
An American Alternative

1. See Lester Brown, *By Bread Alone* (New York: Pergamon, 1976).
2. See Upton Sinclair, *I, Candidate for Governor: And How I Got Licked.* Published by the author, Pasadena, California, n.d.
3. "The Ohio Plan: 'Production for Use,'" *Self-Reliance,* January-February, 1978, Institute for Local Self-Reliance, Washington, D.C.
4. Sinclair, *I, Candidate for Governor. . . .*
5. Information on North Dakota from Herbert L. Thorndal, testimony before the Committee on Banking, the Assembly, State of New York, April 25, 1975; and *Forbes,* January 15, 1975.
6. See *Fact Sheet for Public Power Systems,* the People's Right to Choose, April, 1978, and other information by the American Public Power Association, Washington, D.C.
7. Cited in *The Real Paper,* Boston, November 19, 1975,

David Geller, "Seven Cures for the State's Economy." See also Ben Achtenberg and Emily Paradise Achtenberg, "BC: Three Years Later," *Working Papers*, Winter, 1976.

## 9   THE LESSONS OF LITTLE ORPHAN ANNIE IN CREATING A TECHNOLOGY FOR REGIONAL SOCIALISM

1. Amory Lovins, *Rutland Herald* (Vermont), October 16, 1977.
2. All Schumacher quotes from E. F. Schumacher, "City Patterns," *Resurgence*, May-June, 1977.
3. Sam B. Warner, *The Urban Wilderness* (New York: Harper & Row, 1972).
4. *Wall Street Journal*, November 15, 1977.
5. Harvey Wasserman, "Pulling the Plug on Solar," *New Age*, September, 1977.
6. Fred Branfman, "California's Fight for the Sun," *The Nation*, June 18, 1977; *New York Times*, October 7, 1976.
7. Ibid.

## 10   MONEY, MUZAK, AND THE SETTING FOR CHANGE

1. SA, 1978; *The Future of Small Business in America* (Washington, D.C.: United States Government Printing Office, 1978).
2. *New York Times*, March 8, 1979.
3. *Business Week*, November 6, 1978.
4. Ibid.
5. *Engineering News-Record*, October 10, 1977.
6. *In These Times*, December 20–26, 1978.
7. Talk at Harvard University, Kennedy Institute of Politics, October 28, 1978.
8. Richard O. Boyer and Herbert M. Morais, *Labor's Untold*

*Story.* (New York: United Electrical, Radio and Machine Workers of America, 1955).

9. Edward Levinson, "Labor on the March" in Aaron and Bendiner, *The Strenuous Decade* (Garden City, N.Y.: Anchor, Doubleday, 1970).

10. *Wall Street Journal,* October 30, 1978.

11. Martin Carnoy, "A Tale of Two Sit-Ins," *Working Papers,* March-April, 1979.

12. See William F. Whyte, "In Support of Voluntary Employee Ownership," *Society,* September-October, 1978; Daniel Zwerdling, "Worker Ownership: What Are the Next Steps?" *Working Papers* (forthcoming 1979); "Asbestos Mine Gets New Management," *Dollars and Sense,* May-June, 1978, Somerville, Mass.; and information from the National Center for Economic Alternatives, Washington, D.C.

13. For a more detailed analysis of worker ownership and worker democracy, see Daniel Zwerdling, *Democracy at the Workplace* (Washington, D.C., Association for Self-Management, 1978). Also contains a useful resources section.

14. *New York Times,* May 28, 1977.

15. Citizen/Labor Energy Coalition, *Policy on Alternative Energy Sources,* April 20, 1978; *Policy on Utility Rate Reform,* April 20, 1978.

16. Letter to President Jimmy Carter, March 22, 1978, Environmentalists for Full Employment, Washington, D.C.

17. *New York Times,* December 17, 1977.

18. Ibid., October 16, 1977.

19. *Business Week,* June 26, 1978.

20. Ibid.

# INDEX

279